Forgotten General

Commanding Officer
3rd Battalion, Grenadier Guards, 1930

Forgotten General

A Life of Andrew Thorne

Donald Lindsay

Michael Russell

First published in Great Britain 1987
by Michael Russell (Publishing) Ltd
The Chantry, Wilton, Salisbury, Wiltshire

Typeset at The Spartan Press Ltd,
Lymington, Hants
Printed and bound in Great Britain
by Biddles Ltd, Guildford and King's Lynn

ISBN 0 85955 137 7

Dedicated, by gracious permission, to
His Majesty King Olav V,
who, as Crown Prince, was Norwegian Defence Chief
in 1945 when Norway was liberated,
and who has always desired to ensure that
General Thorne's name has not been forgotten in Norway.

Contents

Acknowledgements

In writing this book I have been greatly indebted to the many people who knew or who served under General Sir Andrew Thorne and who generously answered my many requests for information about him. It is impossible to list them all separately and I hope that they will accept this collective expression of my gratitude.

There are, however, one or two who must be mentioned by name. First and foremost is General Thorne's eldest child, the late Miss Diana Thorne, CBE, TD. After her father's death she collected and arranged his papers and further material which she amassed with tireless devotion. Without her work this book could not have been written. The other members of the Thorne family have all met my repeated requests for memories of their parents with exemplary patience. They have been alert in correcting errors of fact; for any mistakes in interpretation I am alone to blame.

I am deeply indebted to Major-General R. H. Whitworth, CBE, for reading the chapters dealing with General Thorne's military career in two world wars and for giving me the great benefit of his knowledge as a military historian.

For the account of the Liberation of Norway I have been dependent upon the invaluable assistance of two men, both friends of General Thorne. Høyesteretts-advocat Hr. Jens Christian Hauge, the leader of Milorg, the Norwegian Resistance Movement, and General Leif Rolstad, the distinguished Norwegian soldier, both gave unstinted help. Between them they spent many hours making sure that I understood the whole Norwegian story, which even the mass of surviving documents among General Thorne's papers could not fully reveal.

Seaford DONALD LINDSAY
October 1982–August 1986

I

Augustus

Thorne is a West Country name in origin and today is still commonly found both as a surname and a place-name in Dorset, Devon and Somerset. Some socially aspiring branches of this large and widely spread family trace a rather tenuous descent from the de Tonis, who in early days crossed the Channel from Northern France. The branch with which this book is concerned made no such claim and by the mid-eighteenth century had settled in London.

Here Thomas Thorne was born on 18 September 1786. In July 1815, a month after the Battle of Waterloo, he married Sarah Atwood of Southwark by whom he had four sons and two daughters, all duly baptised in St Botolph's Church, Bishopsgate. Thomas seems to have had a curiously varied career, for in the baptismal registers he is successively described as a bookseller and newsagent, a coffee-house keeper, a tavern keeper and, on his death certificate in 1868, as a retired dining-room keeper. When his wife died in 1852 he was briefly designated 'Gentleman'. All these pursuits were carried on by him, or financed by him, within the City of London, making him both prosperous and sufficiently acceptable socially to be admitted in 1829 as a Liveryman of the Worshipful Company of Cooks, of which he became Master in 1857.

It was Thomas Thorne's third son, Augustus, who is important in this story, for in due course he would become Andrew Thorne's father. He was born on 16 July 1825 and was sent to his father's old school, Merchant Taylors'. This was surprising because the eldest boy, also called Thomas, who died at the age of thirteen, was said to have been virtually bullied to death for being clever and hardworking. The second son, Joseph, was immediately withdrawn from the school, but although Merchant Taylors' has no record of his entry Augustus went there when of age. On leaving school he wanted to read Law at Oxford, but his father refused, saying that by paying public school fees he had done all that could be expected of him.

So in 1845 Augustus went to Canton, a member of the firm of Gibb, Livingstone & Co., which had been founded nine years previously to exploit the rich Chinese market thrown open to all traders with the ending of the East India Company's monopoly in 1833. The Chinese had tried to exclude foreigners from their empire, but the Opium War in 1842 had forced them to open Canton, Shanghai and three other ports to Western traders and to cede Hong Kong to Britain. The holds of the giant clippers made a highly lucrative trade possible as tea, silks, porcelain and other Oriental luxuries were exchanged for the manufactured goods pouring out from the mills and factories of Lancashire, Yorkshire and the Midlands.

At some date Augustus changed firms and worked in partnership with J. P. Thomas & Co., presumably attracted by the permission granted to its employees to do business on their own account out of office hours, thereby laying the foundations of his own fortune as a pioneer of British trade with the Yangtse valley. Life in China was very enjoyable for a young man of means. Sailing and keeping his own racehorses occupied much of his spare time. He became a Freemason, which increased his social and business contacts, and in 1855 he set up business entirely on his own. Returning home on leave he founded the firm of Thorne & Co. with the help of his brothers Joseph and Cornelius. It was his business flair which guided the firm through early difficulties and made it prosperous. It passed into other hands in 1874.

Before leaving China Augustus succumbed to blackwater fever, then regarded as incurable. He survived but was told that henceforth he must live an open-air life in England and not return to China. For a while he accepted his doctor's orders. He bought a small farm near Battle in Sussex and a house nearby and for a few years became a hardworking sheep farmer. Farming on a small scale – a Board of Trade return in March 1866 records 120 sheep, 38 lambs, 2 milking cows and 1 pig – soon failed to satisfy his restored energies. Treating serious illness as a thing of the past, he embarked on several new careers.

His early interest in the law led him in 1863 to enter the Middle

Temple, and he was called to the Bar in November 1865. He had no intention of practising as a barrister, but he knew that legal knowledge would be of great value to his commercial plans and also to his growing interest in prison reform. In the year that he entered the Middle Temple he began another new venture by holding weekly auctions of tea in Mincing Lane. The tea was advertised as being 'sold without reserve', which meant ignoring the agreed market price in order to undercut his rivals when it suited him. This breach of common practice aroused much opposition in the City, which he disregarded, shrewdly believing that his critics would be forced to follow suit.

Study of the law, control of Thorne & Co., the Mincing Lane auctions and a farm meant leading a very busy life. However, his sense of civic duty encouraged him to take an active part in the affairs of two Livery Companies – the Cooks and the Cordwainers – eventually becoming Master of each. His Mastership of the Cordwainers fell in the year 1896/7 when, as part of the Diamond Jubilee celebrations in 1897, he presided over the banquet at which the visiting Colonial premiers were entertained. In 1870 he agreed to stand as Parliamentary candidate for the Borough of Nottingham, but the radical sentiments expressed in his election address alarmed potential voters. As a supporter of what today would be called 'Women's Lib' he would never have toed the line as a true blue Conservative. As a strong individualist he would have often found it difficult to obey the commands of the Whips, and so when a safer candidate proposed to contest the seat for the Conservatives Augustus tactfully withdrew, thereafter confining his work for the community to the City of London. Here in 1887 he became Deputy Lieutenant for the Tower Hamlets and from 1893 a Councillor for the Borough of Marylebone. At the turn of the century he was invited to be prospective Lord Mayor of London, but he would have been seventy-five on taking office, and as his health was beginning to deteriorate he reluctantly declined the honour.

For over fifty years Augustus remained a bachelor. In 1856 his elder brother, Joseph, had married a very remarkable woman, Isabel Jane Pryer, who became a leading figure in the fight for women to become doctors. That Augustus was no misogynist is clear from the help which he gave her in her struggle. After paying for Isabel's trousseau, which she needed on accompanying her husband to China after the wedding, he greatly furthered her career when she returned to England. In 1864 he drew her attention to classes at the Ladies Medical College, paying her fees two years later for a practical midwifery course at the City Road Lying-In Hospital. He helped her to apply for the Society of Apothecaries examination, and a generous subscription to the Royal Free Hospital was conditional upon the acceptance of women doctors. In 1901, the year of his death, the hospital appointed women to resident posts.

On 6 February 1877 Augustus's bachelor days ended suddenly when, with characteristic impulsiveness and quixotic kindness, he married the thirty-year-old Margaret Blenheim Ochterlony Greig – known as Maggie. At the time of her marriage she was a very sick woman, unlikely to live long. She died three weeks after their first wedding anniversary, probably from consumption, as Augustus in his will bequeathed money to two hospitals for chest complaints. It is impossible to say what prompted this step or what his feelings were towards his young and ailing wife. What is certain is that he kept her memory alive by endowing a bed at the London Hospital to be known as 'Maggie's Cot', and in his will be expressed a hope that his second wife would maintain the endowment, which she did.

Two years after Maggie's death Augustus met Mary Frances Nicol, a girl of twenty-one whom he was determined to marry. He was apt to get his way but had to wait for four years. On 17 November 1883 the marriage took place at St James's Church, Paddington. Once again he had chosen a Scottish bride.

Mary's father, Andrew Nicol, was a colourful character. Born in Banff in 1819, as a young boy he was judged clever but impetuous or, less flatteringly, as 'a royt rogue of a red-haired loon'. In his early teens he travelled widely, reaching Ceylon in the early 1840s to become a coffee planter. He chose an excellent site twenty-five miles from Kandy, but temperamentally he was not the ideal planter for, as a contemporary explained, 'brains are rather an encumbrance to a planter . . . plodding perseverance is more necessary.' Andrew was no plodder. His roving disposition led him to disappear into the jungle for weeks at a time, accompanied only by a few coolies. However, by 1851 his coffee plantation was doing so well that he could afford to employ a manager and to return home to Marnock in Banffshire for the first time with two friends – 'three lively blades' as the neighbourhood testified.

At Marnock he met and in 1856 married Jane Stronach, whose father had been factor to the Earl of Fife. Two years later with his wife and first child he returned to Ceylon. Mary had been born in 1857 and on the voyage had a miraculous escape from drowning. The ship was struck by a sudden freak storm and the child was very nearly sucked out by the retreating wave from the porthole which had been left open. Only the long clothes in which she was sleeping saved her.

Much of Mary's childhood was spent in Ceylon where the family, eventually consisting of five girls, was brought up by governesses. Life was erratic. Andrew, having eaten his customary two peaches for breakfast, would rush out of the house, plant the stones and return to dictate innumerable and often intemperate letters. In 1874 he transported his family around Europe for four or five years as part of their education. In 1880 he settled in London but five years later was back in Ceylon where the coffee-leaf fungus had destroyed his Dimbula estate, forcing him to change to tea planting, an exchange which had proved very profitable by 1890. Mary grew up to be very talented both artistically and musically and was once described by one of her daughters as having 'bags of brains'. She had first met some of the Thornes two or three years before her marriage when she had come over from Eastbourne, where she was staying, to Joseph Thorne's house, Southover Grange, at Lewes and she and one of Joseph's daughters had been bridesmaids to a mutual friend. Despite being over thirty years younger than her husband they were to live together very happily for the next eighteen years.

At the time of his second marriage Augustus was living at Sevenoaks in an unattractive house called Dornhurst, commuting daily to the City. Mary's first child was born on 15 September 1884 and christened Mary Augusta Margaret Nicol, known as Mollie. Almost exactly a year later, on 20 September 1885, a son, Augustus Francis Andrew Nicol, was born at Dornhurst. Mary had been delivered of a still-born son in 1887, but on 10 April 1888 Andrew's only brother, Thomas Fleetwood Joseph Nicol, was born. Three more sisters for Andrew completed the family: Sarah Constance Pellew Nicol was born on 9 November 1889; Frances Helen Rennie Nicol on 14 January 1892; and Anne Dorothea Dyce Nicol on 23 January 1893.

Augustus had a large number of relatives and not every young wife is capable of loving all her in-laws. Mary was a girl of spirit and strong character, who did not greatly like Sevenoaks and who increasingly found life at Dornhurst suffocating, largely because of the constant presence of 'Aunt Church', a widowed sister of Augustus who lived close by in a house which he had built for her. One day Mary told her husband that she could not bear to live there much longer. Augustus had been totally unaware of her unhappiness but anxious to end his wife's distress he went off to London as usual the next day, returning in the evening to announce that he had rented a house in Green Street, W.1 until such time as he found a more suitable house to buy. However devoted to their wives, Victorian husbands were unquestioned masters in their homes and it apparently never occurred to Augustus to discuss with Mary the kind of house she would like or even whether she wished to live in London. Presumably the more important choice of their permanent house, 32 Great Cumberland Place, Hyde Park, was a joint decision. This large and beautiful house remained the family home until some years after Augustus's death. Dornhurst was not disposed of until Andrew sold it soon after the First World War.

It has been said that by 1893 the Thorne family was complete. While this is strictly accurate, in the following year three cousins joined the six Thorne children. Mary's eldest sister, Margaret, had married a Ceylon planter, Ernest Francis Messervy, a Channel Island surname. He had died young in 1893 and his widow with her twin children, Gerald and Phyllis, came home from Ceylon to stay at Great Cumberland Place. Here on 26 March 1894 she died while giving birth to a boy, Ernest Dyce Messervy. Without a moment's hesitation Augustus and Mary made a home for the three orphaned children. Except for never being officially adopted and retaining their surname they became fully part of the Thorne family, cared for, brought up and educated as if they had been Augustus's and Mary's own children.

Only a very wealthy man could have maintained the vast household. To look after himself and his wife and nine children Augustus employed five domestic staff 'upstairs', while 'below stairs' in the basement Mrs Gwilliam, the cook, reigned with a kitchen and scullery maid and an 'odd man' to trim and clean the lamps, polish the shoes and undertake all heavy work. The children needed a staff of their own. The nursery was in the care of the loving and much loved Agnes Zimmermann, always known as Addie, who remained their life-long friend. Two nursemaids helped her, for the children seldom joined their parents for meals in the dining-room much before the age of twelve. Below that age they were usually in the unaided care of their mother for only an hour or so before bedtime. Although Augustus left an estate valued at over half a million pounds at his death – a large sum in 1902 – his children were brought up simply and unostentatiously, never being allowed to think that they could have whatever money could buy.

Augustus, who had reached the age of sixty when Andrew was born, must have been almost a grandfather to his children, an awe-inspiring figure who earned their respectful affection by exerting a grandfather's prerogative of taking no ultimate responsibility for discipline. Addie used later to maintain that he was very unfair to his wife in leaving entirely to her the training and occasional punishing of their children. Something of this relationship was seen on a Sunday morning when after a later breakfast than usual the children were allowed into the dining-room to bowl their iron hoops around the table, despite Mary's occasional protests. Mollie's big hoop was fixed up to represent the Marble Arch through which the smaller hoops had to pass. Augustus sat benignly at the head of the table popping small bits of sardine or sausage into open mouths as the hoops passed his chair. Probably less palatable were the improving sayings to which the children were subjected. 'Love your father every day, for this is the right and proper way' – an unnecessary piece of unctuous advice. 'By industry shall man be exalted' or 'Money in wages is money well spent' at least remained in their minds. These sayings were not confined to Sundays but were apt to be delivered as occasion arose. 'Some put their trust in chariots and others in horses but I will remember the name of the Lord my God' probably reflected Augustus's sincere belief. He and his wife were God-fearing parents and brought their children up in their own uncomplicated faith.

Although of pure English descent Augustus had a deep love for Scotland, fully shared by his Scottish wife. He became especially attached to the small port of Lossiemouth, then quite a primitive place. As he grew older the comparatively flat surrounding country enabled him to continue to stride around the district, walking-stick held with both hands across his back. Family holidays were spent here in rented houses until he decided to build a house of his own on a fine site overlooking the golf links. Dunconusg was finished in 1894, Andrew having cut the first sod when he was seven. It was claimed that from one upper window it was possible to follow the progress of almost a complete round and as the years went by the family became devoted to the game.

The journey from London to Lossiemouth further illustrates the distance which Augustus kept from domestic duties. Mary used to book a whole third-class railway coach for the journey and at King's Cross the family was divided up with Addie or a nursery maid in charge of each compartment. The remaining compartments were occupied by the domestic staff. At Aberdeen no one was allowed out on the platform, but fresh baps were brought to the coach for breakfast. The coach was then attached to the Elgin train and the final stage of the long journey was on the local train from Elgin to Lossiemouth where a great welcome awaited them from Mr Duncan, the station-master. Flys were standing by to deposit the entire party on the steps of Dunconusg. Despite this very privileged method of travel Augustus never went with his wife and family. He preferred to arrive the next day.

The accepted authority of the Victorian paterfamilias combined with what was in effect a generation gap made the relation of Augustus to his family very different from that of a modern parent. It did not mean that Augustus was not a kindly man, popular with friends and acquaintances in all stations of life. He loved to gossip with fishermen in Lossiemouth harbour and when he learned that the local inhabitants were accustomed to wander on Sundays over what was now his land on which Dunconusg had been built, he refrained from fencing off his property for three years. He enjoyed chatting with those whom he met and any who were interested were shown over his house. His love for the town and its inhabitants led him to finance the building of the parish kirk there. To him people mattered, a trait which Andrew inherited to an even greater degree.

2

Andrew: 1885 – 1902

With five brothers and sisters and three cousins Andrew grew up with all the companionship that he could wish. To his younger sisters he was 'a little devil' as he and Mollie ruled the nursery and schoolroom roost. It was infuriating for them to return from a walk in the park to find favourite dolls, teddy bears and golliwogs strung across the room just out of reach. His parents certainly objected to finding the legs of three nursery high chairs sawn off to make them into stools. On the slenderest evidence the head parlourmaid was believed not to mind having the long streamers at the back of her cap shut in the door through which she had tried to pass. He enjoyed a scrap far more than his Messervy cousins and cries of anger and reproach rang throughout the nursery as various pranks were played. Even Mollie remonstrated at times. 'Oh! Debbie!,' she cried, a name which stuck to him for some time and had been her attempt to call the new-born Andrew 'Dear baby!' Nevertheless, the young ones felt a sense of dependence and an ability to rely on the two older ones when necessary. It is clear that Andrew's high spirits and sense of fun were apparent early in his life and there is no reason to believe that he was naughtier than any normal boy of his age. However, he had obviously tried his mother's patience too far at Lossiemouth in the summer of 1891. His punishment was to write a letter of apology to his father, at that moment in London. The letter, dated 8 September, is on a small sheet of paper on which double lines had been ruled to guide his inexperienced hand with a pencil:

> dear Father, I have been so naughty, rude,
> disobedient I am sorry. I must remember. Will you
> forgive me. love from Andrew.

He was not quite six years old.

Whatever lessons Andrew may have learned in the schoolroom

from Addie, his formal schooling began in 1892 when he attended Miss Woodman's Morning Class for the Sons of Gentlemen near Portman Square. This select establishment, which would doubtless horrify modern educational theorists, at least gave him a thorough grounding in the three Rs. But by 1894 Augustus had decided that he needed discipline, which could be best achieved by sending him away to boarding school. Why he chose Mulgrave Castle School near Whitby is not known. The school had only been in existence for less than a year and Whitby was far from London. In the event it proved an excellent choice.

In April 1890 the Revd the Right Hon. Constantine Charles Henry Phipps, Earl of Mulgrave, became on the death of his father the 3rd Marquess of Normanby. Ordained as a young man, he had been vicar of St Mark's, Worsley, near Manchester from 1872. He was a man of great spirituality, vigour, firmness and enterprise, who throughout his long life was first and foremost a priest. Even after the age of eighty he still took four services every Sunday. On inheriting the title he was faced with the problem which had defeated his father, how to save the estate financially. The 2nd Marquess had leased Mulgrave Castle for short periods to raise money but one lease to the famous cricketer Duleepsinghi proved unfortunate. 'Duleep' had a passion for falconry and saw no harm in filling the castle with rats for his falcons to kill.

The new Lord Normanby had enjoyed occasionally coaching boys for examinations and he decided to open a small school in Mulgrave Castle in January 1893. It certainly was a small school: the numbers in any term never rose above thirty-eight and usually averaged about thirty boys; from the time of its opening until it closed when Lord Normanby married in April 1904 a total of ninety-six boys had attended the school. It seems doubtful if it was ever a paying proposition. The staffing ratio was unbelievably generous, with four or five assistant masters and a visiting drill sergeant. The estate carpenter gave instruction in woodwork, and gamekeepers were available to supervise homework. The teaching was good and the boys received little short of private tuition. Andrew used to say that he learned nothing new in mathematics at Eton until he reached the First Hundred. Instruction in woodwork was severely practical and he long boasted that his first achievement was to make a wooden seat for a privy. In a school of about thirty pupils it was difficult to avoid being in the first or second eleven teams but as a naturally good and keen games player he would have found a place in the teams of far larger schools.

Andrew loved Mulgrave. He was there from January 1894 until April 1899 and he became devoted to Lord Normanby, who was one of the formative influences in his early years. One advantage of the smallness of the school was that although Lord Normanby had become a Canon of Windsor in 1891, the school could be transported to a rented house in Windsor during his periods of residence. These he usually managed to arrange for the Easter Term when Windsor in February or March was less bleak than Whitby. Andrew's first meeting with his headmaster was on the night that he reached Mulgrave. Anxious to send a letter home, he knocked on the door of Lord Normanby's study and in language more appropriate to the New Testament asked: 'Please, Lord, can I have a stamp?'

Many of his letters home have survived. They give a picture of a happy life at school but bear all the usual signs of a small boy's laborious efforts to find something to say in his weekly letter. 'I like rabbit chance very much we when yesterday and we caught a lot and we when and saw the dog. We when to church this morning and we may go to church this evening. I wount have time to write any more.' . . . 'I did write last Sunday but I think I must have lost it.'

The future ensign who so much enjoyed a 'rag' with his fellow officers seems to be preshadowed in frequent references to fighting. 'I and the new boy are always fighting.' . . . 'Dear Lennie [his sister] I have much fun and I have just been fighting with Clifford.' It would be wrong to read too much into his accounts of mock battles between two armies. On his side he was a colonel but only commanded his troops when his general was absent. Rather more significant is a request that *Battles of the British Army* be sent to him and his interest in the military careers of some of Lord Normanby's friends who came for the shooting. A more serious pointer to the future was trouble with his eyes. Inevitably his glasses were broken. 'Please will you send me two more pairs.' . . . 'I am wearing my glasses in every lesson except when I forget them which I don't do very often as the masters remind me.'

Money was always running out. 'Please will you send me some money for some things as I don't want to brake into two and sixpence.' . . . 'My dear Mother. Please will you send me some stamps and 5 shillings to get a present for you.' Augustus was more fortunate in not being directly invited to contribute to his own birthday present. As Andrew wrote to his mother: 'I am going to give Father for his birthday present the Certificate I got for First Aid for the injured and I will try to make a frame for it.' This would be a pleasant change in carpentry from making hen coops, to which he had progressed from the privy seat.

Food was always to be important to Andrew and was naturally so to a young boy. 'Please will you send me a box of rock because the boys want some.' . . . 'Please will you send a box of Rose's Lime Juice Jujubs. I want them for after football when I am winded.' . . . 'We are called at a quarter to seven. Prayers are at 25 minutes past seven we are all expected to be down. If we are not it is because we are lazy and so we don't get any hot meat for breakfast.'

One event at Mulgrave of lasting importance to him was his Confirmation in the local parish church by the Archbishop of York on 17 July 1898. He came from a Christian home, and the influence of Lord Normanby in building on this was his greatest permanent gain from Mulgrave. Throughout his life he was to possess a strong and simple, almost a childlike trust in the Christian faith, apparently untroubled by doubt. He had so hoped that at least his mother would come for his Confirmation but 'Father and I are going to spend a quiet Sunday in the country and if possible we shall attend Holy Communion . . . anyhow we shall be with you in thought and prayer, dear boy.' It took three letters to her before responding to his request for 'a remembrance of my Confirmation a little book called 'Before the Alter' [*sic*]'. The delay was probably due to her worry that Lord Normanby was a High Church man and the devotional book was in places too 'high' for her taste. The book arrived in time for his first Communion with the parts approved by herself and her husband underlined and those of which they disapproved – mostly relating to private confession to a priest – crossed out.

A year before Andrew left Mulgrave Augustus transported his wife and the younger children to Brussels for nine months. He had been advised to take a rest from work and this was to be combined with the children absorbing the French language by hearing it spoken around them. Belgium rather than France was chosen for this highly optimistic purpose because of his avowed dislike of the French nation. Andrew and Tommie, who had come to Mulgrave in April 1897, joined the family in the holidays. Far more memorable to them all than a visit to the field of Waterloo was to see their father's hat knocked off his head in the street for refusing, while watching a religious procession, to raise it to the passing statue of the Virgin Mary.

Two or three days before the end of his last term at Mulgrave Andrew received the only letter which his father ever wrote to him. It is written on a narrow scrap of paper torn off from the bottom of a larger sheet:

> Dear Andrew, I have rec^{d} your Post Card (Postmark date 28 March) and agreeably to your request send herewith Postal Order for Five Shillings.
>
> I hope Fleetwood [Tommie] is recovering from his cold and that you have coached yourself up, so as to take a good entrance into Eton.
>
> Your aff^{t} Father
>
> AUGUSTUS THORNE 29 March 1899

One thing which Andrew took away with him when he left Mulgrave in April 1899 and which remained with him all his life was his nickname – Bulgy. Years later he gave what must be the definitive account of its origin. 'My nickname came from a dog whose fondness for buns was only equalled by mine at the age of 8½ years and on the dog's demise the name descended on me. I have never since then been able to escape it.'

Andrew was at Eton for three and a half years from the Summer half of 1899 until December 1902. The choice of Eton was probably at Lord Normanby's suggestion for Augustus had originally thought of sending his sons to Elgin Academy. It is interesting to speculate on the effect on Andrew's career by this change. It would have been far harder in 1903 for a candidate from Elgin to have been accepted into the Grenadier Guards than one from Eton. Although only at Eton for a comparatively short period, he was there in the golden age of the public schools when few questioned their right to exist and when Eton in particular had not yet aroused the jealous hatred of those determined to root out any form of privilege. His headmaster was Dr Edmond Warre, physically a giant of a man and immensely impressive, especially to a new boy. For his first half he was in the uninspiring Revd H. Damon's house, but was fortunate when in September Hugh Macnaghten took over. He was a remarkable man, an exciting teacher of young boys, a minor poet, utterly devoted to his boys though, judged by modern standards, impossibly sentimental about them.

Andrew's Eton career was successful without being outstanding. He was not in any sense a scholar and his achievements were the result of hard work. In his second half he won the Lower Master's History Prize and in the half before he left the 4th Army Class Trials prize. In between his progress was steady if not spectacular. Yet in the end he was to pass well into Sandhurst. Like many another boy his enjoyment of games competed with his need to work and at Eton under Warre athletic success was important. He was already a keen and promising footballer when he arrived, and before he left he captained his house eleven. He had some success in athletics but the hitherto unattempted sports of fives and rowing interested him more. As a 'wet-bob' he spent much time on the river and in 1901 he and his friend D. P. Wormwald won the Novice Pulling Competition. His greatest achievement came in 1902 when he was invited to take an oar in *Britannia* for the Fourth of June celebrations. Dressed, as he wrote to his mother, in a 'straw hat with Britannia in silver letters round the band and two oars crossed in front; a blue short naval jacket; white ducks; skin coloured socks; evening shoes with gilt buckles and a linen shirt, white with blue lines wide apart, starched in front and cuffs and a turn down collar attached', he wore this uniform as proudly as he ever would others in the years ahead.

'A little too fond of playing sometimes at work!!' had been an early report by Lord Normanby on Andrew's high spirits. Eton did nothing to quell them as his letters home show. 'I was smacked today by Ovey. I got nine, they didn't hurt. I got them for shooting peas into Hegate's windows.' . . . 'So far I have only been smacked by the Captain of the House once this term and that was for throwing egg shells onto the roof.' A long letter describes the way that Eton like the rest of Britain erupted with relief at the news on 19 May 1900 from Mafeking which Etonians learned by a two-rocket signal from Windsor Castle. After early morning school 'we rushed off to the shops to get flags. The flags were selling at 2/- for a 3d. flag. I got by main force two huge big red and white flags . . . I and about 4 other boys went to Windsor blowing coach horns. We went into the Castle with flags tied round our hats and our waists and our legs. I had hardly any wind left to yell after blowing my horn . . . The school formed on each side of the road outside the Chapel and threw fireworks at each other. All the carriages that passed were filled with bursting crackers greatly to the alarm of the occupants.' Andrew did not join the Eton Officers Training Corps until half way through his time and for a future distinguished soldier his military prowess was not remarkable. He rose to the rank of sergeant but lost his stripes for firing a pencil at the Adjutant's charger on a field day – an ancient and honourable practice known in most public schools.

'I am very well in myself today and I don't know why I am not allowed up. Dr Hale couldn't even find a wheeze, an event unheard of before with me.' It is difficult to be certain about Andrew's health at Eton. He could not have played football or rowed well had he not been very fit, but surviving letters contain references to colds and influenza and even to part of one autumn spent recuperating at Seaford. In an age before antibiotics boys had to stay out of school for far longer than today and he seems to have been singularly prone to colds and 'wheezes'. Victorian families were notoriously alarmed at a cold and, judging from repeated references to colds in his adult letters, he inherited something of this.

Far more puzzling than Andrew's health was his relationship to his father and mother. As has been said, his father was so much older than fathers usually are that he must often have seemed a little remote. His mother, to whom almost all his surviving letters are written, had the reputation at Lossiemouth of being graciously kind but rather austere. 'Commemoration Day will take place on the 3 June this year. You must dress smartly and Father ought to come down in a frock coat and top hat.' Andrew evidently wanted his parents to visit him, to judge from the rather frantic messages asking at least to know one way or the other. All children need affection and Andrew's natural craving for it met so often with a rather chilling response. 'I am sorry, dear, that y^{r} side did not win y^{r} football match. It w^{d} be nice while you are captain that they sh^{d} do well – but success is not so easily won.'

That Mary Thorne expected impossibly high standards of behaviour from an adolescent son is clear from the rather pathetic letters of apology which Andrew at times felt bound to write. From Brighton, recuperating from mumps, he wrote: 'I am so sorry to give you and everybody so much trouble and worry. I am thoroughly ashamed of myself for spoiling everybody's holidays.' . . . 'I *did* enjoy myself last holidays. I hope I was not a nuisance or very extravagant.' . . . 'I am very sorry for giving you such a lot of trouble during the holidays and I am very sorry for losing my temper on the last day.' This is not the normal affectionate relationship of mother and son, and his later determination to be a friend to his own children, sharing their interests and being with them as much as possible, must have been a reaction against the lack of longed-for affection which his father was too old and his mother unable to show.

Andrew may have shown unsoldierly conduct on a field day but he was regarded as sufficiently responsible to line the route of Queen Victoria's funeral procession at Windsor. His mother had watched the procession in London and wrote an account of all that she had seen to her two sons and their cousins in a rather forbidding style almost worthy of the old Queen herself. 'The Kings and Princes all rode and had such fine horses – but I could not take my eyes off that wonderful gun carriage and its burden . . . Now, dear Sons, I want you never to forget this and try and do y^{r} best as true English school boys – then as you grow up to be brave true Servants of y^{r} Country and y^{r} King . . . every man, every little boy can help and keep our dear Country in its high position – and now that every country is jealous our country needs all we can do to keep in the front!' Like so many others that day she sensed that this was the end of an era and that an uncertain future lay ahead.

In the Thorne family the year 1901 also marked the passing of the Victorian age, for on 28 October Augustus died at Dunconusg. When her eldest daughter became engaged to a man much older than herself Mary Thorne once said to Addie that she regretted this. 'Well, you did it yourself, madam, and were very happy.' Mary agreed but added: 'It was a long time to be left alone.'

Andrew's choice of the Army as his career was dictated by no family tradition. It seems probable that he was drawn towards the Army by the influence of two great friends who 'messed' with him at Eton – Bill Balfour and Chico Leatham. Both were destined for the Guards and despite warnings of the difficulty of becoming a Grenadier he had set his heart on it. In the written examination for Sandhurst he did far better than he had expected, but one hurdle, the medical examination, had to be surmounted. What worried him was not his general fitness but his defective right eye, with which he could see very little. His housemaster wrote on 9 January 1903: 'Please goodness all will be well . . . But if things should go wrong I shall feel it a real blessing for the House – and for myself – to have you back again. As it is I can't face the thought of your leaving but as it is the best for you I wish it.' Somehow he bluffed his way through the eyesight test. Family legend has it that the candidates were examined alphabetically and that when the medical officer reached T he was tired. After finding the left eye perfect he took his word that the right eye was equally good. Throughout his life he was virtually blind in his right eye, a potentially serious disability which he overcame with skill and good humour. A family friend wrote to him on hearing of his acceptance at Sandhurst: 'I think that apart from pecuniary advantages the sons of such a father as yours are likely to have inherited qualities which, if used as you no doubt will endeavour to use them, may lead to great distinction.'

3
The Making of a Soldier: 1903 – 1908

A. C. Benson, when a housemaster at Eton, confided to his diary his opinion of his head master, Edmond Warre. His main criticism was aimed at Warre's excessive encouragement of games, so that boys 'became prostrate before athletics' resulting in that 'absence of the development of intelligence of which the disastrous results are now apparent in South Africa'. The Boer War, which had at last ended on 31 May 1902, had revealed disturbing deficiences both at the War Office and in elementary competence on the battlefield. Before peace was signed an official inquiry took place to discover the reasons for the British failure to defeat the small Boer nation as swiftly and decisively as had been expected. One very necessary part of this inquiry was the Government Committee on the Education and Training of Officers of the Army, consisting of three Members of Parliament, three serving officers, and the Head Master of Eton and the High Master of St Paul's.

The Committee's report found that all concerned with the running of Sandhurst had sacrificed efficiency to economy. Excessive time was devoted to drill and far too little to the study of military technology. During the meagre sixty hours allocated to tactics in the year's course more than half the time was spent indoors and in the final examinations the subject only counted for a possible 450 marks out of a possible total of 3,800. Discipline was lax and there was little inducement for gentleman cadets to work hard in an institution where hunting was as important as study and where an official blind eye was often turned on a cadet's misdemeanours. In the opinion of the Committee the time spent at Sandhurst needed to be doubled to allow serious study of military history and of French and German or, for those hoping to serve in India, of Hindustani. On the practical side the Committee proposed an annual summer camp, lasting for a month, with full-scale manoeuvres and field training.

Andrew's entry to the Royal Military College at Sandhurst in January 1903 was at an opportune moment for one intending to take the profession of arms very seriously and whose whole career was to earn him a reputation as a forward-thinking officer. The arrival in September 1902 of a new Commandant at Sandhurst was of greater immediate importance than the report of the Committee, whose recommendations could only be implemented by increased expenditure, not at once forthcoming.

Colonel G. C. Kitson came to Sandhurst from being Commandant of the Canadian Royal Military College at Kingston. He inherited a state of considerable indiscipline among the cadets. Serious disturbances in Camberley during a fête at the Foresters' Inn involving a large number of cadets and a series of unexplained fires had caused his predecessor great anxiety. Stern measures quickly restored discipline and Kitson could turn his attention to urgently needed reforms. Irregularities in the use of College funds were detected and corrected; bad messing arrangements were improved; and lecturers were curtly informed by the Commandant that too much of their work was insufficiently prepared. By the end of the summer term 1903, that is at the end of Andrew's first half year at Sandhurst, Kitson could report to the War Office that good discipline had been maintained, rifle shooting had markedly improved and that the Company system, which he had introduced in January 1903 at the moment that Andrew had arrived, was an unqualified success. Valuable practical training had resulted from the month's camp on Salisbury Plain and he had even wrung an annual grant of £50 from the War Office for the officers' library. Hitherto books of a professional character had seldom been regarded as having any value in training a British officer.

It was thus Andrew's good fortune to begin his military career at a moment when a sense of serious purpose was being injected into Sandhurst, and his years as a subaltern were to coincide with the transformation of the British Army as a result of the reforms carried through Parliament by Richard Haldane, the Liberal Secretary of State for War, a man with an invaluable knowledge of Germany and the growing might of its army.

For it was not only the Boer War which had led to this fundamental questioning of the efficiency of the British soldier. It was the growing realisation from the turn of the century that Germany rather than France was Britain's 'natural enemy'. The overwhelming of Austria in 1866 and of France in 1870 were slowly heeded warnings of what might be ahead. In May 1903 Erskine Childers's exciting novel *The Riddle of the Sands* was published. It achieved a sensational success, fortuitously aided by its appearance at the moment when Anglo-German naval rivalry was becoming serious. By a curious coincidence Childers had made his first sailing voyage along the north German coast in 1897 when German plans for an invasion of England were being laid on lines which fitted remarkably well with Childers's imagination. The plans had in fact been abandoned as impracticable by 1903, but military as well as naval minds were affected by the novel. Generals were no longer content to accept the age-old belief that the defence of Great Britain lay solely with the Royal Navy. The novel appealed not only to those who enjoyed a good spy story or were keen yachtsmen but it confirmed national fears that war with Germany was a growing possibility and that for her defence Britain must not look to her 'moat' alone but must train and equip an efficient army.

From such weekly letters to his mother as have survived we can gain a sufficiently clear picture of Andrew's fifteen months at Sandhurst, though his infuriating habit of dating most letters 'Sunday evening' makes chronology difficult. Later in life he became meticulous in his dating, often recording the exact time that he began to write. Despite social and athletic activities he worked steadily and at the end of his first six months was placed 44th in order of merit, his conduct and character being pronounced 'very good'. Riding, shooting, signalling and gymnastics were all part of the curriculum, which pleased him, and they kept him busy and fit.

The summer camp, instituted by Colonel Kitson, was at Tidworth Pennings, which was reached after a four-day march with reveille at 4.40 a.m., kit bags packed by 5.25 a.m. and a 6.00 a.m. start. Lunch must have been very welcome after marching some thirteen miles. 'I think I shall enjoy camp even though I don't get a bath for a month,' he told his mother. He gave her details of the heavy programme of field exercises, musketry, drill and frequent inspections involving 'extra special cleaning for one hour'. Unfortunately bad weather set in and 'the clothes which I was wearing got soaked through as I had to crawl through a field of clover on my tummy to reach the road, unseen by the enemy in a field of clay', but 'I have never been in better health than I am now'. His one regret was his inability to lose weight. 'I get thin during the day but I eat such a lot of bread and butter that I make up for the loss during the day.' He had hoped at the end of camp to be promoted to the rank of corporal but before this could occur the rank was abolished. His reward came with promotion to sergeant in September 1903.

One characteristic which he never lost was his infectious enjoyment of living life to the full. As a future officer his keenness to play football, golf and tennis were encouraged, though his defective eye was a handicap in tennis. Frequent visits in spare moments to see Tommie and Gerald Messervy at Eton enabled him to play games there also. He seemed to thrive on an exhausting programme of lunch, tea and dinner parties though he disliked the waste of valuable time spent in paying subsequent formal calls on hostesses.

He was occasionally the guest at tennis parties of the ex-Empress Eugenie whom he first met 'presiding over a huge tea party of foreigners and a few English' at Farnborough Hill. Once she enlivened her party by including four attractive young actresses, among them 'a Miss Gladys Cooper, the most beautiful woman I have ever seen'. He always loved the theatre but the Commandant had put London theatres out of bounds as part of his tightening of discipline. The likelihood of being caught seemed negligible, and he decided to take the risk. The occupant of the next seat was one of his instructors, who markedly turned his back on him throughout the performance. Dancing was another of his loves, and a Sandhurst cadet became increasingly courted by his girl friends as the end-of-the-year dance approached. He had no hesitation in placing his elder sister, Mollie, at the head of his list despite his mother's pressure to invite a daughter of a family friend.

'Can you send me some money as I am broke to the world?' Similar cries for help regularly punctuate his letters to his mother. Life was good but good living was expensive. No cadet was expected to live on his pay and it was assumed that aspiring officers were blessed with ample private means. Augustus had died a wealthy man, seemingly unaware of the difficulties which his tightly drawn will would create for his family. Mary Thorne inherited £1,000 per annum together with her share of the marriage settlement, an income far too small to educate and provide for a large family. Since she inherited none of her husband's property, which passed to Andrew from the age of twenty-five, she was forced to start her widowhood by buying from the trustees of the will all the furniture in her house. Andrew and his brothers and sisters inherited £500 a year each but, again, not until reaching the age of twenty-five. On entering Sandhurst Andrew was only seventeen and a half and until the age of twenty-one was dependent on his mother's ability to extract money from the trustees. Between the ages of twenty-one and twenty-five he could make direct application himself, but the trustees had complete power to give or to withhold and they believed that Augustus had expected them to keep a tight control over his children's finances until at last they became twenty-five.

Augustus had died without knowing that Andrew had set his heart on joining the Brigade of Guards. If he were to maintain the standards expected of him and live up to fellow officers who would at least be comfortably off, a shortage of ready money would be peculiarly awkward. As his time at Sandhurst began to draw to a close he realised the keen competition which he must face to achieve his hopes. 'I do not know if I told you,' he wrote home, 'there are three vacancies in the Grenadier Guards and eleven in the Scots.' On the eve of the final examination he wrote: 'Everyone is working hard today: I've been turned out of several rooms by their occupants who are all working. I personally always get muddled if I try and learn up the subject the day preceding the exam.' Although never a natural linguist, he had done well in the colloquial French examination a day or two earlier, and all went well with the final examination. On 2 March 1904 after taking part in the Sovereign's Parade with its moving traditional ceremonial, he was commissioned and posted to the 3rd Battalion Grenadier Guards.

The British Army when Andrew was commissioned and up to the end of 1914 was small and highly professional. With no compulsory service to swell its ranks until 1916, its smallness gave it an entirely different character from that of a Continental conscript army. Its regiments, composed of long-serving soldiers who became known to each other more often than not by nicknames, developed distinct personalities of their own affecting every aspect of its life. Regiments vied with each other in professional and sporting events and in standards of discipline and personal conduct. This was true throughout the Army but especially so in the Brigade of Guards. The Grenadiers were then recruited exclusively from young men reared in the more famous public schools and were expected to afford a style of living considered appropriate to membership of the senior British infantry regiment. Dress, which was costly, had to be correct to the minutest detail if punishment in a 'subaltern's court martial' was to be avoided. An officer must only travel first class on the railway and never be seen laden with parcels or carrying a suitcase. As an officer and a gentleman he was expected by his behaviour to exemplify the English aristocratic habit of never appearing to take anything seriously.

Andrew joined his battalion at Aldershot, the first officer to join after the Boer War, and over the next four years was stationed either in London or Windsor, thus saving him from being cut off from social and intellectual life, the all too frequent lot of young officers stationed in remote places in days when the motor car was still something of a rarity. It was not a very arduous life. In the Brigade of Guards the peacetime regimental training was largely run by the Adjutant and the Regimental Sergeant Major. Officers were on parade when required but had little difficulty in obtaining leave of absence to indulge in various sporting activities, especially hunting, with the active encouragement of their seniors. In the autumn of 1904 Andrew acted as fourth whip with the Drag and on 1 February in the following year the *Household Brigade Magazine* recorded one 'regrettable incident, Thorne coming to grief at the first fence and cutting his eye badly. He, however, sustained no serious injury and was enabled to continue the run.' In itself this was of little importance but is an early instance of an accident-prone Andrew's determination to carry on regardless of pain.

He had an almost obsessive need for exercise, partly to keep his figure in control but mostly to be completely fit so as to do his job as well as possible. Regular games of golf, often against his commanding officer Lord 'Fatty' Cavan, which he was occasionally tactful enough not to win too easily, were supplemented by rowing in the Household Brigade Regatta, which he had helped to organise. Like any good officer he encouraged his men to play games and was an enthusiastic supporter of his battalion's prowess at football. He rode whenever possible and his love of horses took him frequently to race meetings. At the Ascot Meeting in 1906, thanks to some useful advice from an Eton master, he won a sufficiently large sum to finance a two-month holiday at the end of the year. He and his great friend Chico Leatham hired a yacht in Corfu and sailed across to Albania to shoot duck. The reluctance of his father's trustees to advance enough money to allow him to live the life which his regiment expected inevitably left him in debt. They did, however, fully approve his wish to follow Augustus by being admitted in June 1907 to the Worshipful Company of Cordwainers.

This full sporting and social life in no way interfered with Andrew's main purpose of making himself and the men under him first-class professional soldiers. In the early summer of 1905 he was posted to the School of Musketry at Hythe, successfully passing the Advanced Course. During that summer he was Camp Adjutant at Bisley where the National Rifle Association had initiated a course in elementary rifle-shooting for boys from secondary schools which did not possess a uniformed cadet corps – a sign of the need to train young men to repel a possible German invasion. In the same spirit, when he came of age on 20 September 1906 his mother marked the occasion by presenting a boys' club in Lossiemouth with a miniature rifle range and a challenge cup.

Following the Bisley Camp Andrew was promoted to lieutenant in August 1905. For an officer convinced of the necessity for practical training, to be based in a London barracks presented a difficulty. Pirbright was too far away when motor transport did not exist. So he used to take his men for skirmishing exercises in Hyde Park, teaching them to gain what cover was available from trees and bushes before they advanced across open country to the delight of excited children and the alarm of attendant nursemaids. In March 1908 he was appointed Assistant Adjutant 1st Battalion Grenadier Guards (London District).

While still a very young officer he and another officer were sent off by the War Office to East Anglia to report on what local obstacles existed which might hinder a German invasion force. As a wide area of country had to be covered they were each generously provided with a bicycle. Since the best views were obtained from the top of church towers they used first to call on the local vicar to obtain his consent. One vicar was curious enough to inquire why two parties should be sent round Suffolk on the same task with only a brief interval between their visits and why the first party had arrived by motor car while he and his friend were on bicycles. Andrew informed the War Office of this strange duplication of policy. To the chagrin of the War Office it eventually transpired that his predecessors were Germans. This experience marked the start of his reluctant admiration for the superiority of German military Intelligence.

Devotion to his regiment did not lessen his sense of responsibility to his family, especially after his father's death. It was pleasant to give away Mollie at her marriage in June 1905 to Robert Campbell-Preston, even if as he advanced up the aisle in a new frock coat with his sister on his arm he overheard an aunt say: 'They look like a couple of children.' Yet as the eldest son he appears at times to have been surprisingly weighed down with family cares, probably intensified by the barrier of inhibitions which prevented an easy relationship between mother and son. He always found it easier to confide in his old nurse, Addie, to whom he wrote in September 1907: 'It rather upsets me to find I am the brother to four strapping young women . . . I suppose I am getting older though even when I was hardly out of the nursery I felt the whole weight of the world on my shoulders – and when for relief I became childishly young people merely thought or said: Poor fool.' The letter may to some extent explain the period of so-called bad behaviour which had led to his letters of apology but is more likely to have been written at a moment of temporary depression. For in the course of the same letter to Addie he mentioned that he had been staying with the Cornish family of Vivian at Bosahan, their house near Falmouth, and it was through the Vivians that about this time he met Margaret Douglas-Pennant.

4
Margaret: 1886 – 1907

Andrew might occasionally feel weighed down with the cares of a large family but in size and complexity of relationships the Thornes were no match for the Douglas-Pennants.

On 20 June 1800 Frances Douglas, elder daughter of Edward, 2nd Earl of Harewood, and wife of John Douglas, younger son of James, 16th Earl of Morton, gave birth to her third son, Edward Gordon Douglas, the grandfather of Margaret Douglas-Pennant. As a young man Edward had served for a short time with the Guards, but most of his life was divided between the family business and valuable public service. From 1841 to 1866 he was Tory Member of Parliament for Carnarvonshire; he was also commander of the county militia, a justice of the peace and lord lieutenant. His famous herds of shorthorns testified to a genuine interest in farming. In addition he was a first-class fisherman and a keen collector of paintings, especially by Spanish artists.

Edward was twice married. In August 1833 he married Juliana, elder daughter and co-heiress with her sister of George Dawkins Pennant of Penrhyn Castle in North Wales. George had inherited a considerable amount of property from his cousin Richard Pennant, the first and last holder of the Irish barony of Penrhyn and developer of the valuable Bethesda slate quarries near Bangor. As a result he added the name of Pennant to his original surname of Dawkins and later increased the complications of the genealogical tables by marrying as his second wife Edward's first cousin, Elizabeth Bouverie, a marriage fortunately irrelevant to this history. In 1841, through his wife, Edward became the possessor of 26,000 acres of estates around Penrhyn and the slate quarries. Since the estates yielded an annual rent roll of £67,000 and in a good year the Bethesda quarries brought in some £150,000 Edward had become immensely rich. In view of this inheritance Edward followed the example of his father-in-law by adding Pennant to his surname. A year later after having borne him five children Juliana died of consumption at Pisa. In 1846 Edward Douglas-Pennant, as he was now styled, married Lady Maria Louisa Fitzroy, daughter of the 5th Duke of Grafton. He saw no need for a second honeymoon and his bride was transported at once to his Northamptonshire home at Wicken Park to encounter her five stepchildren drawn up in line to receive her. In 1866 in acknowledgement of his great public services Edward was raised to the peerage as Baron Penrhyn of Llandegai – 'to please his daughters' as he maintained.

Edward ruled his estates and the quarries as a benevolent despot, much concerned for the welfare of his tenants and workpeople but refusing at Bethesda to have any truck with new-fangled notions of trade unionism. In 1874 a strike by the quarry men in protest against his paternalist methods was a foretaste of more serious trouble ahead. Advancing years, however, caused him to relax his grip and management passed increasingly into the hands of an elected committee of men who by 1885 had brought the business to the verge of bankruptcy. In the last year of his life Edward virtually surrendered the running of all his affairs to his heir George Sholto Gordon Douglas-Pennant, who in 1886 became the 2nd Baron Penrhyn.

George, who had been born in 1836, was educated at Eton and Christ Church, Oxford. He had wanted to make the Army his career but in deference to his father's wishes devoted himself to the family business interests. He succeeded his father as Member for Carnarvonshire from 1866 to 1868 and 1874 to 1880. His chief outside interest lay in horse racing and hunting. For some years he took over the Grafton Hunt, running it as a private pack and paying all expenses. Neighbours hunted by invitation. A Tory of the old school, he managed his estates with stern justice tempered with generosity. He was a man of great strength of character, scorning popularity, whose courage was severely tested as the unions grew in power.

On his father's death George had repudiated the authority of the workmen's committee and had restored the prosperity of the quarries. However, among a section of the quarrymen there was deep resentment, inflamed by outside agitators, at their exclusion from management. In 1897 when a prolonged strike occurred in the Bethesda quarries George immediately closed them. A debate on his action was held in the House of Commons but George refused to yield or to tolerate any outside interference. The men ultimately capitulated, but three years later a strike which was to last even longer began. Again the quarries were closed. Accused in a newspaper article of cruelty to his workmen, George rode the storm and won £500 damages for libel. Gradually the quarries reopened but only with non-union labour. Throughout the long and bitter struggle he acted with what he believed to be absolute fairness and in the best interests of all employees who had not joined a union. His concern for them was shown in 1907, the year in which he died, when he awarded them a ten percent bonus because bad weather had interrupted their work and caused them hardship.

Like his father George was twice married. In 1860 he married Pamela, daughter of Sir Charles Rushout, owner of Sezincote, the famous house in Gloucestershire built in Indian style, by whom he had one son and six daughters. This annual presentation to her husband of a token of her affection killed Pamela, who died in 1869. Six years later in 1875 he married Gertrude, daughter of the Revd Henry Glynne, rector of Hawarden. By this second marriage two sons and a further six daughters were born. Into this formidably large family Margaret Douglas-Pennant was born on 3 April 1886, her mother's sixth and her father's thirteenth child.

Margaret was born at Wicken Park, near Stony Stratford, and always used to declare that with her mother unwell at the time only two adults attended her baptism in the village church – her nanny and the coachman who had driven them. Doubtless George had become over-familiar with the service. Her entire upbringing would have led a modern psychiatrist to predict more serious effects than the shyness which she never fully conquered. She knew from an early age that she was the plain member of a good-looking family and later was to hear her father declare that it would be quite safe for her to go to Newmarket, though not safe for her sisters, as she would not attract Edward VII's roving eye. It would be hard to imagine a more cruel remark. 'Never mind, Mar. You were the first to be born an Honourable' was her nanny's form of comfort.

In their anxiety to prevent their children from being spoiled by the family wealth George and Gertrude went to absurd lengths. One penny a week was bestowed on each of them in their younger days, out of which they were expected to buy Christmas and birthday presents for each other – a daunting thought in such a large family. The weekly dole could be supplemented by making copies of their father's business letters if handwriting was neat; the younger ones picked up acorns in the park for the pigs until it was realised that they were depriving the poorer tenants who needed the money more. To the same end they were dressed in such plain and serviceable clothes that they were locally known as the 'Charity Children'. When Margaret's half-sister Ina was married she refused to have any of her stepmother's daughters as bridesmaids because they were so poorly dressed. An infuriated Gertrude retaliated by dressing her daughters so beautifully for the wedding that they eclipsed the bride and her attendant train. There was very little love lost between the two halves of the Douglas-Pennant family; the gap between the eldest and the youngest was too great. The younger family bestowed on the older family the collective but inaccurate title of 'The Steps'.

Margaret, like her sisters, received little formal education. As boarding school was never contemplated by her parents, governesses were inevitable. The family moved regularly each year between their three houses: Wicken Park near Stony Stratford was the children's favourite, where they could enjoy the freedom of the countryside with marvellous riding, and Margaret grew up to be an accomplished horsewoman. Penrhyn Castle near Bangor was, not surprisingly, the least favoured. Here on a beautiful site her great-grandfather had replaced an attractive Wyatt house with a gigantic replica of a Norman castle. The great hall was modelled on the nave of Durham Cathedral and the whole building must have been impossible to heat. The children's quarters were well away from sight and sound at the top of the keep – and for major events such as the visit of the Prince and Princess of Wales they were sent right away. The third house was in London. Mortimer House in Halkin Street was occupied by the family for the London Season, and, as some recompense for the loss of Wicken, the horses were brought up from Northampton so that riding could continue in Hyde Park. Christmas was always spent at Penrhyn where Margaret found the wet Welsh climate very depressing. During the time that her father was breaking the strike the castle had to be guarded by the militia, which cannot have made it a more cheerful home. Nor when the whole family foregathered in their father's or their mother's sitting-room were there sufficient chairs, and Margaret early grew accustomed to sitting on the floor. The only break in the routine progress from house to house came with the annual visit to Scotland. Years later Margaret used to tell her own children that she was convinced that each summer she walked from North Wales to Scotland because at every hill all were made to leave the carriages and walk to save the horses.

Margaret like all girls of her class was brought up to draw and paint but apparently music was not included. Her most useful 'accomplishment' in later life was her knowledge of German, as a German governess was in frequent attendance. As she grew up in the security and opulence of Edwardian England she accepted as natural constraints which a modern girl would find stifling – rigid social conventions and the prescribed pattern of the London Season. It probably accounted for the fact that in later life she put great store on manners, dress and civilised behaviour. She greatly disliked anything which she regarded as second-rate. But for the wealthy it was an enjoyable life with its formal dinner parties, its round of country house visits and race meetings.

Life changed suddenly when George Penrhyn died in March 1907, allegedly from setting an example by being vaccinated. He had been obsessed, when making his will, by the need to maintain the Penrhyn estates intact at all costs and he felt it impossible to make generous provision for his widow and his fifteen children. Gertrude found herself in much the same position as Mary Thorne when Augustus died, having no right to continue living in any of the family houses. Immediately on George's death, according to custom, the family, dressed in deepest mourning, toured the Continent for six months before returning to a new life. No. 37 Lennox Gardens was bought as a London home and various houses in Shropshire and Worcestershire were rented in the next few years. The change did not prevent Margaret's country house visits and the name of Mr Andrew Thorne began to appear among her lists of fellow guests.

5

Andrew and Margaret: 1908 – 1914

The exact date of Andrew and Margaret's first meeting is unknown. What is certain is that Andrew at once fell in love with her and only her father's death prevented an earlier proposal. He waited until 29 October 1908, when they were both guests of the Leathams in Gloucestershire, and was accepted.

The news of the engagement came as a total surprise to both families. Mary Thorne wrote to Andrew two days later: 'My son, you have taken my breath away! Am I very blind – very unnoticing?! because I certainly thought you heart-whole last week! but as Father always said "The unexpected most frequently happens."' She went on to regret that Andrew had not confided in her before the proposal, but 'I am not going to spoil what should be one of the happiest days of your life by even a tiny reproach.' A day later, having had second thoughts, she wrote again to remind him that he could not inherit his share of his father's estate, and thus afford to marry, for another two years, which 'is a long time to ask a girl to wait. So much can happen in that time. I've been looking at it as fairly as I can from both sides and I can't help feeling that an *understanding*, leaving both free, would be better than an engagement. You are young, dear. Margaret Pennant, tho' I think younger in years is – being a woman – older than you now. In two years she may prefer an older man, let her be free to do so. You know I liked her [when she stayed with them in Scotland] so that I am thinking of her as well as of you!'

With Andrew totally unknown to the Penrhyn family Margaret received even less encouragement. 'The family took the news quite well but Mother is obdurate and won't hear of anything of the sort for another year . . . She is prepared *not* to hate you.' When they met, Lady Penrhyn liked him and found him 'socially acceptable', but she wished for a man's judgement on his suitability as a son-in-law. So he and Margaret went to stay at Mereworth in Kent with her sister, Kathleen, eldest of the Steps, who had married Viscount Falmouth, then Colonel of the Coldstream Guards. Andrew passed this second test but was told that he was far too young to marry and must wait for another two years. Both mothers did, however, agree reluctantly to permit the formal announcement of the engagement. Even so, Mary Thorne felt compelled to write to Margaret early in 1909: 'Don't think me a horrid old woman if I preach prudence and patience . . . Andrew is fairly level-headed as a rule but a man in love is capable of anything.'

For the first three weeks in December Andrew and a friend were travelling in Germany. His main purpose was to learn the language and he also hoped to study German military progress. This latter aim was declared impossible by the British Military Attaché, but he made progress with the language and found plenty of time to listen to music, especially opera – *Tannhäuser*, *Siegfried* and *Hansel and Gretel* – in Berlin and Dresden. Back in England he began to experience the frustrations of a long engagement, and his military duties seemed to be merely obstacles to his meetings with Margaret. He was in trouble with his Commanding Officer for 'sending the Battalion out wrongly dressed. I could hardly see for temper.' Heavy snow in February 1909 made him more irritable: 'It's perfectly beastly especially as I shall have to go and stand about in *flannels* for 2½ hours during this horrible Bayonet Fighting competition.' His carefully laid plans for meeting Margaret one weekend were prevented by official duties. 'I'm angry with everyone and everything. I'm not going to play golf as I wouldn't be able to play properly I'm in such a temper!'

He was also heavily in debt. A request to his trustees for £400 to meet outstanding bills had met with a chilling response until some friendly pleading by Margaret's half-brother, the new Lord Penrhyn, made them a little more sympathetic. Married life would inevitably increase his expenses and at moments he even considered leaving the Army, believing that civilian life would be less costly. Both he and Margaret found the insistence of Lady Penrhyn on strict chaperonage infuriating. 'Whoever invented all the ridiculous system of chaperonage deserves hanging,' wrote

Margaret. 'It does make me so angry', he replied, 'to think that we should be treated like babies or wild beasts. I do hate being subjected to a thousand and one horrible conventions all because *people might talk*. Heavens, it makes me mad!' There were moments when in the Penrhyn household that he needed to keep a tight control over a naturally quick temper as a young man. 'What aggravated my bad temper was the thought that your people hated me, or, rather, disliked me.' Margaret tried to comfort him: 'They *all* approve of you. But honestly you mustn't be like Sunday afternoon too often as it does give me too fearfully livid blue funk.' She had caught a glimpse of the frightening effect of Andrew's silences when angry.

The irritation of chaperonage did not prevent frequent meetings. They rode together, went to race meetings and played golf. 'Do tell me *why* I can't manage to make the ball go up in the air beautifully like you do . . . but it *does* go much more in the direction that it's meant to now!' It was difficult to be engaged to a man with a natural eye for a ball. They shared to the full his delight in what in Edwardian language he called 'going to the Play' and both loved dancing. He arranged for his dancing shoes to have specially thick soles so that when stationed away from London he could travel back from a dance on the milk train and walk the remaining miles to barracks in time for the morning parade.

A letter from Andrew to Margaret in April 1909 illustrates his formidable energy. 'What I hope to do is to bicycle over to The Chase before lunch on Thursday with my evening clothes tied on somehow like a tourist: I can then stay all day at The Chase – changing there for dinner and then biking back at night to the Barracks. The next day I would ride over, lunch there and go on with you to the races. We could ride round a bit afterwards. Then I would go back to The Chase, leave you there and go back to change at Barracks into my mess clothes – taxi back to The Chase – dine there and go on to the dance. I would then go straight from there to Barracks.' He was taxing his strength to the limit, and twice in his life he would have to learn that his body could not for ever do all that he demanded of it.

Margaret with some reason was constantly worried about his eyesight. 'Mother told me . . . that you were frightened you would be letting yourself in for a blind husband . . . To be truthful my eyes *haven't* improved as Mr Fleming prophesied, but I'd *never never* let you marry me . . . if I was going blind. I'm not quite such a cad as that. As it is I am afraid that you are engaged to an awful crock. I don't know if you have ever heard the whole list – 1½ eyes, a broken nose, 30 shot in various portions of me [following a shooting accident] and parts of my "innards" squashed when I had my horse (5 years ago) on top of me.' The reference to the riding accident was a discreet avoidance of the full truth that he had had to undergo an operation for a crushed testicle. This in no way affected him but gave him an excuse for not indulging in the cruder sexual activities sometimes expected of young Guards officers and which, without in any way being a prig, he found distasteful.

In the meantime negotiations were proceeding between his solicitors and those of the Penrhyns which were to remove the financial barrier to a marriage in 1909. Andrew was to insure his life for £20,000 on marriage until on his twenty-fifth birthday in 1910 he would receive the £40,000 promised from his father's estate. It would be expensive, but as far as his debts were concerned his trustees were slowly becoming more amenable and were paying off some of his bills. A general dislike of long engagements had eventually reconciled both mothers to an earlier marriage than they had originally approved. So on 29 July 1909 Andrew and Margaret were married in the Guards Chapel, Wellington Barracks. Margaret, with a train of eleven bridesmaids, was given away by her half-brother; Andrew's best man was Chico Leatham. Newspapers, which then found space for such things, printed not only the list of guests but details of their presents, which to a modern married couple would appear overwhelming in their number, variety and opulence. Andrew, relieved of immediate financial embarrassment, gave Margaret a diamond tiara and in return was given by her and her family a small yacht.

For nearly fifty-eight years they were to live together, as devoted to each other in old age as on their wedding day. Superficially they were an oddly assorted couple. Her upbringing had not helped her to share his enjoyment of art galleries or concerts. Although they were great companions, he could enjoy visiting a museum or exhibition on his own: she was lost without him. Her innate shyness made her much more dependent on him than he was on her. She had little real interest or understanding of nature but when he was gardening she would want to be beside him; later in his career when he worked late at night on his papers she would be content to remain curled up on the sofa, just being with him. She would never allow the slightest criticism of him within the family circle and she disliked his sisters teasing him. On the other hand she was a very amusing raconteur, with entertaining stories about people and the minor accidents in every married life. While Andrew had a great sense of fun Margaret had the more highly developed sense of humour. Despite, or perhaps because of, great differences between them it was a wonderfully happy partnership – 'Even if Andrew was a Turk I would have married him!'

Originally Andrew had hoped to spend the honeymoon travelling to China on the Trans-Siberian railway but this demanded a longer period of leave than his military duties permitted. Instead he rented a house at Salcombe in Devon where he sailed his yacht with the aid of a hired crew consisting of an allegedly reliable skipper and a boy. On one occasion when a storm suddenly blew up the skipper lost his nerve and begged the boy to lash him to the mast, where he prayed for their safe return. Either his prayers or Andrew's helmsmanship brought them safely to harbour. Margaret was never very happy in a sailing boat but always felt that it was better to be drowned with Andrew than to be left at home to survive him. By contrast her nervousness would not later extend to driving a car or to flying. She enjoyed driving fast and became a better driver than he was. After the war they used frequently to fly over to Le Touquet for a game of golf, sometimes almost on the spur of the moment.

Before returning to routine military duties Andrew went again to Germany to continue his study of the language and also of mathematics. Margaret, accompanied by her lady's maid, travelled with him and thanks to her former German governess she became quite fluent in German, an admirable asset when a quarter of a century later Andrew was posted to Berlin. Back in England early in 1910 they rented 24 South Eaton Place, a convenient base for Andrew who was quartered at Chelsea Barracks. The death of Edward VII in May and the coronation of

George V a year later inevitably added to the ceremonial duties of the Brigade of Guards, and he took his turn as one of the officers on guard at the Lying-in-State of the late King in Westminster Hall. In June 1910 George V inspected the Grenadier Guards in the garden of Buckingham Palace, and Andrew acted as Brigade Major for the royal review of Haldane's recently created Officers Training Corps at Windsor on the day after he had been a member of the winning eight in the Household Brigade regatta.

Of much greater importance for his future career was his determination, once the Coronation ceremonial was safely over, to start working for entry to the Staff College. In this he was joined by his friend 'Fat Boy' Gort, the future Field Marshal and holder of the Victoria Cross. They were still young for selection, but they were ambitious and they arranged for special tutoring. In the event the outbreak of war was to mean the postponement of the realisation of their hopes. However, Andrew was promoted captain on 22 March 1913.

Meanwhile, Andrew and Margaret were living a full and demanding social life. They loved entertaining their friends generously either in London or in the houses which they rented each autumn for two or three months for the shooting. Margaret had had no experience of running a household and at that date it was unthinkable that they should not have an adequate domestic staff. Unfortunately she never acquired Andrew's happy ability to be quickly on friendly terms with those who served him. She had never needed to keep careful accounts of her expenditure and relied heavily on him for help. He had never as a bachelor been a prudent manager of his own affairs, but 'I've just invested in three volumes of a financial classic – *A Primer of Book Keeping* . . . and the man who chose it for me said it wouldn't be above my comprehension.' He soon became a meticulous keeper of the family accounts, but an accurate knowledge of his affairs did not often lead him to adopt a simpler style of living.

In September 1910 Andrew at the age of twenty-five inherited his share of his father's estate, and together with Margaret's personal income they were for a time comfortably off. This was fortunate, for they both had expensive tastes and moved among wealthy friends. It was in 1911 that they rented Guisborough Hall in Yorkshire from September to December, becoming responsible for eighteen indoor servants, nine gardeners and six men to look after the shooting. Presumably the Grenadiers managed without him. Had he not been married in 1909 he might have had to wait for some considerable time as he was due to become Adjutant, which would have postponed marriage and prevented his autumn shoots. Soon after receiving his inheritance he bought his first car, a 15 h.p. Napier, at a cost of £578.12s.6d., exchanged a year later for a more powerful Napier. The Penrhyns had possessed a car almost from the start of motoring and Margaret had vivid memories of frequent stops to replenish the radiator with water from nearby ditches.

In addition to meeting the cost of a very comfortable life-style Andrew and Margaret started a family. On 1 June 1910 their first child, Diana, had been born in London, the choice of her name leading to a protest from her grandparents who deplored a 'pagan name'. Her parents were far more concerned not to saddle their daughter with the sole initials D.T. and she was given the additional name of Mary. On 1 July 1912 twin boys, Andrew and George, were born. Diana's birth had left Margaret seriously unwell and her doctors – a profession whose members she disliked nearly as much as clergymen – after conflicting diagnoses eventually removed her gall bladder and appendix. The operation took place in their new home, Heckfield Place in Hampshire near his mother's home at Highfield, which Andrew had rented in place of their London house at the end of 1912. Since the house had seventeen bedrooms, irrespective of the servant's quarters, there was obviously sufficient space for a room to be turned into a temporary operating theatre. All went well, though for some years she suffered from internal pains and tensions only partially relieved by regular massage.

By August 1913 it became clear that hard work at his profession, his social life and family cares were affecting Andrew's heart. He was ordered to remain in bed for a fortnight, followed by a period of sick leave which enabled him and Margaret to go on a recuperative Mediterranean cruise in October and November. He returned fully recovered, and at the start of 1914 the family moved from Heckfield Place to Farnborough House, Farnborough. This was the official residence of the Commander of the 1st Guards Brigade but was not at the moment wanted by General Maxse, who allowed him to rent it for what turned out to be the duration of the war. It was in this house on 6 August, two days after the British declaration of war on Germany, that their fourth child, Peter Francis, was born. A week later Andrew was in France.

6

The First World War: 1914 – 1916

In the 1920s the light-hearted question 'What did you do in the Great War, Daddy?' became a common saying, popularised in magazine jokes, music hall repartee and family banter. For Andrew the truth would have been that he was three times awarded the DSO and seven times mentioned in despatches. Time and again he was in the thick of the fighting, seeming to bear a charmed life. For two years he commanded a Guards battalion and at the age of thirty-three became one of the youngest brigadier-generals in the British Army. Since all who knew him were unanimous that modesty was his outstanding quality, he would have evaded such a parade of his achievements. In later life he spoke comparatively little about what came to be re-christened the First World War. When he did recall some of the experiences he used to insist that it was not the horrors of trench warfare that had left the deepest impression: it was the wonderful spirit of comradeship born of shared danger that remained uppermost in his mind.

In the remarkable correspondence with Margaret, which she fortunately preserved, we can gain an insight into his most intimate hopes and fears, as well as learning as much of his activities as the censor would permit. It is sad but inevitable that in a life of constant movement he could not preserve her letters to him. Unless in the heat of battle he wrote to her every day, occasionally twice a day: even in the midst of fierce fighting he usually managed to send home an official printed postcard which told her that at least he was still alive. In the story of the war years which follows, unless otherwise stated, everything in quotation marks has been taken direct from his vivid and often amusing letters.

AUGUST 1914 – AUGUST 1915

On Wednesday 12 August 1914 Andrew said goodbye to Margaret and to his young family. Leaving Farnborough Park at

11.00 p.m. he walked to Farnborough station where he joined Brigade Headquarters as Staff Captain of the 1st Guards Brigade. He saw his two horses, Punch and Judy, safely entrained before finding a seat for himself. The train reached Southampton in the early hours of 13 August, and the waiting Channel steamer entered Le Havre after a smooth but hot and crowded passage. Disembarkation began next day, during which the troops were soaked by a heavy thunderstorm, at first mistaken for the echoes of a naval battle in the Channel. On 15 August, after another drenching during the march to Le Havre station, they clambered into the trains waiting to take them towards Amiens, unaware that as late as 5 August no final decision had been taken by the British Cabinet as to where the British Expeditionary Force was actually to go once it had landed on French soil. After prolonged debate the BEF was ordered to go to Maubeuge and there to take up positions on the left of the French.

The BEF of about 100,000 men was, in the words of the official history of the war, 'incomparably the best trained, best organised and best equipped British army which ever went forth to war'. While this was undoubtedly true so long as the war was a war of movement, the BEF was totally unequipped to meet the new kind of trench warfare which developed towards the end of the year and which military planners, both British and German, had not foreseen. The first phase of the war, however, was highly mobile. The German Schlieffen plan of an attack through Belgium and a wheel to the east with a final assault on Paris was the traditional war of movement which was defeated by equally mobile Allied armies. The trouble came when neither side could advance.

Materials for siege and trench warfare were at first non-existent. There were only two machine guns for each battalion. The entire British Army only possessed a mere eighty motor vehicles, with the result that all guns and supplies had to be drawn by horses and all messages carried by officers on horseback, as Andrew was quickly to discover. Unlike the Navy, the Army possessed no wireless equipment, and no field telephones were at first available. In command of this army was Sir John French, a man whose mood varied alarmingly from unjustified exuberance to deep depression and near loss of nerve.

Throughout the night of 15 August and all next day Andrew

travelled in an overcrowded railway carriage from Le Havre to Le Nouvion, near Étreux. 'At every station where we stop the inhabitants pursue us with fruit, flowers, wine, cigars etc.' By 20 August the British were in position and were ordered by Sir John French to advance into Belgium alongside his French ally. Three days later two British divisions faced six German divisions at Mons and beat off their attack. So miraculous did this engagement seem that the British success was popularly attributed to divine intervention in the form of the Angels of Mons, whose numbers were variously reported as two or even a complete platoon. It was, in fact, the good training, equipment and discipline of the BEF which largely caused the failure of the German plan for a quick knock-out blow. French had intended to hold his position, but Joffre, the French Commander-in-Chief, decided to withdraw, forcing the British to comply, and the long retreat from Mons began. On 26 August the British turned to face the Germans at Le Cateau, checking the enemy's advance at this point: 'We were all very frightened and excited yesterday when we came under shell and rifle fire. It was most unpleasant for your excellent husband, who is by nature a coward though he tries to hide it.' Apart from this first experience of enemy fire, he admitted to being exhausted with excessive marching and riding long distances with messages from headquarters. The retreat continued behind the River Marne, which the Germans crossed on 5 September. Next day the Allied counter-attack began. The Battle of the Marne (5–10 September), one of the decisive battles in history, ended German hopes of destroying the French army before the Russians advanced on the Eastern Front. By 14 September the Germans had been driven back behind the River Aisne. 'I regret to say I have worn the same underclothes, boots and everything now for over a week. I have sometimes managed to air them for half an hour while we wash and shave but otherwise they have remained on day and night.' However unwashed, BEF officers jubilantly predicted an end to the war by Christmas, a prediction which was suddenly proved false.

The Germans were ordered to halt their retreat and to hold the line of the Aisne. It was at this moment that, almost accidentally, a new truth about modern warfare was discovered: men in trenches, armed with machine guns, could beat off all but the most overwhelming attacks. As both sides dug themselves in, the war ceased to be one of movement. Fortunately for morale nobody could realise that the rival lines of trenches, stretching before the year was out from Switzerland to the Channel coast, would not vary in position by more than thirty miles for the next four years. Trench warfare, the characteristic form of fighting on the Western Front, had begun.

During the fierce fighting on the Aisne Andrew's headquarters were in a cave, familiarly known to its inmates as the 'Old Funk Hole'. 'At night we go and sit in the mouth of the cave and keep ourselves warm by our kitchen fire. We have straw on the ground. Our dining table is an old door with heaps of stones for legs.' Of the actual fighting he could tell Margaret little save that he had had 'a very hard and anxious week'. He had been made a censor and so had to be additionally circumspect, though he could assure her that he was reasonably comfortable and well fed. 'The most curious thing is that the best place to obtain farm produce is a village exactly half way between ourselves and the Germans. Our patrols and theirs go in at various hours and come away with milk and a chicken or two . . . The only bother is when the patrols meet and then both have to go away empty handed.'

The position of the BEF on the Aisne, wedged between two French armies and some distance from their Channel ports supply lines, led Sir John French to persuade Joffre that if the British moved north into Flanders they would be in a more effective position to outflank the enemy. As late as 12 October Andrew was still in the Old Funk Hole, which 'smells strongly of the disinfectants we threw about yesterday. It effectually stopped my hay fever which was something good.' Three days later he was on the move. During the advance into Flanders 'I had been reported (unofficially) as killed and a vivid description had been given of my decease as well.' By 22 October he had clearly arrived in Flanders 'where English, French and German are useless'.

Antwerp fell to the Germans on 10 October and two days later British and German forces met in headlong collision, with the Germans intending to outflank the British and capture the Channel ports and the British determined to retain their lifeline with England by outflanking the Germans. What became officially known as the first Battle of Ypres was fought from 12

October until 11 November, the first battle to be fought on a narrow front with each side pouring in reserves to replace appalling casualties for little or no territorial gain.

With woefully insufficient forces – fourteen Allied divisions against twenty German divisions – the British after some initial success were forced on the defensive as 80,000 fresh troops were hurled against them. On 29 October the Germans, with their Emperor present, began a supreme attempt to break through to the coast, following an intense bombardment in which the British trenches were mercilessly smashed. The fiercest fighting, in which the 1st Guards Brigade bore the brunt, took place around the village of Gheluvelt, some four miles south-east of Ypres. For three days the battle raged at its height, the most dangerous moment for the British being between two and three o'clock in the afternoon of 31 October. After superhuman feats of endurance the line of the Guards was broken and a great German victory seemed inevitable. It was at this moment that Brigadier-General Charles FitzClarence, commander of the 1st Guards Brigade, on his own initiative sent an urgent order to the 2nd Battalion The Worcestershire Regiment to fill the gap and recapture Gheluvelt. The staff captain whose highly dangerous task it was not only to carry the message to the Worcesters but also, having delivered the order, to guide them to the position where they could best help the Scots Guards, was Andrew. His horse, Judy, was shot under him, not 'just as I had got off her', as he purposely minimised his danger in his letter to Margaret. 'Then I had a spent bullet on to my cap. It didn't even make a hole in the cap but it has given me a niceish bump on the head.' FitzClarence's initiative and the courage of the Worcesters saved the day.

The Germans had failed to break through to the coast but the battle continued for another eleven days. 'We are having a hell of a time of it now . . . The strain is continuous, every hour of day and night.' The 1st Guards Brigade had suffered heavily. 'Whatever losses we suffered the poor Germans had more than double as many – it was a horrible slaughter.' A day or two later he referred casually to a 'very exciting run between two lines of Germans about 400 yards apart . . . But you needn't worry about my looking for glory. I'm not that sort. I find doing my duty is quite as much as I want; volunteering for more trouble is not likely to be my besetting sin in the future; it hasn't in the past.' Doing his duty was as dangerous and exhausting as any man could imagine. The fighting was 'twice as strenuous as the Battle of the Aisne'. 'I am a dirty creature at the moment. I haven't been to sleep or washed the last 48 hours and to top it all I fell last night just before the night attack into a very filthy farm pond and got properly soaked to the waist. I am practically dry now but very offensive and uncomfortable.' By 11 November the crisis was over, and though spasmodic fighting continued until the 16th both sides were utterly exhausted. 'The mud round our house is perfectly horrible and in the trenches it is simply like a brine bath only perhaps a little thicker. The men do all their sleeping standing up.' In the Flanders mud neither British nor Germans could move. The Channel ports had been saved at an Allied cost of 50,000 casualties. The British regular army had been shattered, leaving only a framework for the new mass armies which would be raised. As Andrew wrote: 'What are left of us are all very well.'

One fact about the fighting around Gheluvelt he only learned twenty years later. Among the German troops in the List Regiment was a *Meldegänger*, a runner who carried messages between company and regimental headquarters. He was not actually in the trenches, but, as Andrew would have agreed, it was a dangerous enough task, for which the young corporal in December 1914 was awarded the Iron Cross, Second Class. The corporal's name was Adolf Hitler.

As a keen professional soldier, Andrew could not help admiring the courage and skill of the enemy. 'I must say the German officer is most splendidly brave and he gets his men on with him somehow (as often with threats as not) but when he [the officer] becomes a casualty the old German infantry man doesn't like it a bit and generally runs.' Accurate shelling of key points behind the British lines increased his admiration for German Intelligence which 'is really magnificent. It must have been organised for years with consummate skill.' Telling Margaret of how British wounded were rescued by Germans he added: 'The more one goes into the stories of German barbarities the less one is inclined to believe them. I have a sneaking regard for the

Germans, I must confess, and certainly admiration for their staff work which has been superb.'

Andrew would have been less than human had he not secretly nursed the hope that his service since landing in France and especially at Gheluvelt might receive some form of recognition. 'I was very naughty yesterday [in his previous letter] when I grumbled I was not "mentioned". I ought to be so thankful to be alive, it was only wicked pride. I had been so bucked when Maxse sent my name in as I had hoped it would go through and then if anything happened and I didn't come back the Bratties need not know what an arrant funk I was.' Further representations on his behalf were made by Colonel Corkran. 'He has on 4 occasions to my knowledge behaved with the greatest coolness and gallantry under heavy fire.'

The DSO, which he had richly earned, eluded him in the 1915 New Year's Honours. 'I am still wishing that I had something tangible for you and the Bratties, to show I was not always a useless cove.' It was not inconsistent with his innate modesty to be aware of his own military achievements, and the admission of his private hopes was only made in letters to Margaret, never to fellow officers. However, he had not long to wait for the first of his seven 'Mentions'. On 14 January 1915 Sir John French praised Captain A. F. A. N. Thorne of the Grenadier Guards for 'gallant and distinguished services in the Field'.

After the fighting around Ypres Andrew was delighted to get a brief ninety-six hours leave at home towards the end of November. He fully understood the strain under which Margaret laboured throughout the war. Both of them faced the possibility, almost the probability, that he would be killed. 'If love could effect it I know I will come back to you. But at present it seems so impossible when one considers the others who have come out and are no more. It will almost be a reproach to have survived the war.' 'You must never forget that whatever happens to me it will always be for the best . . . our bodies may die but if love lives on then all is unchanged. That is what is meant by God is Love.' It was harder for her, who would be left behind, to face such a future with his Christian serenity. In addition to this nagging fear, she had four young children to bring up, a large house to manage and responsibility for Andrew's finances. Remembering the great difficulties which both his mother and mother-in-law had experienced when first widowed, he had arranged for Margaret to have control of his affairs while he was away. She was only twenty-eight years old, shy and unaccustomed to personal responsibility. She had never lived without servants, who became harder to obtain as the war continued.

Early in the war Margaret and her family had gone to live at Highfield Park with her mother-in-law. It quickly proved an unwise decision, and as relations between them became more and more strained she returned to Farnborough Park. Andrew understood the problem and approved the return. A very revealing letter throws a clear light on his feelings for his mother and by contrast the passionate love which he and Margaret felt for each other. 'I am sorry you find Mother hard to get at. You know I think it is because she was cheated out of the love we have lived in and has never really been alive, or if she was, something has made her cover herself up and keep herself for Father's memory and doesn't dare let anyone else in. She and Father could never have had the same feelings of absolute union, the disparity in years must have prevented it. The most wonderful affection which is the best they could have attained to doesn't come within a patch of what we have enjoyed of love . . . it is only when the union is spiritual, mental and *animal* that real love exists . . . Please go on trying to be more than mere friends with Mother. I honestly think she is shy of showing her feelings. You see I have never shown mine really to her and I think she is just a bit jealous that you should have succeeded so quickly where all maternal love had previously failed.'

The combination of strains on Margaret probably accounted for her constant references in her letters to being unwell, which so worried him when away from her and about which he could do nothing but sympathise. Only once in his letters does he feel that worries about servants were of trivial importance compared with the far greater difficulties which Margaret faced. 'Even though there is no one there [Farnborough Hall] to meet you the end of the world is not at hand. You should see how the women out here are putting up with a very different sort of life – plenty of hardship and discomfort.'

Back in France after his tantalisingly short leave Andrew was clearly cheerful and relaxed. 'I am beginning to get more sleep at night or rather I don't have so many bad dreams of attacks etc.' He passed on to Margaret the more repeatable salacious jokes which he heard in the mess, and even the boredom of censoring had its lighter moments when letters became capable of misinterpretation through total absence of punctuation: 'God bless you and save you from your loving husband.' Comforts for the Brigade poured in from home and he feared 'that some of the worse characters will be selling these good clothes for half a glass of brandy . . . it has happened in one or two places.' As Christmas approached he felt sad at having no personal presents to send home to his children. 'Some people are sending home German trophies, helmets, swords etc; personally I would rather not unless you particularly want them. I do not care to strip even the dead of their things and certainly not as presents for home.' On Christmas Eve he wrote: 'I hope to be able to attend Holy Communion on Christmas Day but if I can't I know you will have taken me with you into God's presence.'

Towards the end of January 1915 fighting began again in Flanders despite unrelenting rain over Christmas which, if possible, made the mud worse. 'It took four hours for one man to be dug out the other day.' Andrew had hopes of a longer spell of leave in January but on 26 January 'the poor old Brigade took rather a knock yesterday and our casualties were unfortunately very heavy' and immediate leave seemed unlikely. However, he unexpectedly was granted a few days at home before on 12 February becoming DAA & QMG of the 1st Division, a post which he held throughout French's disastrous spring offensives until August. He felt qualms of conscience at being relatively safe 'but considering I have been at it for six months on end I almost think I am entitled to get away from shells and bullets just for a little at any rate'. Nevertheless, it was often a dangerous and always a very arduous post as he was responsible for the supply of food, ammunition, stores and water. He was also charged with preventing waste. 'The men are always so appallingly stupid and inconsiderate. They will cheerfully wash in the only supply of drinking water.' His task was made more pleasant by the arrival of the Prince of Wales to assist him. The Prince, himself a Grenadier and angry that his position kept him from active fighting, became a close friend, a friendship which lasted until the Abdication in December 1936.

On 10 March French launched an assault at Neuve Chapelle. In a three-day battle the German line was pierced, but closed before British reserves could arrive to exploit the success. Two months later, from 21 April until 25 May, the Germans began what became known as the Second Battle of Ypres, an engagement in which they first used poison gas, an example followed by the Allies. On 9 May an Anglo-French attack began at Festubert which achieved little, but which Sir John French explained away by complaining of an insufficient supply of shells.

The heavy casualties at Neuve Chapelle, which had been a purely British effort, moved Andrew to offer to return to his regiment, but he was ordered to remain where he was. Margaret's brother, Henry, had been killed and buried near Neuve Chapelle and Andrew knew how anxious she must be as she read accounts of the fighting in the newspapers. 'You can't possibly know when I am in danger or not and there must be heaps of times when you are suffering at home and I am here probably out of danger, riding on Punchie or basking in the sun.' . . . 'If it is meant that I should die I should much rather do it out here feeling I was doing it for my best Beloved and her Bratties than being killed off in some rotten taxi cab smash or something in London.'

In July 1915 Kitchener, as Secretary of State for War, decided that the battalions of the Grenadier Guards and the Irish Guards and the Welsh Guards still stationed in England were to be sent to France to join the Guards battalions already in France to form a new Guards Division. Rumours of this impending change had caused misgivings which Andrew shared, feeling that the Guards in their traditional formations had proved their worth. However, the appointment of Lord Cavan as the first Divisional Commander removed many doubts, and Andrew was very anxious to obtain a worthwhile post in the new organisation, rightly believing that there were not many with his experience of administrative work on active service. As the days passed and no appointment for him was announced he grew increasingly despondent. 'I have now very nearly completed twelve months active service and I am the only staff officer who has earned no promotion, no award and only had one rise in appointment. From its military aspect it is not encouraging, lamentable I call it; but on the other hand I am very thankful to be alive when most of my contemporaries have gone west. I fear I am a very unpopular creature with the Brigade of Guards.' He wrote this on 9 August. Six days later he learned unofficially that he was to be DAQMG Guards Division and on 17 August he was ordered to take up the appointment next day with the Prince of Wales as his assistant. This post Andrew held until March 1916.

AUGUST 1915 – DECEMBER 1916

In the first Battle of Ypres the BEF had fought heroically, but the heavy casualties meant that it had virtually fought itself out of existence. Kitchener set about the task of raising seventy divisions to replace the BEF and in the first week the famous poster with the pointing finger brought 175,000 recruits. By the time that conscription was introduced in March 1916 some 2½ million volunteers had enlisted. Despite all their courage and enthusiasm the new divisions could not arrive in France as fully trained as men of the BEF had been. Even the newly formed Guards Division made Andrew's work 'particularly exacting as I have to start a show with raw material, half of which won't roll up until they are absolutely necessary'.

Sir John French entered on the autumn offensive of 1915 with misgivings. After Neuve Chapelle and Festubert he had neither sufficient men nor munitions for a successful attack. With some reluctance he bowed to his ally's arguments that a combined attack would relieve pressure on the Russians and might regain the valuable coal mining district around Lens. The result was the Battle of Loos, which, after a preliminary four-days' bombardment, raged from 25 September to 13 October. In the first day's fighting the British troops were wholly unsuccessful, with the result that the Guards Division, intended to be kept in reserve until becoming the spearhead of a victorious advance, had to be employed in recapturing important points, such as Hill 70. It was in the assault on Hill 70 that Andrew's brother, Tommie, was killed on 28 September.

At Mulgrave and Eton Tommie had been the golden lad who excelled at games, winning every conceivable athletics prize and

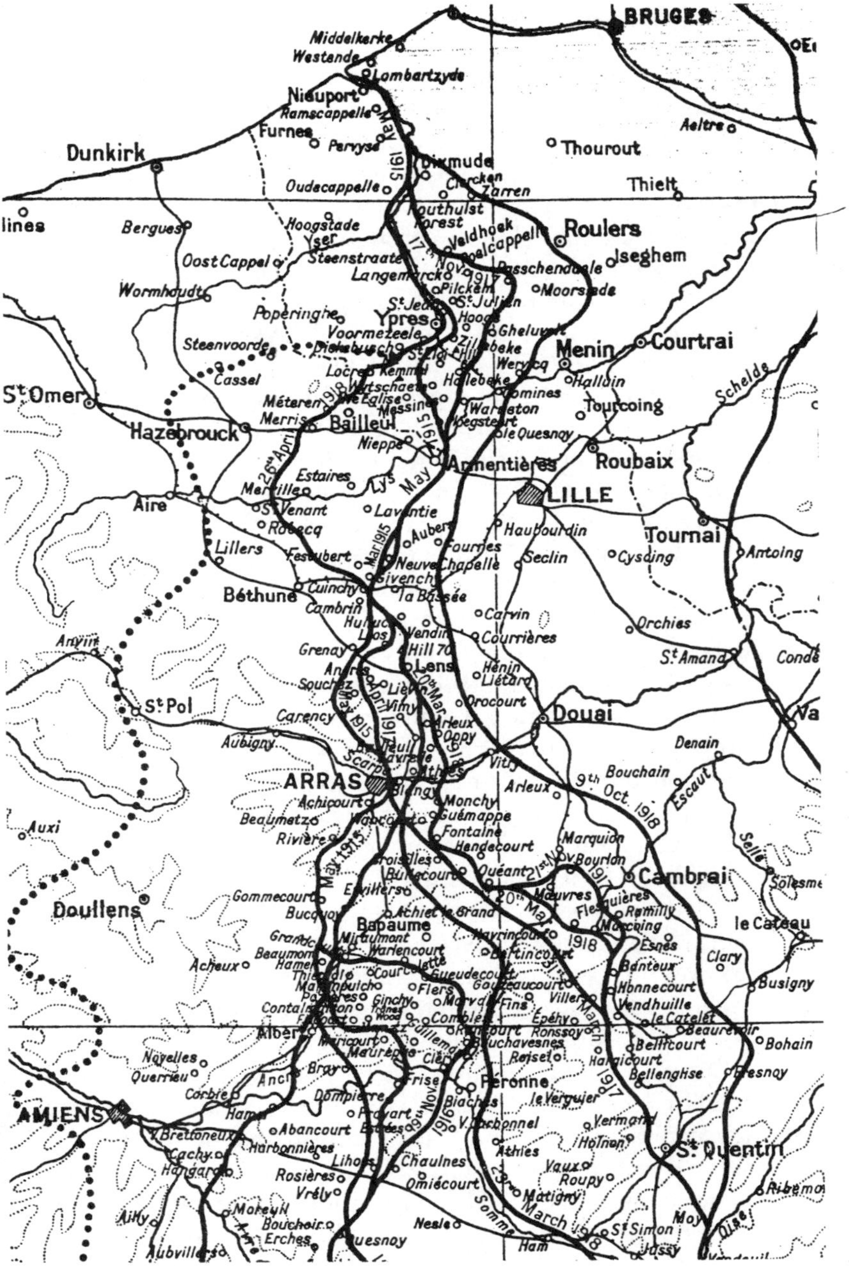

BRUGES
Middelkerke
Westende
Lombartzyde
Nieuport
Ramscappelle
Furnes
Pervyse
Dunkirk
Dixmude
Thourout
Aeltre
Thielt
Oudecappelle
Zarren
Bergues
Hoogstade
Yser
Houthulst Forest
Roulers
Oost Cappel
Steenstraate
Poelcappelle
Veldhoek
Passchendaele
Iseghem
Langemarck
Wormhoudt
Pilckem
St Julien
Moorslede
Poperinghe
Ypres
Hooge
Voormezeele
Gheluvelt
Steenvoorde
Dickebusch
Zillebeke
Menin
Courtrai
Wervicq
Halluin
Cassel
Locre
Kemmel
Hollebeke
Comines
St Omer
Méteren
Messines
Warneton
Tourcoing
Schelde
Merris
Bailleul
Ploegsteert
le Quesnoy
Hazebrouck
Nieppe
Armentières
Roubaix
26th April 1918
May 1915
Estaires
Lys
LILLE
Merville
Aire
St Venant
Laventie
Robecq
Aubers
Haubourdin
Tournai
Lillers
Festubert
Fournes
Neuve Chapelle
Seclin
Cysoing
Antoing
Mar 1915
Béthune
Cuinchy
Givenchy
La Bassée
Cambrin
Carvin
Orchies
Anvin
Grenay
Courrières
Hill 70
Lens
Hénin Liétard
St Amand
Condé
Souchez
Liévin
Vimy
Drocourt
St Pol
Carency
Douai
Arleux
Oppy
Aubigny
Denain
Scarpe
Vitry
ARRAS
Bouchain
Achicourt
Monchy
9th Oct. 1918
Beaumetz
Guémappe
Escaut
Auxi
Rivière
Fontaine
Hendecourt
Marquion
Selle
Bourlon
Cambrai
Quéant
Solesmes
Gommecourt
Mœuvres
Flesquières
Doullens
Bucquoy
Achiet le Grand
Ramilly
Marcoing
Bapaume
Havrincourt
le Cateau
Miraumont
Warlencourt
Bertincourt
Esnes
Beaumont Hamel
Clary
Acheux
Gueudecourt
Banteux
Flers
Gouzeaucourt
Honnecourt
Busigny
Villers
Vendhuille
Contalmaison
Ginchy
Combles
Fins
Épéhy
le Catelet
Albert
Ronssoy
Beaurevoir
Bouchavesnes
Bellicourt
Bohain
Novelles
Querrieu
Maurepas
Hargicourt
Ancre
Bray
Frise
Bellenglise
Fresnoy
Corbie
Dompierre
Péronne
AMIENS
Hamel
Biaches
le Verguier
Proyart
Vermand
Abancourt
Harbonnières
Athies
Holnon
St Quentin
Cachy
Lihons
Chaulnes
Hangard
Rosières
Vaux
Roupy
Vrély
Omiécourt
Matigny
Ribemont
Somme
Moreuil
Ailly
Bouchoir
Nesle
March 1918
St Simon
Moy
Oise
Erches
Quesnoy
Ham
Jussy
Aubvillers

straining his heart in the process. From Eton he had gone to Christ Church, Oxford, where he had a large circle of friends, male and female, of not all of whom his brother approved. He had hoped after a few years in the Army to enter politics but he got caught up in the war. In the first months there were signs that he had overstrained himself in trying to emulate the remorseless energies of his brother, and Andrew feared that Tommie was having a breakdown. He was certainly not proving a success as Adjutant to the 4th Battalion, and his Commanding Officer, Colonel Gilbert Hamilton, had spoken to Andrew of his dissatisfaction. 'He complains Thomas is always resting or goes to bed early when he (Gilbert) would like him to be getting the Ensigns to play rounders or ragging about. It looks very much as if Thomas has taken on too much of a job.'

Not until 2 October was Tommie officially posted 'missing – believed killed'. 'The strain of not knowing is so much worse than the definite knowledge he is dead.' Gradually Andrew learned what had happened. Colonel Hamilton having been gassed, the command passed to Major Myles Ponsonby. During the last part of the advance Ponsonby was badly wounded and Tommie remained with him although only twenty-five yards from the Germans and himself wounded in the head. Seeing how serious was Ponsonby's condition Tommie gave him morphine tablets and supported him in his arms until he died early next morning. Tommie hoped to get back to his lines after dark, but on the way he came across two young drummer boys who had been acting as orderlies. One was dead, the other was wounded in the leg. Knowing that if he left the boy he would be killed, he put him on his shoulders and began to carry him back. At this moment the Germans put up a flare and seeing Tommie opened fire. Both he and the drummer were killed.

'It was a very fine performance . . . I am ever so proud of him . . . As the Corporal [whom Andrew had interviewed] says, old "Tatters" could certainly have got away without the wounded drummer.' In a later letter Andrew repeated his hatred of the deep black mourning then considered obligatory for widows and near relations. 'It is wrong in every way. If anything should be changed in one's clothing it should be for the scarlet of the Resurrection.' The telegram officially announcing Tommie's death was delivered at Farnborough Park to Margaret, who for one terrible moment must have thought that Andrew was also dead.

Andrew was fortunately too busy during the Battle of Loos to indulge in useless grief, though he felt the loss of his brother keenly. 'That the big attack wasn't a gigantic success was simply because two Divisional Q Staffs failed to get food up to the men. And as I am responsible for food, ammunition and bombs I've plenty to think about . . . Unfortunately I am also responsible for supplying horses, transport and all routine returns have to go through me.' One consolation came to him at this sad time. Two days after Tommie's death he was promoted to the rank of major. He also found the burden of work eased by having the Prince of Wales as his assistant. He 'is such a good fellow but extraordinarily young in every way but a most determined creature when he had made up his mind'.

Fortunately for the Prince, he shared Andrew's ceaseless need for violent exercise. Together they had long rides in the course of duty, and when much of the day had been spent at a desk they went for walks and runs. Exercise was also essential to offset the effects of living in the Divisional Mess. 'Salmon and grouse have descended in clouds on us.' Next day four-a-side football or 'a six mile run with the P. of W. to see the 2nd Brigade' was imperative. A fortnight before Christmas Andrew with the Prince and a friend were like a trio of preparatory schoolboys enjoying a midnight feast in the dormitory. 'I don't think I ever confessed to the "sock" we had four nights ago. P. of W., Davidson and I were munching a midnight biscuit and drinking mere Vichy; when suddenly we discovered the glass of preserved strawberries. With a flash of inspiration the P of W dashed onto the verandah where the cream was standing and before we knew anything more we had poured the strawberries and cream into wine glasses and we had most splendid strawberry messes. Weren't we pigs!'

The Battle of Loos destroyed whatever little belief Kitchener still had in French's abilities as Commander-in-Chief, and he was in constant communication with Haig behind French's back. Haig, who replaced French at the end of 1915, was a far more stable character than French, unperturbed by the strains of command. He had been a brilliant staff officer, a master of railway timetables, and now was completely confident that he could win the war, though he never actually divulged how this would be achieved. Another casualty in high places at this time was Winston Churchill, made the scapegoat for the Dardanelles failure. Demoted from the Admiralty to what he termed a 'post of well-paid inactivity' as Chancellor of the Duchy of Lancaster and excluded from the War Council in Asquith's Coalition Government, he decided in November to resign and join the Army as commander of an infantry battalion. This had been promised him by French, but Haig refused to implement the promise until Churchill had displayed under fire the necessary qualities and character. Churchill readily agreed to this testing and he arrived at Guards Divisional Headquarters on 20 November.

It fell to Andrew's lot to conduct Churchill to the front line north of Neuve Chapelle and introduce him to Colonel Jeffreys in command of the 2nd Battalion Grenadier Guards. Before setting out Churchill bluntly asked why a young and fit major was doing an administrative job which could equally well be done by a man too old for active service. Andrew protested that the post needed a fit man and that he had already had a good share of being shot at. Churchill was unconvinced but his attention was diverted elsewhere.

'The reception of "Winnie" by the 2nd Battalion was very cool but Cuthbert Headlam is quite convinced that by ten days time they will be swearing by him.' 'I never asked to have you,' was Jeffreys's greeting. He 'has got Winston stone cold. They took over the trenches about 6.0 p.m. and walked him about the line until 1.0 a.m. They then went to bed, pulled out again about 7.0 a.m. and walked till 9.0 a.m. when Winston was too tired even to eat his breakfast. It will do him no harm as he is looking very bloated.' Three days later 'Winston is already laying down the law about the trenches and will shortly be commanding the 2nd Battalion if only he can oust Jeffreys!' However, Headlam's prophesy was correct and Winston won the battalion's respect before returning to Headquarters where Andrew 'spent two hours instructing Winston in the theory and practice of supplies. I think I must have been very clear in my instructions as he went away saying he thought it such a very simple affair.'

It had been decided to withdraw all Indian troops from service in France during the winter months; therefore, shortly before Churchill's visit the Guards Division had taken over the northern part of the section allotted to XI Corps with Headquarters at La Gorgue, a short distance north-west of Neuve Chapelle. For men in the trenches the Ypres Salient was the most unpleasant and often the most dangerous part of the British Line. The countryside was completely waterlogged and the Germans, occupying higher and drier ground, dominated the British on three sides. Prolonged serious fighting was unlikely: the British often waist-deep in water could not easily advance, while the Germans would have been foolish to abandon their positions of vantage for the Flanders mud.

For Andrew life at Headquarters was strenuous and responsible but comparatively safe and comfortable. There were moments when he felt uneasy about the privileged life which he was enjoying but 'they won't let me go back [to a Battalion] as 2nd in Command as I am supposed to be more valuable here.' A week before Christmas there had been a big dinner party in the mess. 'When the Generals left about 11.30 p.m. we carried on into wild rags until about 12.30 a.m. I then came home in the P of W's car with a skinned elbow and various bruises; none at all serious. I really thoroughly enjoyed it all and feel much younger for it.' 1916 began well for him. On 15 January when the New Year's Honours were published he learned that he had been awarded the DSO, with which he was decorated by the King at an investiture during leave in April.

Constantly immersed in his duties and always anxious for the welfare of a deeply loved wife and their four children – 'it is simply so splendid how independent and self-reliant you are becoming' – Andrew found it difficult to sympathise with his mother's moods. 'I know how very trying she can be . . . unreasonable is not the word.' In fairness to Mary Thorne it must be remembered that she had lost her younger son, her elder son was in frequent danger, and her two Messervy nephews, Gerald and Ernest, familiarly known as Gub and as Boy or Kummel, were both on the Western Front. Gerald was a Gunner and Ernest with Andrew's help had transferred from the Army to the Royal Flying Corps in which he was an observer.

Nor had Andrew much time for the various troubles of his many sisters-in-law. He believed with some justification that his Penrhyn in-laws had not as yet greatly taken to him, an opinion which he reciprocated. 'It is really rather a good thing that your family should be so keen about the new cure [which rejoiced in the name of "the fruitarian doctor"]. It is splendid that they can raise any enthusiasm at all – it is their "negativeness" which is their worst crime.'

In mid February the Guards Division joined Cavan's XIX Corps and moved into Flanders north of Ypres, with headquarters in 'a damp and deserted Château' near Wormhout. As the Guards were not at first needed in the front line the opportunity was taken to send each brigade in turn into camp in Calais for training and recreation. On 21 February the Prince of Wales wrote to Andrew describing life in camp; it also shows the close friendship between the two men.

My dear Bulgy,

I thought you might like to hear how we are getting on. It is ripping to get back to a Br[igade] again . . . But it is a chilly life this, tents in February and when it isn't blowing a whole gale it rains!! . . There's no ground for training but a small common so that we can only practise bombing and then we route march!! But we are free by 3.00 always and Calais isn't such a bad town and we go in to dinner! . . . Then it's grand to be on sand instead of mud and this would be a heavenly life in Summer; but it isn't Summer and we know it . . . It's too bloody cold at night but I suppose it's healthy and hardens one! . . . I wish you could have been here; we could have had lots of exercise and there is a long canal and deserted roads to run on!! And the sea air would do you good!!

Yours ever, E.

New responsibilities now fell on Andrew. At the end of February he learned that he was to be second-in-command of the 1st Battalion, an appointment confirmed on 17 March. 'The Staff is being so much changed that I don't really mind leaving it, particularly now that the P of W has gone . . . Having run, walked and lived with him since August last I should feel his absence quite a lot.' He had only one regret: he did not greatly like or respect his Commanding Officer, Colonel St Leger Glyn, an opinion irreverently shared by the Prince of Wales in a letter to Andrew written on 20 April from the Canal Zone in Egypt.

> I hear you have got back to the 1st Battalion all right but I fear you have got a pretty bloody C.O. but perhaps I shouldn't say this!! . . . Poor you. I do feel so sorry for you as I fear you are having absolute hell in that bloody Salient. It's too splendid of you to be going back to a bn. [battalion] when it's not in the least necessary, for you know what a fight you had!! You'll forgive me for saying this, won't you? But I *do* mean every word. All the news you gave me was most interesting but made me feel a worse shit and shirker than before, having a fat, comfortable and pleasant time out here!!

Andrew's immediate reaction to his new post was characteristic: 'I do hope I won't let anyone down by my ignorance or funk. I feel just like a small boy at the prospect of going to his private school after having indulged in a tutor.' Before leaving Divisional headquarters he made his Communion at Talbot House, the famous Toc H at Poperinghe. The Guards Division went into Ypres Salient early in March, the 1st Battalion reaching Ypres on 16 March. It was a peculiarly grim assignment with constant casualties and no compensating gain of territory. The normal procedure was for a battalion to be in trenches for two days and to be withdrawn for two days' rest. After very heavy fighting the battalion retired to billets for a longer period of rest and training. Early in May the 1st Battalion came under heavy fire. 'At night my toilette consists in taking off my coat and putting a woolly on instead. My legs I put into [empty] sandbags (to keep the blankets clean) and so to sleep . . . It is only in Reserve that I can get into pyjamas.'

On 12 May Andrew temporarily took over command while Glyn was on leave. 'I hope I will do it properly and not botch the show.' Although the most modest of men he knew that he had the ability to command. 'I do wish Leger would stay away. I honestly think that I am no worse than he. Still, I must be loyal and learn all I can from his mistakes.' A week later the battalion moved out of the line and was in billets for much of the next month, giving an opportunity for greatly needed training when so many men were newcomers, sent to replace casualties. Battalion sports were organised and 'I managed to win the officer's race fairly easily. They all accused me of making the race 150 yards instead of 120 yards so that I could tire them all out. After the Sports were over we had wrestling on each other's shoulders . . . Dude and I defeated Copper and R. Lambert and threw them into a large cow pat.'

During June and July Andrew had several spells of trench warfare. 'Crawling about in wet breeches is poor sport . . . It is almost impossible to realise the number of rats and mice that abound in these parts . . . They are becoming very bold and treat me with very little respect. The trench cats (who are practically wild) have no end of a good time hunting them.' He gained a reputation for remaining unmoved when rats ran across his body when he was lying down: he believed it right to reserve his energies for things which really mattered. To his great joy Major Mark Maitland on 9 July took over command from Colonel Glyn. It was an important change, as the summer offensive on the Somme had begun on 1 July.

Haig had hoped to attack in the north, which would help his communications, but he was ordered to accept Joffre's directions for a combined Anglo-French offensive, not least to ensure that the British bore a full share of the fighting. In the event they bore the brunt of the battle, as ever since February the French were desperately holding Verdun against the German assault and it was hoped that an attack north of Verdun might draw off German troops.

The point chosen for the attack was on the River Somme, strategically useless but chosen as the area where the British and French armies linked up on the Allied line. On 1 July thirteen British divisions attacked in waves. On that day alone 19,000 were killed and 38,000 other casualties sustained. Despite the total failure of the initial attack Haig maintained his offensive until 16 November. It is true that the Germans retreated for some miles after the British had inflicted enormous damage on them, but the strongly fortified Hindenburg Line awaited them. For the loss of 400,000 men the British had gained only a sea of mud.

The Guards Division remained in the Ypres Salient until 27 July when they moved south 'without regret', reaching the Somme battle area early in September. 'We are going to have Battalion leap-frog to get the stiffness out of the men. The last few days marching after so much standing in the trenches have left them all very stiff and weary, but the leap-frog should put them all right.' . . . 'We are just on the eve of the Great Adventure . . . I am not cast to play a very distinguished rôle. I have been attached to the Brigade Headquarters to be used as the Brigadier thinks fit – until I am required to replace a casualty . . . if anything should happen to me and I don't come home I just want you to remember what I have said so often before and that is that we will not really be parted. We have belonged to one another too much for that.' . . . 'In the event, we have been very lucky and got off comparatively cheaply. The Battalion are very well and cheerful but like the officers very tired.'

On 18 September Andrew's great chance came. He received a telegram appointing him Commanding Officer of the 3rd Battalion Grenadier Guards. 'I am too excited and proud to realise for the moment how "much" I shall have to be fit for its responsibilities. I do pray that I may not let the Battalion down.' He reached his Command headquarters next day and 'am feeling very strange as everyone now calls me Sir the whole time'. A day later, 20 September, was his thirty-first birthday. 'As it was my birthday and as we are shortly going up again to try a throw with the Boche I went to H.C. at 7.30 a.m. I am now walking about today with the badges of rank as a Lieut.-Colonel.' The day before his Battalion went into action 'I had a route march of 6 miles. It sounded a monstrous thing for a Sunday afternoon but I wanted to give myself the pleasure of seeing what a splendid command I have. I always think that a Battalion on the march gives one a better feel than anything else I know of.' They were in the thick of the fighting for ten days and although 'the Division are very pleased with themselves it is appalling the number of one's friends that have been killed or wounded.' In later years his devoted servant Guardsman Arthur Bines, recalling the Somme and subsequent desperate fighting, used to confess: 'I was always scared stiff when shelling started, except for when I was in touching distance of the Colonel.' To Bines Andrew appeared to bear a charmed life: he undoubtedly possessed the infectious courage which helped all around him to conquer their fears as he had conquered his.

As the Battle of the Somme slowly came to a halt Andrew told

Margaret that 'I really don't feel I should go on leave when I have just got the Battalion'. However, he was able to spend forty-eight hours at the Ritz Hotel in Paris, where with a special pass, Margaret was able to join him. Perhaps some of his officers and men at Christmas time wished that their CO had taken prolonged leave. On Christmas Eve 'I have had great fun today making specimen trenches – only officers and NCOs working. A lot of them will be very stiff tomorrow I'm afraid. It will otherwise do them no end of good.' Next day 'I am off to see the Companies but not to wish them a merry Christmas, one hasn't the heart to do it out here.'

7
The First World War: 1917 – 1918

1917

Kitchener's army perished on the Somme: with it perished the idealism and excitement which had inspired the volunteers. The two remaining years of war were marked with a bitterness of spirit and a grim determination to hang on till victory, but with fading hopes that victory would bring to birth a brave new world which would justify the appalling loss of life. In contemporary literature this change of feeling is the theme of C. E. Montague's novel *Disenchantment* and is expressed even more passionately by the later war poets. A world of difference lay between the work of Rupert Brooke, Julian Grenfell or Laurence Binyon's 'For the Fallen', and Wilfred Owen's 'Anthem for Doomed Youth' or Siegfried Sassoon's poem 'Attack', with its agonised cry 'O Jesus, make it stop!'. For the British people 1917 was the year of greatest strain. There seemed no hope of a decisive breakthrough on the Western Front; on 31 January the Germans announced the start of unrestricted submarine warfare, leading to severe food rationing which undermined the will to resist, a will deeply shaken by the lengthening casualty lists; the March Revolution in Russia was the beginning of the end of Russian participation in the war, removing from Germany the danger of having to fight the war on two fronts.

For the moment Andrew did not share the general depression. He unashamedly enjoyed the responsibility of command and he spent much time ensuring the highest standard of fitness and efficiency. Christmas dinners, postponed until Twelfth Night because of a spell in the trenches, were to be followed by 'a nice steady route march on 8 January to settle us all down again'. He never doubted that the courage and steadfastness of the Guards in battle stemmed from the hours spent in drill on the parade ground and from regular periods of military training. However, the U-boat warfare altered his opinion of the Germans as a race. He never lost his respect for the fighting qualities of the German soldier but 'if anything else was necessary to complete one's dislike of the Boche the sinking of the hospital ship [the *Asturias*] . . . will certainly not fail to do so . . . They are *proper* swine as a nation.' Just before the delayed Christmas celebrations he privately told Margaret of his disappointment that his work had not been recognised. All the names which he had sent in had received their 'Mentions' and it was galling to 'have now been left behind by everyone of my own standing. I'm the only one that has not got either two decorations or a decoration and a brevet.' This was a letter written at a time of some anxiety for Margaret, who was awaiting the imminent birth of her fifth child. Fortunately he was granted a well-earned month's leave from 15 January, and he hurried home to Farnborough Park, where on 17 January Margaret Helen, always known as Poppy, was born.

During 1917 Andrew and his battalion were strenuously involved in three separate offensives. At the start of the year he was fighting on the River Ancre, steadily pressing the enemy back and confirming Ludendorff's decision to withdraw all his troops behind the Hindenburg Line. On 16 March he was in command of the whole of the centre of the line. 'This phase of the war is very interesting . . . After 31 months of continuous active service with a Division I do not have quite the same idea or illusions about war, but I must confess that I have been wildly excited with the business of war these last three days.' For the next two and a half months he was hard at work supervising training for the summer offensive and directing and often taking part in the heavy tasks of making roads, truck loading and laying the foundations for a railway. He hardly needed Major-General Fielding's April reminder that it was an established custom in the Guards for 'officers to take their coats off and work with their men'. 'It is the greatest fun training . . . I am just off to do a bit of digging at the back of our huts to make a place for wrestling.' Early in May his passion for exercise suddenly took its toll.

While playing football he had received a severe hack on the leg which was not only very painful but caused the leg to stiffen. An X-ray on 11 May revealed a bruised and choked vein. The doctors fearing a thrombosis moved him to hospital. 'I am so annoyed that I have spoiled my record for never having gone sick during the war, and now to come in here because of a hack got in a football match is more than I can stand.' It quickly became clear that a week in hospital would not effect a cure and he began to dread being sent to a base hospital and losing his command. His letters reflect his alternating hopes and anxieties. The good news was that 'Boy' [Ernest Messervy] had won his 'wings' and that Lord Cavan had been greatly impressed by the march discipline of Andrew's battalion. He worried at the news that 'very shortly doctors will become so short in England that they will be unable to go round their patients but that the latter will have to attend at some central point like an old-fashioned show booth of the travelling quack'. Foreknowledge of the National Health Service would have delayed his recovery. He was far more depressed by the failure of his name to appear in the latest list of 'Mentions'. 'It is, I suppose, that my services are being rated at their value now. Still, it does begin to make me feel a little less confident in my own prowess.'

There was at least a chance to read, and he got through a large number of light novels as well as books by Kipling, Wells, de Maupassant and Anatole France. In his rather depressed state he might have been wise not to dip into partially understood books by Havelock Ellis. He must have completely lost his sense of proportion when he wondered whether some eye trouble which Diana had experienced 'has anything to do with some hereditary taint of syphilis'. His most serious reading had begun before going into hospital when, with the help of his much admired Chaplain, the Revd F. W. Head – inevitably known to the Guards as 'Tail' –he had tackled William Temple's great philosophical treatise *Mens Creatrix*. Poor Margaret, never a bookish person, who was at the time dutifully wading through some work on Commonwealth problems, was advised 'in small but thorough doses' to try to understand the product of Temple's giant intellect. Even Andrew with 'Tail's' help had had to admit to finding the work 'testing'. 'Reading *Mens Creatrix* . . . has made me realise how ill-developed mentally I am.'

Although back from hospital by 24 May he could only command the battalion from the Orderly Room and it was clear that as yet his leg could not stand the strain of training, let alone of battle. However, he was cheered by the award on 30 May of the Croix de Chevalier of the Legion of Honour. Even better news came from a personal visit by Major-General Fielding on 6 June, who promised Andrew that if he were back in France within three months he would not lose command of his battalion. The news came at the right moment. A slight thrombosis had developed and prolonged treatment was needed. To Margaret's delight he was returned to England for this and for subsequent convalescence. On 13 July he was back with his battalion in time to take a full part in Haig's summer offensive. He was to retain his command until August 1918.

A week later Boy was shot down and killed. Not until early September did news from Germany confirm that a largely unrecognisable body was that of Boy. 'I shall miss his most cheery presence. He would have been such a jolly sort of uncle for the Brats.'

For the Allies their spring and summer offensives were costly failures. Nivelle, who had replaced Joffre, evolved a plan which he claimed would achieve final victory, to which Haig was ordered to conform. The British were to attack near Arras on 19 April, and a week later the main French thrust would follow in Champagne. The Arras attack, in which the Guards Division took no part, led to the capture by Canadian troops of the long-wanted Vimy Ridge but was unduly prolonged in view of what was happening to the French. Nivelle's offensive was a total disaster and after the terrible losses during the defence of Verdun in the previous year confidence in their leaders evaporated. Some French regiments openly mutinied and refused to advance; others came near to mutiny. Nivelle was dismissed and Pétain was given the task of restoring order. In this he slowly succeeded, but for much of the rest of the year the French army was convalescent and the brunt of the 1917 fighting fell on the British.

Nivelle's failure allowed Haig to pursue his own plan for winning the war by another Flanders offensive – preferably before the Americans, who had entered the war on 6 April, could arrive in sufficient numbers to share the credit. The British were to break out of the Ypres Salient, advance to the Belgian coast and then turn eastwards to roll up the entire German line. There was only one difficulty: Haig was uncertain how his troops would actually break out of the Salient. The battle would have to take place in an area, much of it below sea level, which the preliminary bombardment must turn into an impossible morass. Lloyd George only assented with the greatest reluctance.

On 31 July the Third Battle of Ypres – better known by the horror of its final stages as Passchendaele – began. Everything went wrong. The bombardment destroyed the Flanders drainage system, and in Haig's determination to reach Passchendaele at all costs men fought waist deep in the mud, the guns sank and tanks were useless. Not for four months was failure admitted. When the attack was finally called off four miles of territory had been gained with the loss of 324,000 British casualties compared with 202,000 of the enemy. The loss of officers was even more serious – three British to every one German. At no point of the battle did Haig visit the battlefield. When the battle ended a highly placed officer from General Headquarters, who had been an important adviser to Haig, arrived on his first visit to the battle front. As his car approached the swamp-like edges of the battle area he broke down and burst into tears, exclaiming 'Good God, did we really send men to fight in that?' His guide replied that the ground was far worse ahead.

On 21 July Andrew's battalion had taken over the line near Boesinghe. The immediate obstacle to the British advance was the Yser Canal. Beyond it lay open country across which ran the Ypres to Staden railway line, passing farmhouses and outbuildings, each likely to have been converted into a strongly defended pillbox. During preliminary training a dummy representation of the Canal and of the German trenches had been elaborately constructed so that as far as possible each man knew what was expected of him. About a week before the offensive was due to be launched Major-General Fielding learned that in the daytime the German trenches were only thinly manned – to avoid casualties from shells. He decided to send forward strong patrols from the Coldstream to cross the Canal in broad daylight with no preliminary warning bombardment. This audacious scheme succeeded and a foothold was established on the far side.

On 30 July Andrew moved his battalion up to the Canal and at 5 a.m. next day they started to cross. Despite the success of the early crossing it was a difficult and dangerous operation to get large numbers of men across. Hastily constructed lines of old petrol cans had to serve as a bridge, and he gave his officers some latitude in deciding where to cross. To his surprise the battalion reached the far side without any casualties. From then on as they stormed their way up the railway line it was a very different story. 'I have been frequently frightened since this morning,' he managed to scrawl on a postcard late that day. Rifle fire was useless against the concrete of pillboxes and each strong point had to be attacked with bombs. By the capture of the Pilcken Ridge, which enabled him to reach the River Steenbeck, some two miles of territory had been won but at heavy cost. Throughout the day Andrew had been in the thick of battle controlling his share of the operation. Years later, in 1941, a friend wrote to him: 'I shall always remember you at Passchendaele on July 31st when we went over to visit a unit on our flank, a very dispirited unit, beat to the world. You were a wonderful inspiration to those poor tired troops. I shall never forget the effect of your visit. You will always live in my memory as the finest leader of troops in battle that the Brigade of Guards produced in the last war.'

Torrential rain added to the general misery and delayed the next attack until 16 August. In the area on the left of the battle where Andrew operated the attack was again successful but on the strategically important right flank little was achieved on the Menin road. Haig's refusal to accept the overall failure of his offensive led to further attempts to advance in late September and October. On 7 October the 3rd Battalion took part in the crossing of the River Broenbeck and the very stiff fighting which followed. In the whole canvas of the Passchendaele struggle the battalion's achievement under Andrew's leadership stands out as very remarkable. Thereafter for the last ten days of the month and the first week in November the battalion was in good billets at Moule. For them the Battle of Passchendaele was over, but equally severe fighting lay ahead before the year was out.

On 10 November the battalion began a long march south. The reason for the move was strictly secret and some of the wilder spirits suggested that they were off to Italy to avenge the Caporetto disaster. After a fortnight's hard marching they reached Ribecourt, some six miles south-west of Cambrai, and took up their positions on the edge of Bourlon Wood facing the village of Fontaine-Nôtre Dame. Four days earlier on 20 November 381 tanks rolled forward in the half light of early morning followed by a comparatively small body of infantry. There had been no preliminary warning bombardment, and complete surprise was achieved. The tragedy of the Battle of Cambrai was that Haig's insistence on prolonging the Passchendaele battle prevented the arrival of sufficient reinforcements to exploit the success of the tanks. On the positive side it had become clear that in the tank the Allies had the key to victory.

For the moment the Germans were able to mount a formidable counter-offensive which the 3rd Battalion had to try to stem. It was only on reaching Ribecourt that Andrew learned that his task was to be part of the Cambrai offensive which his General – Major-General Fielding – had strongly opposed. His orders were to attack Fontaine-Nôtre Dame on 27 November.

The capture and temporary holding of the village was one of the great tests of Andrew's leadership and of his battalions's courage. The weather was bitterly cold with snow and sleet, but the greater part of the village was captured. At this point ammunition and bombs were in dangerously short supply, but Andrew encouraged his men to stand firm and await the expected reinforcements. Some help came from tanks, but they could do little within the village where so many undamaged houses held snipers and effectively concealed the enemy's movements. Andrew tried to hold the village from three centres of resistance, but with enemy numbers increasing and no reinforcements for his men the situation became desperate. In the end there was no alternative to fighting their way back to the original line. Their gallantry had been wasted by the failure of the higher command to give wholehearted support to the Cambrai offensive. For the first four days of December the exhausted battalion, who 'did most magnificently', were in trenches at Gauche Wood without coats or blankets in icy weather until relieved. The 1917 offensives were over. Only in one letter, written on 16 July, had Andrew included a criticism of Haig. 'Best of all news is that about Sir D.H. Perhaps he is to be retired for good in September from C in C! Anyhow I pray that it is so.' There is no hint in the letter why the rumour had arisen. It seems possible that the failure of the Passchendaele offensive to reach the Flanders coast quickly had caused general disillusionment and lack of belief in Haig's leadership.

As Margaret's letters to Andrew have not survived it is only possible to guess at their content from his replies. She was never physically strong like him and undoubtedly suffered from having to bear her ailments alone. The strain of the continuing dread of hearing that he was dead was sufficient to make her occasionally neurotic about her health. Moreover he was unwittingly a very demanding husband. Almost every one of his letters contained a request for some item of clothing or equipment, and Margaret was given minute instructions and measurements to be passed to tailors and outfitters. He would ask her for a new pistol, a strong pair of wire cutters, an electric torch, a pocket size copy of Shakespeare's plays and 'a really good khaki waterproof to keep the wet out and the warmth in'. She also sent him regular food parcels, which he and the mess greatly appreciated, but after experiencing the discomforts of 1917 food rationing when on leave he began to feel guilty and asked her to cut down the amount sent to him and to cancel his standing orders for Devonshire cream, sausages and butter.

Margaret was also expected to keep meticulous accounts and to watch the household expenditure all the time. 'I feel that in course of time you may have to reduce the household at Farnborough Park or else undertake work as a substitution – say as a clerk in the HQ office under General Ellis at Aldershot on Saturdays and Sundays.' She had become an enthusiastic motorist and it must have been a little depressing to be told that 'you should only use petrol as a treat or when it is convenient or necessary to motor . . . What you save in petrol etc. during the months ought to go into War Loan in the Bratties' names.' There was an austere, almost a Scottish puritan, streak in Andrew's make-up. He saw considerable virtue in the enforced austerity the U-boat successes were imposing on British life. 'How very wonderful England will be after the War . . . If they [the Germans] had given in to our terms last January [1917] they would not have made us ration ourselves or submit ourselves to any self-restraint or discipline.'

'After the War . . .' Andrew's letters frequently refer to plans for the future. At moments they are only day dreams to forget the horrors around him. Thoughts of renting an island off Scotland took his mind off the mud and the rats. 'We would rough it and go without a retinue of servants. We would spend our time working at natural history, flowers, birds, geology, everything like that.' It is not difficult to guess at Margaret's reply to such a suggestion. Of far greater interest is Andrew's uncertainty about remaining in the Army. 'Unless all our companies go phut we ought to be able to live comfortably after the War but we shall have to take up something useful like farming or gardening for profit.' There had at one time even been a suggestion that he might like to become a Member of Parliament. Margaret wanted soon to find a permanent home, but Andrew was unwilling to buy a house until his future was settled and he knew where it would be most convenient to live. He was certain that he would sell Dornhurst, the Sevenoaks house in which he was born, and when the time was ripe three other properties which he had inherited from his father. Despite his words of caution about their financial position, his ideas about the right kind of home were scarcely modest. In her search for a possible house Margaret was not to consider any property which did not have a large garden, surrounding fields and stables. At one moment he had an even grander idea. An architect should design a large house for themselves and the children with a separate house for the servants but also containing bedrooms for relatives and friends who came to stay. He saw the need to make domestic service more attractive than it had been in pre-war days, and women servants would only be required to wear overalls over their ordinary clothes. He pictured a happy community in which master and mistress would be as concerned with their servants' welfare as he was in the welfare of the men of his battalion and their families.

1918

On New Year's Day Andrew learned from Routine Orders that he had been awarded a bar to his DSO, news which came as a much-needed tonic, for there were increasing signs that he was tired out. Although there was no large-scale operation on either side for the first two months of the year, fighting continued all along the line in bitterly cold weather. It was difficult not to fall in the frozen trenches and he was 'bruised and chipped all over'. Inevitable encounters with barbed wire had a devastating effect on his uniform. 'My breeches are completely indecent as my drawers appear as I walk along.' He badly needed a complete month's leave, and although this was promised it did not come until February, as in mid-January he temporarily took over command of the brigade. His tiredness was partly due to the cumulative effects of nearly four years in France and partly to anxiety about his career prospects. What he wanted more than mentions in despatches was a brevet, enabling him to remain at least a lieutenant-colonel and not having later to revert to the rank of major. He confessed to Margaret to having bouts of depression when he wondered if his belief in himself as a dedicated and highly professional soldier was an illusion. Four weeks at home were a great help, and he returned to his battalion on 17 March, four days before the opening of what proved to be Ludendorff's final offensive.

For much of the next three or four months Andrew was either directing his battalion in battle or organising the next withdrawal. It was deeply disheartening during the long retreat to give up territory which had been won at great cost. 'It is very sad to see how the Bosche has managed to push right through the Allied line at the Aisne. It is all through the country that we retired and advanced through.' . . . 'Very soon we'll be back in England because the Bosche won't let us stay here at all . . . I would rather return for more honourable and more pleasant causes.' . . . 'It is appalling when I think of the number of officers and other ranks who have been through the Battalion since I took command. Still it would probably have been the same even if I had not been commanding. It might even have been worse!' In the heat of battle, as ever, he appeared imperturbable. After Andrew's death Sir John Aird wrote of him: 'Bulgy and I first met in the early hours of a March morning in 1918 when the Germans had broken through . . . I had been sent up to him with some Machine Guns which, as usual, I had sited in the wrong direction. While he was putting this right he kept on admiring the Huns whom we could by this time see, saying, "What good soldiers they are trying to get round our right flank." This thanks to the way Bulgy commanded us they never did; but I well remember thinking "I wish this man would think more about us and less about the soldiering ability of the enemy."'

On 7 April Andrew had received his fifth 'Mention', though he did not hear the news until the end of the month. He was naturally pleased but 'I do wish I could have got a Brevet. I regret so much having allowed myself so much longing for it!' Fortunately there was no time for idle regrets. He was again temporarily in command of the brigade from 21 to 24 April, and in June he learned that he was second in line for a permanent command and 'likely to get it soon' – a slightly over-optimistic forecast. In spells of so-called relaxation out of the trenches he did everything possible to make his battalion ready for the next bout of fighting. Early in July he enjoyed himself 'quite enormously. I drilled or rather tried to drill the Battalion for about ninety minutes. They worked awfully well and it was a real treat. It is wonderful to get 800 men in a fairly confined space to work as one man for an individual.' He worked himself even harder. On one day 'I had an excellent forty minutes physical and bayonet fighting from 6.30 until 7.10 . . . I dug between 3.40 and 4.30 p.m. and from 5.30 to 7.30 p.m.'

'I am sure that this Battalion is in need of fresh blood . . . The absurd thing is that I am and look in the best of health. It's only my head that is fed up and stale! It was never my strongest member!' His most depressed letter was written on 17 July, the day before the start of Foch's counter-offensive. 'I am afraid that I am always doing the wrong things and only take precautions when boldness should be the policy. Evidently other people think the same, otherwise I should have been promoted some time ago. All through my "career" I have come to a stage when I suddenly cease to be considered any good and everyone else goes by me. It has happened at Mulgrave, Eton, Sandhurst and in peace time in the Regiment and now the same fate has overtaken me on active service. I suppose it is that I am not quite all out!' There is not a shred of evidence to justify this comment on his 'career' and it is not a picture of the man which his brother officers and men under him would have recognised. He was simply and solely exhausted; but fierce fighting between 21 and 23 August had to be undergone before any relief could come.

The August fighting was part of the Allied counter-attack which was to lead to victory. The 3rd Battalion attacked on 21 August in thick fog, making it almost impossible for companies to keep in touch and to locate their objectives. To advance on a compass bearing necessitated the removal of steel helmet and respirator and even then the compass was not entirely reliable. So thick was the fog early in the battle that Andrew's battalion headquarters were charged by the Scots Guards in the belief that they were attacking a German machine-gun post. To keep control of his part of the attack was Andrew's greatest difficulty, but on the second day of the battle a German counter-offensive was brilliantly driven off under his direction. 'I have seldom been so desperately dirty or sweaty as I have been since 5.00 a.m. yesterday. The higher authorities seem pleased with our efforts which is gratifying,' he scrawled in a pencilled note to Margaret. And next day: 'I have now three days' growth on my chin and there seems little chance of removing it for the present . . . I have sweated beyond all possibilities or conception. All ranks have done most wonderfully and I am damned proud of them.'

The day before the battle started Andrew learned that he was shortly to leave the battalion to command the IX Corps School and that his second-in-command, Viscount Lascelles, would succeed him. In his autobiography, *Old Men Forget*, Duff Cooper, then a second lieutenant, drew an interesting comparison between Thorne and Lascelles as commanding officers. Referring to Thorne's departure on 1 September he wrote: 'I used to want this but, like so many things one wants, as soon as it happens one regrets having wanted it. He (Thorne) was a man who had no thoughts except for soldiering and the energy which he displayed and expected was very tiresome in our hours of ease. But he had the great quality of a commander, the power of inspiring confidence. Everyone felt safe when he was there or at least certain that the best would be done for them . . . Lascelles is far more human . . . but one feels that on the day of battle he would be of less help. It is the difference between the professional and the amateur.'

When the time came to leave the battalion Andrew felt the parting acutely. Having made his Communion 'to return thanks for the victory on the 21st, 22nd and 23rd', he wrote 'I am thankful I did not miss those three days. I feel now that I can go away from the Battalion with less shame . . . I have never enjoyed battle fighting so much . . . It was a glorious finish to two years of command.'

Andrew's period as Commandant of the IX Corps School was not intended to be more than a way of giving him a brief rest before his next posting. He did not much enjoy his six weeks at the school, feeling relegated to the position of an onlooker as the Allied advance continued. 'The wonderful comforts of my room [in a luxurious château] and the absence of shellfire etc. do not make up for all I have lost in the Battalion. The Instructors seem very nice but they are all here because they have been badly wounded or are not properly fitted for work in a Battalion. The NCOs are the same. Think of my feelings as a fighting soldier!' Furthermore, for one who appreciated good food and drink the change from a Guards battalion mess to his new mess was an unpleasant come-down. 'Everyone here is so very poor that it is difficult to do much except to try to improve the cooking.'

On 1 October Major-General Mathieson announced that Andrew had been awarded a second bar to his DSO. Swearing her to secrecy – the award was not gazetted until 2 December – he proudly told Margaret that this latest honour 'is as far as I know the first double in the Regiment and in the Brigade of Guards'. Yet proper pride still did not remove the hankering after a brevet. 'I am so sorry that you wish to insist on my staying in the Army . . . it is *à cause de* my determination to leave that I was put in for a Bar instead of a Brevet.' As Commandant he had been permitted to retain his temporary rank of lieutenant-colonel: he wondered how long this would last. The answer came a fortnight later. On 14 October he learned that in three days' time he was to command the 184th Infantry Brigade with the temporary rank of brigadier-general. He was just a month over his thirty-third birthday. 'I do hope I won't be a dreadful failure.' He held the post until March 1919.

Although he did not hear the news for ten days, Gerald Messervy of the Royal Field Artillery, who had won the MC in September 1917, had been killed on 9 October, his twenty-eighth birthday. General Peel, a former commander of 'Gub's' Brigade, told Andrew that Gub had been a first-rate battery commander, who should have been promoted earlier. Of the four younger members of the Thorne-Messervy family only Andrew was still alive. He was very worried about the effect of this latest loss on his mother, though she later came to recognise that 'if three had to go it was best for Andrew to be the one to come back to Margaret and the children.'

The war had only a month to run when Andrew assumed command; it was a moment when his brigade was in need of the energy and drive which he could supply in good measure. Although he had not been given command of a Guards brigade he was well pleased with his officers and men. 'The material in the shape of the men is very good and makes one long to command them as a Battalion Commander instead of as a Brigadier General. One cannot get at them except through their COs and I feel I could run their show so much better than they could!' During the last few days of October and on 1 and 2 November he was once again in the thick of the fighting. 'I am a bit sleepy, damp and dirty but the Brigade has had another good show and has once more been congratulated by the Corps and Divisional Commanders.'

On 4 November Andrew wrote: 'I have started slight thrombosis in my left forearm.' Phlebitis was diagnosed and three weeks' complete rest was ordered. It was cruel ill luck to succumb with victory in sight and when prolonged rest might threaten his command of the brigade. He hoped that strict obedience to his doctor would ensure a speedy cure. 'I am *ordered* port twice daily at least and as much food as I can manage as he [doctor] thinks I am run down. You can imagine how suitable I consider his treatment to be!' As the war drew to its close he could modestly tell Margaret that 'I was given a brigade when my name was still a long way down the list of prospective Brigadier Generals . . . At any rate I finished up the war by commanding the 184 Brigade and having two good little battles on my own.' He could also gleefully pass on to her the story of a convalescent fellow officer whose wife was able to visit him in his private room and who was persuaded that it was quite safe to join her husband in bed. In the midst of their reunion there was a gentle knock on the door. Framed in the doorway was an awesome figure in toque, long overcoat and leaning on an umbrella. Queen Mary gasped in horror and beat a hasty retreat.

At 11 a.m. on 11 November Andrew wrote at some length to Margaret a letter which merits full quotation.

> I am trusting that at this very moment some very high dignitaries are signing a very valuable document which will put us on the road to peace. I don't mean physically as I am lying very contentedly in bed but I mean mentally. I have concentrated all my available faculties on the war and it now seems to me that I have got to get an entirely new orientation. I know perfectly well that I shall be here on service for months yet and there is always the possibility that we might have to go and restore order in Russia or the Balkans; but at the conclusion of that period there are quite different conditions to be faced. As a pre-war professional soldier I don't expect that I shall be allowed to leave until demobilization of the civilian population is completed but after that to what am I to aim? One prays and feels that there will be no more war in our generation. Well, if that is really so I cannot imagine that I shall be able to continue training soldiers year by year for a war which I do not believe will materialise in my generation. Personally I don't feel that I could compete in the Army on those terms considering my age. If I had more service and was more than forty I doubt if I should be so keen on trying my hand at some other employment. As it is I am only just 33 and I feel that I am still sufficiently adaptable to pick up new ideas and habits.

For a day or two everything seemed strange until he realised he was no longer hearing the guns. 'However far one is behind the line one could always feel if not hear the reverberations. Now it is quite still!'

Like everyone else Andrew always longed for the war to end quickly, but he believed that it would be wrong to end it before Germany had been totally defeated, whatever the cost; otherwise 'Sandy, Gork and Peter will all be doing the same as I am in another twenty years or so.'

8

Uncertain Future: 1918 – 1921

The six months following the Armistice of November 1918 was a time of great difficulty and often of unhappiness for both Andrew and Margaret. Both were in a sense temporary war casualties. Although Andrew had miraculously emerged unscathed from the war, over four years of great responsibilities and constant danger had left him in a state of nervous exhaustion, aggravated by phlebitis in his arm and the consequent likelihood of losing command of his brigade. To have been a general on very active service at the age of thirty-three was bound to have taken its toll. For Margaret the care of five children and all the problems and frustrations of civilian life in wartime, the loss of her two brothers and of what were virtually three brothers-in-law, so closely knit were the Messervys with the Thornes, and the seeming impossibility that Andrew would survive is sufficient excuse for minor personal misunderstandings between them. When the war ended she was only thirty-two and, thanks to her upbringing, she had none of the self-reliance of a modern woman of that age. At rare moments Andrew, seriously unwell himself, could not adequately sympathise with her ailments, telling her that she was taking too many pills. Would it not be better to have them 'all lumped together and just have one tonic instead of this multitude which must be having a hell of a battle inside you?' He did, however, fully realise that they were both suffering from a reaction from the strain of the war years. How far she was comforted by being sent by him a book on war neuroses can easily be guessed.

It was his own uncertain future which most seriously worried Andrew. Phlebitis entailed a long and slow cure, and not until Christmas was he transported by ambulance to Brigade Headquarters where, under strict medical supervision, he was allowed to return to duty. He managed to visit all units over Christmas and he particularly enjoyed a dinner with the Ox and Bucks, though forbidden to 'rag'. 'It is a great deprivation as I do love a good rag when one throws other people about and in turn gets thrown by them!' A month's leave early in 1919 was marred by the return of the phlebitis with the inevitable loss of his command and the cruel return to the rank of major on 3 March. In April he was pronounced fit for regimental duties, returning to the 1st Battalion as second-in-command to Colonel Sergison-Brooke. Six days later he suffered a further indignity: he succumbed to chicken pox.

During this difficult time the prospect of remaining in the Army became increasingly unattractive. Almost all of his closest friends, who had enjoyed army life with him, had been killed. The twins always remember being shown their father's collection of photographs of his Eton contemporaries of whom eighty percent had died in the war. Furthermore, his peacetime placement was likely to be so lowly compared with the rank which he had held and the responsibilities which he had shouldered that future prospects were disenchanting. Demobilisation was to begin in early January and the Army would be cut down to a size determined by civilian politicians. As he had written on 11 November, the thought of devoting himself at thirty-three to training men for a war which he did not believe would occur in his lifetime was depressing.

Andrew's sixth mention in despatches had been gazetted three days before the Armistice, but the longed-for brevet lieutenant-colonelcy was denied him in the New Year's Honours. The uncharacteristic bitterness in a letter to Margaret on 2 January 1919 reflected his postwar exhaustion and his unresolved worry about his future career. 'I was stupid enough to be annoyed that I had not got my Brevet, though I felt that the Mention had done it in. *All* my contemporaries have got them and now lots of fellows junior to me . . . My God! I must be pretty rotten that I am not even worth a Brevet. I must certainly leave [the Army] as I am not fit to shovel the proverbial shit!'

Fortunately there were times when he could feel that he had not been finally consigned to the scrap-heap. On 16 March he had been mentioned in despatches for the seventh time. Six days later he rode alongside Viscount Lascelles at the head of the 3rd Battalion in the 2nd Guards Brigade in the Triumphal March of the Household Cavalry and Guards Division, proudly watched by Margaret and the family from a window at Cordwainers' Hall. His return to regimental duties had been hailed by his Lieutenant-Colonel as the best news he had heard for ages but Andrew was still very far from certain that his future lay in the Army.

Suddenly on 6 May he received a telegram which unexpectedly opened up new possibilities. General Keppel-Bethell invited him to come to Washington as his Assistant Military Attaché. The American post offered Andrew what at the moment he sorely needed – a complete break for about two years with new responsibilities and worthwhile scope for his energies. It would also give him plenty of time to decide whether or not to retire from the Army on his return to England. On 24 May the War Office gave formal approval to this temporary appointment. That the odds were heavily in favour of resignation is clear from the June Birthday Honours in which it was announced that Andrew had been awarded the CMG for 'services rendered in connection with military operations in France and Flanders'. Only later did he reveal that he had been offered a choice between a military CMG and the long-coveted brevet. His surprising choice of the decoration was explained by his virtual certainty that he would soon leave the Army and that the brevet would in no way help him in a civilian career. It had come too late. The decision was ultimately to prove a big mistake. Once he had decided to make the Army his permanent career, loss of seniority mattered and in 1939 was to give him a less important command than he would otherwise have gained.

Farnborough Park had been given up when the war ended and early in 1919 the family moved to a rented house near the seafront at Eastbourne. Andrew planned to go ahead to Washington leaving the family to follow as soon as he had found a house for them. On 18 June, accompanied by the faithful Arthur Bines, he sailed from Liverpool in the Cunard liner RMS *Orduna*. Four other members of the Military Mission sailed with him: the Military Attaché, Major General H. Keppel-Bethell, familiarly known as 'The Beetle'; Major J. O. C. Marriot ('Child') of the 48th Foot; Captain W. L. Palmer ('Pedlar') of the 10th Hussars; and Captain E. D. Wallace of the 2nd Life Guards, for whom his Christian name of Euan sufficed – a congenial team.

Enforced leisure during the eight-day voyage gave him time to think about the emotional stresses of the past few months. A week after sailing he wrote to Margaret begging her forgiveness 'for my appalling selfishness since January . . . I have tried to square my conscience by telling it that I was a victim from war strain. Actually it was my self-pity that produced the war strain!' For both of them it had been a difficult time, as in moments of depression each had thought that the other no longer cared. The voyage restored his balance, and his longing for Margaret and the children to join him in Washington showed that a temporary shadow had passed. On 30 June Andrew officially took up his new appointment and joyfully reported to Margaret that 'I have just been turned into Lieutenant-Colonel once more!!'

From the moment of his arrival Andrew loved the United States, and during his time at the Embassy he had several thoughts of settling there or in Canada. He found Washington impressive and exciting despite the almost unbearable heat and humidity in mid-summer. Until he found a house for the family he had quarters in General Bethell's house, and his position in the Embassy gave him the entrée to two leading clubs. Some 250 visiting cards had to be left soon after taking up his post but fortunately the social season in Washington ended with the hot weather. On 4 July he and Palmer went to Atlantic City to experience Independence Day celebrations. A postcard to Diana claimed that he was staying in the biggest hotel in the world. After bathing until his shoulders were scorched, the day ended in merry-go-rounds, swing boats and the giant racer.

Life was full and enjoyable but worryingly expensive. The exchange rate meant a loss of 13½% on all money sent from England, and his pay was totally insufficient for the life he was expected to lead. He discovered that it was equivalent to that earned by an American chauffeur who only drove but did not clean the car. In his letters he harped on the financial problems facing them when Margaret and the family joined him. He advised Margaret to bring out silver and linen and, if possible, to persuade Mrs Bines to come with them as a housemaid and also to bring a young kitchen maid. 'Cooks cost £120 a year and will only work an 8 hour day! Black servants invariably live out as no white servant will occupy a room after a black servant has lived in it!' They were each of them going to need a car, and it would be wise for Margaret to get some experience driving a Cadillac. 'I realise that I will have to clean the car myself and it looks as if I shall have to clean my boots etc. as well!'

His financial anxieties were aggravated by his own rather grandiose standards of living. It was fortunate that the 'ideal' house which he found in August was not available under a three-year lease. Fifteen bedrooms, five bathrooms and sixteen acres of garden would have been larger than was strictly necessary. Nor could he resist joining the exclusive Chevy Chase Club, justifying it on the grounds that tennis and golf professionals were available to members. By August he had bought a car, but until more money arrived from England he could only pay for half of it. In September he signed a year's lease on a smaller but attractive house, built in the old colonial style with an imposing portico – 'Greystones', on Klingle Road in Rock Creek Park.

As Assistant Military Attaché Andrew's main task was to gather as much information as possible for his General about the political and military scene in America. General Bethell's Mission had arrived in Washington at a moment when the United States was about to turn its back on Europe. What Americans frequently designate as the War of 1917–18 had been the most popular war in their history while it lasted and the most hated after it was over. The intense patriotic fervour of 1917 had been followed by bitter reaction. For most of the American Expeditionary Force the war had ended almost before it had begun. Less than half of the armed forces who landed in France had seen action. A triumphal march into Berlin, unconditional surrender by Germany and the hanging of the Kaiser, promised by politicians, never happened. Isolationist feelings, always a force in the United States, gained new strength, and it quickly became clear that the American Senate was unlikely to ratify the Peace Treaty, which President Wilson had unwisely insisted should contain the Covenant of the League of Nations. On 25 September 1919 Wilson was largely incapacitated by a stroke, and for the remainder of his term of office the country was effectively governed by his wife and his doctor, who alone decided what letters he should see and whom he should be allowed to receive. On 19 March 1920 the Senate finally refused to ratify the Treaty, and in the Presidential election of November the nation sent Harding and his cabinet of crooks and vulgarians to the White House. It was not an easy time for those in the British Embassy to build a strong and active relationship with a nation which believed that it had won the war for an effete Europe, reluctant to repay its huge financial debts to the United States.

Gathering information involved endless conversations with political and military figures as well as with anyone able to make him understand the contemporary American scene. Andrew soon discovered that he learned more in New York than in Washington, but he did not confine his study of America to the East Coast and moved West to Chicago and Clearmont in Wyoming, where he watched his first game of baseball and saw the famous Barnum and Bailey circus. 'The Brats would almost have died of excitement and pleasure.' It was hard work and at times bewildering. His mind, as he told Margaret, became confused much 'as my speech is before your mother or others of awe-inspiring natures'. 'I have my eyes, ears and *mouth* open, drinking in all the information I can.' At the end of his first tour: 'Lord, how I have enjoyed my time here! I must have eaten too much corn as I had fierce dreams of the capture of Windsor by the Bosche!'

One of his earliest duties was a visit to Government House in Ottawa. Here he met Harold Macmillan, who was spending a year as ADC to the Governor General, the Duke of Devonshire. He was able privately to assure the Duke that Macmillan's record in the Grenadier Guards of bravery on the Somme was something of a legend in the Regiment and that the Duke could happily accept him as a worthy future son-in-law. Of more immediate importance was the forthcoming tour of Canada by the Prince of Wales. Most of the arrangements had been completed, but because of his personal friendship with the Prince he became involved in plans for the subsequent visit to the United States. While in Canada he took the opportunity of visiting Montreal where his conversation with Sir Robert Borden, the Prime Minister, was largely confined to discussing French adaptations of Greek plays for the French stage, a somewhat recondite subject. In Quebec he climbed the steep track from Wolfe's Cove to the Plains of Abraham and was delighted to find in a nearby village a postmaster who was also the local accoucheur, whose premises bore the sign 'Letters and Ladies safely delivered'. Military conversations with leading officials were easier and more productive than similar talks in the United States.

He greatly enjoyed Canada but was surprised at the lack of social distinctions. The official servant accompanying him and Pedlar was treated in hotels 'as an ordinary guest. He has the next room to me on the ground floor!! "Service" is not obtainable as such in America. A few people have English servants but for the most part everyone looks after themselves.' He was contemptuous of the prohibition laws in both Canada and the United States when there was plenty of drink in private houses. 'The chief results of "prohibition" have been to increase the difficulties in obtaining drink, to encourage moral hypocrisy and to increase the number of Bolshevists.'

There were still signs that he had not yet completely recovered from the war years. These took the form in his letters home of admitting to lack of self-confidence and of embarrassing shyness. 'It is dreadful how bad I am at all the social tricks that are necessary and essential for a "diplomatist".' And a few weeks later: 'I am still painfully self-conscious and therefore stupid . . . I am too painfully mediocre "at most everything" (this is pure yank!). There isn't a game of cards, any sport etc. at which I shine and as all military affairs are now rightly taboo, any virtues I possess in that line are at a discount.' His belief that he was no dancer can only have meant that he had not learnt the new dances popular after the war. So 'I went to a dancing lesson from 4.20 – 5.20 p.m. I believe I learned all six movements of the Fox Trot in that time.' Yet he felt that he badly needed Margaret 'to take me in hand . . . I feel I am entirely gauche . . . and am terrified without your support.' Happily for him Margaret, with their five children and a nanny, Ellen Jefferies, who was seasick for the entire voyage, sailed for New York in October. His largely imaginary anxieties were soon at an end.

The family settled down quickly to the new life. He had arranged schools for the three elder children and immediately after breakfast on their first morning in Washington Diana was taken to Holton Arms School and the twins to the Friends School. Diana had an easy first day, but when the twins were collected in the afternoon they explained to their mother that their dishevelled state was caused by 'fighting for England'. This they had done most successfully by standing back to back while holding the natives at bay with their trouser belts. This bellicose attitude cannot have lasted long for in June 1920 Sandy was awarded a certificate for 'high standing in scholarship and deportment'.

Margaret was the greatest help to Andrew in the demanding social life which those attached to the British Embassy had to live. They very much enjoyed the visit of the Prince of Wales to the United States following his successful tour of Canada, and when the Prince visited Australia and New Zealand in the following spring Andrew was responsible for his proper reception when HMS *Renown* passed through the Panama Canal. Members of the Military Mission were personally popular in the United States and he made a great number of friends among serving officers and civilians alike. This popularity did not always extend to Britain, and in the great cities, especially in New York, the large number of Irish and German inhabitants were hostile to any suggestion of help for Britain. A powerful section of the population opposed all things military, especially during the debates in Congress on the introduction of some form of conscription. General Bethell in a long report to the Foreign Office, with which Andrew must have been closely involved, explained that conscription was likely to be rejected on three main grounds: ignorance among those untouched by the war; fear of high taxation to maintain the Services; fear in the Southern States that military training would raise the standards of physique and education among the coloured population and thus increase their influence. Under Harding America was hell-bent on returning to 'normalcy'.

Andrew's original belief that family life in America must inevitably be a life of strict austerity did not long survive the family's arrival. He was not good at practising austerity and he wanted Margaret and the children to gain from the experience of a year in the United States. In August and September 1920 he rented a holiday bungalow at the fashionable West Virginia resort of White Sulphur Springs where among other activities the three elder children began to learn to play golf. A local newspaper cutting throws some light on the standards which he maintained in Washington. In a reference to the arrival of the Thornes and 'their adorable children', the columnist stated that the family 'live in state in a fine country place . . . and have quite a staff of sedate British retainers, including a tutor, two governesses and the most impressive-looking butler.' 'Colonel Andrew' was hailed as one 'who had smelt powder from the very first moment the English went to the relief of Belgium until the Armistice'.

Financial considerations alone would have made it impossible for Andrew to keep Margaret and the family in Washington for more than a year, but there was a far more important reason for their return home in October 1920. He had decided to remain in the Army. The decision had not been made without much heart-searching, though it was what Margaret had always hoped. American or Canadian life on a civilian's salary was tempting; in May 1920 he had received a pressing offer from the Duke of Devonshire to become Military Secretary to the Governor-General. At about the same time he learned that if he remained in the Army he was likely to be selected for a Staff College course. It would appear, however, that it was a long letter from General Bethell, whose advice Andrew had sought, which helped him to come to a final decision.

On 25 June Bethell wrote setting out the comparative advantages and disadvantages of a business career and a continuing life with the Army. While admitting that financial inducements favoured joining the business world, he felt strongly that Andrew's future lay in the Army. 'Now, Bulgy, you should stick to the Army. You are already classified A.1. It is a career that I know appeals to to you and, mark you, it is one's everyday life that counts; the great gallops are few and far between . . . I know of no one in the Army of your age who has a more promising future; nor of anyone younger than you, for though they have some of them done wonders and collected many souvenirs, they have not graduated out in the to my mind supreme test, commanding in the field for a considerable time. You are much fitter than the average for your age. These two facts together make you a hot favourite . . . Get all possible out of America, then all possible out of the Staff College . . . You are top selection for the Staff College next year.' With the news reaching him in September that he had been selected for the next Staff College course after his return, provided that he agreed to remain in the

Army for at least three years after the conclusion of the course, his mind was made up. The family were sent home and he planned to follow early in 1921.

Before leaving the United States he went on a most enjoyable and informative tour of the South West. It was not all hard work. He found time to visit the Grand Canyon where he learned at his hotel that the record of 6¼ hours down to the bottom and up again was held by a waitress. Such a record could not be allowed to stand unchallenged. Starting at 8.20 a.m. he went down 'knees bent and at a trot' reaching the river bed at 10.10 a.m.. He paddled in the icy water and started the upward climb twenty minutes later. It was hard going but 'my heart must be in good shape as it only gave me trouble once and a few minutes rest on my back put it right'. He completed the total journey in 5½ hours.

Shortly after this feat of endurance he wrote a letter to Margaret which suggests that the strain of the war years was still taking its toll. He was understandably worried about his deteriorating eyesight. He had only twenty percent vision in his right eye but his hitherto normal left eye had weakened and he was prescribed reading glasses. 'I am not despondent or discouraged, but I feel at present that I have shot my bolt and there are no more in the locker . . . It is a horrible thing to feel that I used up most of my nervous energy during the war in fighting down craven fear which dogged my footsteps so relentlessly . . . I did my best to atone for it but the account was too big to square. Without your inspiration I don't know what I should have done. What I do pray so hard is that the Brats will not be predisposed to fear. We must do all we can to strengthen their minds and courage now.'

No man could have been more wrong about his past military service. That he knew fear, like any sensitive man, makes his achievements all the more courageous. Nor could he have been more wrong about his future. There were still many more bolts in the locker.

9
'Our Dwindling Army': 1921 – 1931

At the end of 1921 Andrew received a letter from Colonel (as he then was) John Dill: 'I don't suppose you have any idea of how much you did yourself to make the running of the show easy. Mind you stick to our dwindling Army. The smaller it gets the greater will be the need for good men.' The 'show' to which Dill referred was the year which Andrew was just completing at the Staff College in Camberley. He had been a member of the third and last 'crash' course for those who had survived the war and who in normal times would have been at the College many years earlier. Andrew and his fellow students must have been almost the most decorated body in the College's history and their instructors must have been hard put to it to tell them anything which they had not already learned from experience.

During his year at Camberley Andrew lived in the College while the family stayed at Highfield with his mother. In October he bought 37 Lennox Gardens from his mother-in-law, Lady Penrhyn, which gave him and the family a London base for a few years and some much-needed stability in a life of constant movement. In later life George used to say that to him 'home' meant two familiar armchairs and a sofa. On 1st February 1922 it was officially announced that Andrew had passed out of the College with distinction, his military prowess being more marked than his skill as an actor. In the students' entertainment at Christmas 1921 he was allotted the parts of 'Confused Noise Off' in Act I and 'A Thunderstorm' in Act II. Doubtless what mattered more to him at the time was the birth of his sixth child, Pansy, on 16 December. The family was complete.

The decade between leaving the Staff College as a student and his arrival in Berlin as Military Attaché was, compared with the previous decade, a period in Andrew's life outwardly lacking in excitement or sensational events. There must have been moments when he questioned the wisdom of his decision to remain in the Army. However, as time passed the high hopes that the war had been 'the war to end war' gradually faded and serious-minded professional soldiers like Andrew or his friend Lord Gort, as well as many others, came to believe that it was their task to maintain in the face of every difficulty and discouragement the highest possible standards in what the politicians had seen fit to leave of the British Army.

As his year as a Staff College student drew to its close he was concerned about his next posting. He had learned in August from General Jeffreys that he was earmarked to join him at Headquarters London District as GSO 2, an appointment which did not please him overmuch for he had hoped to return to regimental duties after an absence of three and a half years. Towards the end of the year he was sounded about becoming Military Secretary to Lord Lytton, the Governor-designate of Bengal, but he was not attracted by the suggestion. He was far more interested in a confidential letter from General Godley in mid-December asking if the appointment to London District was really agreeable and hinting that an alternative posting to Aldershot under Lord Cavan was possible. His reply was carefully drafted: 'I am really not anxious to be appointed GSO 2 London District but if it is considered to be in the interests of the Service that I should take up the appointment I will accept it if offered to me. I hope you will not mind my putting it in this way but I thought it best to tell you quite candidly my feelings on the subject.'

Unfortunately at the end of the year Jeffreys learned of the correspondence and wrote tersely to Andrew: 'The Brigade of Guards is supposed to be a branch of the Service in which Officers do as they are told but I regret to say its potential Staff Officers are acquiring a reputation at the War Office for raising difficulties on every possible occasion. Your wish to return to Regimental duty is entirely laudable but when Officers go to the Staff College they thereby express a desire for Staff employment and must expect to be selected accordingly . . . I came to the conclusion that there was less reason for you to return to duty (to command a Company) than for any other eligible Officer.' Jeffreys ended by asking him for an immediate acceptance of the London posting. In his reply he sent Jeffreys a copy of his very innocent letter to

Godley, who tried to smooth things over with Jeffreys, at the same time assuring Andrew that he was free to reject the London posting without in any way prejudicing his career. Andrew felt it wiser to do as Jeffreys had asked.

He expected to remain at Headquarters, London District for up to four years, but after little more than a year he was back at the Staff College on 1 May 1923, this time as an instructor, a post which he enjoyed and which he held for the next two years. In his life of Alanbrooke, Sir David Fraser wrote: 'If the Staff College is a place of student friendships perhaps the strongest ties and mutual assessments are formed between those who form the Directing Staff.' Andrew's colleagues included Gort, Brooke, Adam, Paget, Anderson, Riddell-Webster, Neame and Montgomery. The strange rules governing Army ranking, which appear to a civilian akin to a game of snakes and ladders, made him once again a lieutenant-colonel: he was never to be demoted. He was able to write in almost identical terms to Margaret and to his mother: 'I was very surprised to read in the Gazette of 29th December . . . that I have been made a Brevet Lt. Colonel. It is too late in the day to do me any real good but it is nevertheless pleasing to get it now.'

That Andrew had come to be regarded as a forward-looking officer was implicit not only in his selection as a Staff College instructor but also in other ways. In his letter to his mother about his brevet he told her, 'I am off to London to-morrow for a meeting to discuss 'Psychology' as a future manual to be studied in the British Army.' The subject had fascinated him for a long time and he believed that some basic training in and understanding of psychology was essential for future Army Officers. In 1926 he was invited to set one of the 'Training for War' papers for the Staff College Examination and, of greater importance, from 1929 he was among a small group charged with the task of bringing up to date the second volume of *Infantry Training*.

On 30 April 1924 Andrew's mother died. As his letters clearly show his relationship with her had not always been easy. Tommie had been her favourite son and it had seemed at times as if Gub and Boy had meant more to her than Andrew. She had never found it easy to show him the affection and understanding for which he longed, but as the years went by and Margaret came to make allowances for a difficult mother-in-law, Andrew's letters to his mother show them growing closer together. On her death he inherited Dunconusg, the house which meant much to the whole family and to which in old age he would have liked to retire.

After leaving the Staff College in 1925 Andrew enjoyed a ten-months' spell of duty at the War office as Military Assistant to the CIGS, Lord Cavan. Much of Cavan's military career had been spent on active service and Andrew, whom he had liked and respected ever since Andrew was an ensign, was able to supply the experience of staff work which Cavan lacked. For men devoted to the Army and aware of the need for its being kept abreast of modern ideas, it was a frustrating period. Ever since Lloyd George had told the Service Chiefs in 1919 that they had no need to plan for a major war within the next ten years this same message – 'the ten year rule' – was repeated annually until 1932. Thus both Conservative and Labour politicians were in agreement that money spent on men and equipment was unnecessary. Britain in the mid-twenties was in a stronger position than she had been for centuries and the Army inevitably suffered. Nor was there very much for it to do other than guard RAF bases in the Middle East and quell the occasional civil disturbances at home and abroad. So at the time when Andrew was Cavan's Military Assistant there was thought to be no justification for creating the Army of the future.

When Cavan ceased to be CIGS in February 1926 he wrote to Andrew expressing his gratitude and added: 'I do hope the work will have given you a new interest and insight into all that lies before you.' What immediately lay before him was a happy return to regimental duty as Second-in-Command of the 2nd Battalion, Grenadier Guards at Aldershot. Within three months of taking up this appointment his battalion, as part of the 1st Guards Brigade, took part in maintaining law and order during the General Strike in May. Their particular task was to defend such part of London's food supply as was unloaded at the docks. In the event no action was needed and on 18 May the 1st Guards Brigade returned to barracks in Aldershot, exercising on their way to Waterloo Station their right to march through the City with the Lord Mayor taking the salute.

In September 1927 Andrew proudly took command of the 3rd Battalion, Grenadier Guards, a task in which it was widely recognised that he did a magnificent job whether on ceremonial occasions or on military exercises. Perfection in drill was to him the essential training for discipline under fire and after the Trooping the Colour in June 1929 Gort wrote to him: 'The palm for drill should go to the 3rd Battalion. The only blot was the fact that the Commanding Officer's horse was the worst mannered quadruped on the parade – or perhaps it was due to an excess of zeal and loyal emotion!' Later that month at the Aldershot Tattoo the 3rd Battalion was responsible for a display of historical drill. 'There was nobody within a hundred miles of them,' was Guy Rasch's enthusiastic comment.

In the more serious mock warfare of large-scale manoeuvres Andrew made sure that his battalion was both reliable and competent. For one who had seen so much of the real thing it cannot have been easy to encourage his men to take seriously a 'battle' with coloured flags representing machine-gun posts or non-existent enemy forces. There were not enough real tanks still operational for each unit of command and most units had to make do with dummies. These consisted of two bicycles connected by a wooden framework and covered with a hospital sheet painted green. On the sheet were various external markings to represent caterpillar treads. Those propelling the tanks were said to develop huge calf muscles. Whenever the 'tanks' charged across the 'battlefield' the umpire had to decide whether or not the 'foe' had been decimated.

By 1931 it was becoming clear that Andrew's future career was likely to be one of increasing importance. On 10 January he handed over command of the 3rd Battalion to his Second-in-Command, Major Pilcher, on being selected to attend the Fifth Course at the Imperial Defence College in Buckingham Gate. The College had been founded in 1922 on the recommendation of a Cabinet committee presided over by Winston Churchill, then Colonial Secretary. Courses lasted for a year and were attended by hand-picked officers of all Services and from the Dominions. In September of that year Andrew was promoted to the rank of full colonel with seniority backdated to the end of 1927 when he had assumed command of the 3rd Battalion. Shortly before his course ended he learned on 10 November that from the following April he was to be Military Attaché in Berlin for three years, a post which also included being Military Attaché in Stockholm, Oslo and Copenhagen. It was an exciting prospect, with Hitler on the verge of becoming German Chancellor.

The past ten years had been outwardly devoid of exciting events in his career but they were years of steady advancement in his profession. They were also years in which for almost the first time in his life he was with his family for a prolonged period.

10
A Family Man

No portrait of Andrew is complete which concentrates solely on his military career and thereby omits a very important side of his life – the part which his six children and ultimately his grandchildren played in it. Throughout his married life he was determined to give his children what by reason of his father's age and his mother's difficulty in showing affection he felt that he had been denied. He was convinced that unless parents remain close to their children 'they will never attain any closer intimacy than Mother and I have done and that is so *very* unsatisfactory.' At first he could do very little. During four years of war he was only at home for brief spells of leave and his anxious concern about his children's upbringing was enhanced by his awareness that at any moment he might never see them again. The best he could do was to pour out in his letters to Margaret his hopes for their welfare and advice on how they might best fulfil these hopes.

He was quite clear about how he wanted his children to grow up. 'I don't want the Bratties [they became Brats as they grew older] brought up as prigs but to be taught that certain things are not done, such as sneaking, lying or any such underhand things because they are not fair or playing the game and the best way to play the game is to be a good, hard sporting Christian.' They should be trained 'so that they can play in a garden near water without supervision. They must be brought up adventurous and full of pluck . . . proficient at such things as swimming and riding.' Like many a young father he was unconsciously portraying himself: not that his would be a bad example to follow 'though I was not altogether a child to be copied, at least so they say!' He felt that his own and Margaret's childhood had been too sheltered. 'You and I were much too much looked after, which was a great mistake, and always I was most keen to be allowed to do things myself and always I was prevented.'

Margaret undertook the children's early schooling and Andrew sent copious advice on the content of their lessons. In this he was often in danger of being over-serious, forgetting how young they were during the war. At moments Margaret mildly resented his comments on her teaching of history and geography. He had pointed out to her that while dates and facts were important the causes which led to the facts mattered much more. Geography should be learned through plasticine models to enable an early appreciation of the structure of the land. Everything possible should be done to kindle an interest in nature study and this should be supplemented by examining the skeleton of a rabbit. Physical education was essential and he wondered if it were not time to arrange for some physical drill. 'I am certain I could arrange for an instructor to come from the Gym at Aldershot or Sandhurst. Do they swing on the parallel bars in the garden?' Poor Brats! However, it is probable that lessons were not quite so earnest as his letters imply.

On sex education Andrew totally endorsed Margaret's encouragement of the Brats to ask any question they liked. 'If thanks to this healthy education they will afterwards see no shame in love and human desire you will have done the greatest service that a parent can do. God! – how I hate the way the ordinary creature is brought up either to shun sexual life as a sin or else to indulge in it in a more or less secret way.' He was determined that his children should not undergo what he had been through in adolescence 'quite unnecessarily and only because I had no one I loved I dared ask, because I felt that Mother would not appreciate my troubles.' When he had needed it most, sex education was virtually unknown in schools and often confined to an embarrassing talk with a housemaster at the time of Confirmation. In desperation he had been reduced to the furtive purchase of books which 'explain the why and wherefore of our feelings'. These, he told Margaret, she would find locked away in his bureau and they might help her in answering the Brats' questions.

Formal schooling for the boys did not present any great problem. It was still an age when the education of sons was generally regarded as of much greater importance than that of girls. It was a view to which Margaret subscribed and to which her upbringing had accustomed her. Her three brothers had been treated as a race apart from their twelve sisters, and, with no modern notions of the equality of the sexes, she held that boys must have the best of everything. Pansy years later recalled her mother's apologies to her that she was a girl and told her the names she and her father had chosen for her as an expected boy. At the same time when Andrew was away at the war she felt it her duty to him to ensure that her three sons were not softly brought up.

Inevitably the three boys were destined for Eton and it was only the choice of preparatory school which had to be decided. In the end they went to West Downs at Winchester, Kenneth Tindall's well-known school. At Eton they had early been entered for Geoffrey ('Tuppy') Headlam's house. He had been an Eton contemporary of Andrew and during the war a Coldstreamer. The twins had from early days indulged in constant bickering and rivalry and in later life Sandy wondered if it would not have been better to have separated them if not in different schools at least in different houses. Fortunately for all of his sons Andrew's Eton career had been sufficiently undistinguished to save them from feeling that they had an unattainable standard to emulate. All three boys left Eton a little earlier than might have been expected – the twins to study German and French in a Viennese family and Peter to join his father in Berlin – before going up to Trinity College, Oxford.

Diana went to Parkfield, a school run by Miss Beveridge, which moved out of London to Potter's Bar. Early in her life either Margaret or Nanny had impressed upon her the duty, as the eldest, to look after the younger ones, a remark which she took very seriously to heart. A shy and high-minded girl, who Andrew felt needed more care and understanding than her brothers or sisters, she was a model pupil who became head girl. She used to admit that eventually her parents removed her because she was becoming too 'bossy' and sent her to a domestic science school at Aldeburgh. Poppy began at Parkfield but her more rebellious nature found girls' boarding schools in the nineteen twenties too restrictive, and she sampled a number of schools. This caused her parents some anxiety but did not forfeit their understanding. Pansy's schooling did not begin until the end of the twenties. Both she and Poppy had the usual fear of what their mother would wear when she visited them at school, but Margaret's dress sense and her care to be in the fashion banished any worry when she arrived.

Andrew naturally took a close interest in the family's schooling and did not take too seriously Headlam's strictures on the twins' allergy to Latin. 'They both regard the whole thing as an inexplicable and evil conspiracy.' What mattered to him was that by 1930 Headlam could write that all three 'are excellent boys who can look after themselves.' Formal education was the school's business, but Andrew by giving all the time that he could spare to be with the family gave them what no school could give. In their young days he made a point of postponing all his paper work until late at night so that he could enjoy their company before they were packed off to bed. As they grew older, when he could take his leave in school holidays, he became the life and soul of their activities. The man who had a genius for training his soldiers loved to teach his children to share his enjoyment of playing games, teaching them to sail, to ride, to shoot, to find their way across country with map and compass.

Golf was very much the family game. The three eldest had begun to play in Washington and as they all grew up innumerable games were played between them. One of the great joys of summer holidays at Lossiemouth was that Dunconusg was on the edge of the golf course. Mixed hockey, which Andrew had occasionally played with the Roosevelts in America, was possible at Lossiemouth when a host of cousins came to stay or when local acquaintances could be conscripted. The children of Ramsay MacDonald were regarded with disfavour for declining to play when it was known that they were free to do so. In early days a summer holiday at Mudeford in Hampshire had provided a chance of learning the elements of dinghy sailing in water only three feet deep. Later, serious sailing did not have to be confined to holidays, for Warsash was in easy reach at a weekend and club boats could be used. Margaret enjoyed sailing less than her family, so on windy days one member played golf with her while the remainder 'beat up' the Solent and discovered how easy it was to run aground in the Hamble river on a falling tide. If Margaret was not a natural sailor, she was a natural horsewoman and shot. She had a remarkable knowledge of horses and as a girl had early ridden astride. At Camberley when Andrew was an instructor at the Staff College a miniature air-rifle range was rigged up in the billiard room and she surprised occasional visitors and made the family envious by her marksmanship.

It will be clear that all these activities were very much a family affair. The Thornes were to a large extent by virtue of their numbers a self-contained group with no need to rely on others for their enjoyment. Years later when Andrew commanded in Scotland one of his ADCs said that when the family were present in force he felt they were like a rather exclusive military unit. That they enjoyed the family life there is no doubt; holidays remained with all the children – except, perhaps, for Pansy – as a time with the happiest memories. Pansy, having been born eleven years after Diana, could not easily share in the games and skills and was inevitably a little apart from the rest. Furthermore, she was the only member of the family born without an eye for a ball and, according to her own account, very squeamish, afraid of water and far too nervous to walk along the harbour wall at Lossiemouth. She maintained that as a child she was afraid of her father and had a clear recollection of his pretended threat to drown her if she would not try to swim. It was, however, characteristic of him that when Pansy grew up and devoted herself to work with the 'unattached' youth for whom little was being done, he was as interested in her doings as in those of his other children.

Andrew tried to instil into his children his belief that it was important never to be content with one's standard of playing a game; one must always strive to improve. In the week before he died he had golf lessons, remarking hopefully: 'one day I may be able to play properly.' His physical aliveness was communicated to all with whom he came into contact. The unforgivable sin was to loaf around, and to the end of his life he found it impossible to understand why everyone was not agog to make a compost heap, to light a bonfire or to cut down a tree. Pansy's future husband when coming to see her found that he was expected to help make a road. This was the most natural thing for a man to want to do. A family activity was scrub clearing at 'The Plot', a fourteen-acre former nursery garden near Bagshot, which Andrew had bought in the late twenties as the site on which to build a family house. Working parties of family and friends, armed with saws, slashers and billhooks attacked the fast-growing birches and rhododendrons with professed enjoyment until the scheme was abandoned. At times it must have been slightly exhausting to live up to him – but he was always an encourager of anyone trying their best.

His grandchildren in their turn experienced the same unconcealed delight in the achievements of his family. They admired his unflagging spirit of adventure and his modern outlook; even in his immaculate dress he always kept to the fashion of the day. The grandchildren took it for granted that, however old, he would naturally want to fish with them, play golf, or dive, when over eighty, into Poppy's swimming pool. It was the greatest joy to him that three of his grandchildren went into his old regiment. For on one point he was biased: to him it was inconceivable that a Thorne could be other than a Grenadier.

After Andrew's death General Sir David Fraser wrote to Poppy: 'I always remember the first time I ever had a real conversation with him was at about the age of fifteen . . . and I sat next to him. I had never met anybody before who had talked to me as he did – interestingly, energetically, with enthusiasm, understanding and as if to a contemporary. It's the most wonderful God-given endowment, I think, to transcend the generations completely as he did that night.'

11
Berlin: 1932 – 1935

Andrew's appointment as Military Attaché in Berlin surprised him. Recently he had a little rashly declined a post in India on the grounds that his family's education would suffer. Moreover his hopes had been set upon commanding the Regiment before long, but the post became vacant during his year's course at the Imperial Defence College, which made him ineligible. It was a coveted position which he was never to hold. However, the prospect of three years in Berlin when Germany was in turmoil was exciting.

After touring key military installations at home so as to find out what information about the German Army was most needed, Andrew officially succeeded Colonel (later General Sir James) Marshall-Cornwall on 16 April. Four days previously he had been formally introduced to the Reichswehr Minister and the leading members of his staff with whom he would be dealing. A home was found in the Charlottenburg district of Berlin, at Berliner Strasse 33, where a month later Margaret and Pansy joined him.

Andrew took over as Military Attaché at a tense moment in the tragic story of the Weimar Republic. Brüning had become Chancellor in March 1930 to face an ailing economy, which demanded drastic financial sacrifices by the German people if it were to be remedied. These he hoped to make more palatable by a foreign policy aimed at ending the payment of reparations, only to find his efforts deliberately frustrated by the malign opposition of Pierre Laval in France. Brüning had also to grapple with a deadlier danger caused by the growing division of Germans into those who despairingly saw the sole hope of salvation in the Communists and those whose hopes increasingly rested on the Nazis. The Weimar Republic's experiment in democracy had never won the wholehearted support of a nation accustomed to strong rulers demanding before all else obedience. In the general election of September 1930 the Nazis gained 107 seats in the new Reichstag, compared with 12 in the old. Brüning's attempts to arouse European statesmen to the dangers threatening all Europe from the impending German disaster met with polite interest but no action.

A critical moment came on 10 April 1932, a week before Andrew's arrival, when a Presidential election had to be held. With the greatest difficulty Brüning persuaded the octogenarian Hindenburg to oppose Hitler's candidature by seeking re-election. Although his weak position in the Reichstag had forced him to govern by Presidential decree – permitted under the Weimar constitution – he saw in Hindenburg's retention of power the sole hope of maintaining some form of democracy in Germany and of saving the country from making the terrible choice between Communism and Nazism.

On the day of the election Brüning issued a decree dissolving the two most dangerous Nazi organisations, the Sturmabteilungen (SA), the Stormtroopers, and the Schutz Staffeln (SS), the defence squads. The SA were not just a disguised army reserve but were political troops trained to assist in the capture of political power. At this time they numbered about half a million men, for the most part brutal thugs, who delighted in street brawls whereby they terrorised citizens – and especially Jews. The SS became Hitler's personal guard and were later to develop into an elite corps in the Army. Brüning's dissolution of these two bodies – the SA Brownshirts and the SS with their black jackets – followed the discovery that in the event of Hitler's Presidential victory a coup d'état would ensure supreme power for the Nazi Party. In the event, Hindenburg won the election by a handsome majority, and Hitler, shrewdly seeing that the time for force had not yet arrived, forbade SA violence.

For a time Brüning enjoyed a rare but deserved popularity when a press leak revealed that, as a result of his negotiations in Geneva, there was a likelihood that Germany would be allowed to increase her armaments proportionately as the former Allies decreased theirs until parity was achieved. Once again French intrigues and open opposition defeated Brüning, who was forced to resign in May, to be succeeded – to general astonishment – by the superficially amiable but largely inept Count von Papen, who inherited the reward of Brüning's efforts in July, when reparations were ended at the Lausanne Conference. Von Papen had rescinded the ban on the SA and SS, with the inevitable increase of street fighting. Another general election on 31 July resulted in a doubling of Nazi seats in the Reichstag and an offer to Hitler of the Vice-Chancellorship, which he rejected. Nothing short of total power was acceptable.

What struck Andrew on arrival in Berlin was that the Nazis were winning the support of the Army. This judgment was based upon the 'marked disapproval' within the Army of Brüning's banning of the SA and SS. As he reported to the Ambassador, Sir Horace Rumbold, a diplomat of wide experience whose blimpish features belied a shrewd mind: 'The Officers as a whole feel that the Nazi movement is the best available means of disciplining the youth of the country, for whom no service in the Army is possible [under the terms of the Treaty of Versailles] and that it keeps them out of the Communist ranks; in addition it is an attractive method to the Germans as a whole of expressing their devotion to their country.'

The war years had not left Andrew with an undying hatred of the former enemy. He had appreciated the ability and courage of Germans on the battlefield and he had subsequently studied their military history and their theories of war. In pre-war years his travels in Germany had resulted in several friendships and a love of German music, especially opera. He came, therefore, to Berlin with a friendly understanding of Germany's problems and some sympathy with German resentment of the Treaty of Versailles. In return the high-ranking German officers whom he now met admired his war record and enjoyed his company, thus enabling him to get as much insight as was possible into the secret transformation of the German Army, a process which pre-dated Hitler's renunciation of the Versailles Treaty by some ten years. In 1922 at Rapallo Walther Rathenau, the Weimar Foreign Minister, had negotiated a treaty of friendship with Russia at a moment when both nations were cold-shouldered by the major European powers. In addition to the main clauses concerning trade relations there had been a secret understanding, reached a year earlier, whereby potential members of a future German

Army were to be trained in Russia, largely in tank warfare. By the time that Andrew reached Berlin, diplomatic circles were aware of this evasion of the peace terms.

Andrew's task of gathering information had been considerably eased by a change in official policy. Up to the time of his appointment relations between the embassy staff and the German population had been very formal. No fraternisation was permitted. This rule was now cancelled, and diplomatic officials were encouraged to meet and to entertain Germans on the same footing as other friendly nationals. At official parties Margaret was an excellent hostess, speaking German with growing fluency; she was a better linguist than Andrew who, thanks to hard work, could converse adequately in German but never really possessed the gift of tongues. At their first cocktail party Andrew discovered that a German officer to whom he was talking had been fighting in the Battle of Loos in which Tommie had been killed. The officer introduced his wife, who was nearby, with the words: 'You must meet the new British Military Attaché. I think I may have killed his brother.' In 1932 the Germans were still very short of food, and Andrew was advised at his dinner parties to provide a substantial meal which should include meat.

It was a help to Andrew that during his term of office all the family were with him at one time or another, enabling close friendships to be formed with German families who shared their enjoyment of golf and sailing. The Wannsee golf course was much used by them, and in 1934 Andrew was made an honorary member of the Kaiserliche Yacht Club at Potsdam. Here they saw something of the aristocratic families who remained loyal to the old regime. Among them were former members of the German Royal Family, who, although having no longer any status within the Weimar Republic, as cousins of the British Royal Family had to be received with bows and curtseys by members of the British Embassy. This once presented Margaret with a problem. Emerging from a bathe she found the Crown Prince talking to some of the family. Did one or did one not curtsey in a dripping bathing costume?

In the early months of Andrew's appointment conversation at parties or elsewhere was normally free and uninhibited, though the inability of some young officers to remain discreet under the unfamiliar effect of cocktails led to those below the rank of lieutenant-colonel not being allowed to accept British hospitality. With the advent of Hitler to power, conversation became more guarded. The only entirely safe topic being the wonders of the Nazi revolution. In another way the Nazi triumph changed the atmosphere of diplomatic parties. By 1934 Andrew and Margaret found it incumbent on them to entertain notorious decadents like Ernst Röhm, head of the SA, or leaders like Goering, who he always maintained was as cruel as any Nazi, in spite of his outward semblance of geniality. However, as guests in their house the Germans were received with equal charm and courtesy.

During June and early July 1932 Andrew, with Margaret, paid official visits to Sweden, Norway and Denmark. As Military Attaché to all three countries as well as to Germany, he established friendly contacts with his opposite numbers. It was impossible to spare all the time he would have liked with them, for he was bound to be mainly occupied in assessing the rapidly changing situation in Germany. In later years he liked to recall that on a visit to Norway he lunched in Oslo at the Bristol Hotel with the then Defence Minister, Major V. Quisling. His next meeting with the Quisling family was when he had in 1945 to reject Mrs Quisling's plea for her husband's reprieve from the death sentence.

Shortly after returning to Berlin from his first visit to the Baltic Andrew met with a serious accident when he was riding slowly home with Margaret. His horse, on a loose rein and half asleep, stumbled and threw him. Unfortunately he was not thrown clear and the horse trod on him, cracking his pelvis and fracturing the tips of three vertebrae as it got up. With an unbelievable determination to ignore what must have been agonising pain, he remounted and rode back to the car, which Margaret drove back to Berlin. Though in bed for six weeks he made a good recovery, aided by a family summer holiday at Bannsin on Usedom, a small island off Pomerania.

At the end of September Andrew attended the German military manoeuvres at Frankfurt-am-Oder. As he reported to Rumbold, the general public 'who flocked to the manoeuvres from near and far showed such marked interest in the work of the troops that on several occasions machine gun posts etc. were entirely hidden by a circle of interested spectators'. Among these were Margaret and some of the family, armed with a picnic lunch. Despite the crowd he saw enough to convince him that the manoeuvres were far more efficient than his predecessor had witnessed in 1928. 'I have to acknowledge being immensely impressed by the obvious efficiency of the German troops and the high standard of training to which they have been brought.'

Events now began to take a rapid turn, making it impossible to forecast their likely course. A second General Election in October confirmed the Nazis as the largest party in the Reichstag, but still without an overall majority. As the year drew to a close mob violence increased. Von Papen failed to form a government and gave place to the intriguer General von Schleicher. He held office for only fifty-four days, when he became himself the victim of an intrigue and resigned. Hindenburg could only follow the constitutional procedure of offering the Chancellorship to the leader of the largest party; so on 30 January 1933 Hitler achieved his ambition by constitutional means and not by revolution. The Nazi revolution could now begin.

Hitler started by demanding a new election in the hope of winning an overall majority in the Reichstag. On the night of 27 February the Reichstag building was burned down, apparently by a mentally retarded Dutch Communist, van der Lubbe. It was, in fact, the result of a plot concocted by Goering and Goebbels, who were searching for a pretext to smash the Communist Party and used van der Lubbe as a dupe. While minor details of the plot remain uncertain, the fire gave Hitler material for further denunciation of the Communist menace. Even so, the Nazis still only won forty-four percent of the seats. This did not satisfy Hitler, who now persuaded the Reichstag to give him and his ministers complete power for four years. The Weimar Republic and parliamentary government were at an end.

Rumbold had for some time been warning the British Government of the danger likely to arise from Hitler's ability to mobilise the mass of German discontent, even though he was like 'a revivalist preacher with the appearance of a greengrocer wearing an air-force moustache'. His warnings were strengthened by the full and penetrating analysis of the semi-military training of

German youth which Andrew on 25 April had submitted to Runbold for transmission to the Foreign Office.

In this report he pointed out that on 3 April Hitler had transferred control of all youth clubs from private hands to the Ministry of Labour. The clubs had been organised on military lines before Hitler came to power, but the military aspect was now predominant. Andrew warned that to pretend that the instruction received in these clubs was comparable to the Boy Scouts movement would be dangerously wrong. Pack marches of sixteen miles while carrying over fifty pounds of equipment were part of a training which included 'exercises involving scouting, attack and defence, withdrawal and pursuit, surprise and ambuscades, the enemy as a rule being designated either smuggler bands or Communists'. Even groups originally formed to give religious and athletic training to boys of twelve to sixteen had now begun to train them on military lines. The report included a full list of the camps, their equipment and details of their courses. 'The cumulative effect of these measures will be to produce a very large reserve of personnel who will require little further training to take their places in the armed forces of the country on the outbreak of war.' Rumbold, whose diplomatic career was drawing to a close, valued this report as confirmation of his belief, based on his own observations and a careful study of *Mein Kampf*, that perhaps five or six years hence Hitler would threaten the peace of Europe. He retired in July, to be succeeded in September by Sir Eric Phipps, a man known for his hostility to Nazi ideas.

Meanwhile the Nazi revolution was going ahead with gathering speed. The press and broadcasting had been immediately controlled, and in order to subdue the minds of the rising generation every teacher had to accept and proclaim Hitler's lunatic views on history and race, with terrible consequences for the Jews. Textbooks were rewritten, and during May books which the Nazis disliked were publicly burned in city squares and, to the shame of German scholars, in the grounds of the universities. The Nazi Youth organisations had been founded in the early days of the Movement, but now all other youth organisations were banned. Before Rumbold retired all political parties other than the Nazi Party had been abolished, trade unions and strikes forbidden, and the power of the States' governments within the Reich taken over.

In September 1933 Andrew presented his new Ambassador with a very long and interesting account of the development of the SA and the SS. He traced the evolution of the SA from its formation in November 1921 as a body of 'chuckers-out' protecting Hitler's early meetings in Munich up to its reorganisation during 1930–31 by Röhm. 'It is almost impossible for an Englishman to understand the amount of keenness which is shown by the SA men and the subordinate leaders. It must be remembered that most of the men are now expected to pay for the privilege of being in the SA and that about 60% of the men have already done a full day's work before they reach the Sturm Lokal [the beer house which was the centre of local training].' There was a danger that the intense SA training made them too tired to work on Monday after an arduous weekend and that the tempo could not be maintained if war were not envisaged for at least another five or six years. Despite official denials from Hitler and Röhm downwards, Andrew was convinced that the purpose of the SA was changing. Röhm might proclaim that 'the will of the Führer has entrusted us with a high honour and a great responsibility, to be the guarantee of the German revolution', the original political aim of the SA; Andrew, however, insisted that their purpose was to form depots of man power to enable the rapid expansion of the Army. By contrast the SS had always been intended as a *corps d' élite* within the Army, and Andrew had no doubts 'that their units would be fit to take the field the moment they had received their full infantry armament'. What he could not have foreseen was the dramatic events of 1934.

'By far the most important event in the military sphere in 1934 was the struggle between the headquarters of the SA forces and the Reichswehr Ministry for the control of the national defences.' With this sentence Andrew began his official review of military events in Germany during the year. A year after his appointment as Chancellor, Hitler's power was seemingly complete. There was, however, a danger: either the Army might turn against him or a revolt within the Nazi Party led by Röhm and his SA might oust him from the leadership. Therefore in April Hitler made a secret deal with the Army leaders, who loathed Röhm and his ever-increasing SA, now numbering over one and a half million men. Exact details of the agreement have never been known, but the main gist is clear. The Army agreed to back Hitler as head of state after Hindenburg's death – an event which could not long be delayed – in return for the destruction of Röhm and the leading SA figures. Any possible challenge to the supremacy of the Army by the SA must be ended once and for all.

Three weeks before Hitler fulfilled his side of the bargain Andrew met him for the first time in a private interview. He had been studying the history of the First World War in the German War Archives, and Hitler, learning of this, summoned him for a personal discussion. As Andrew wrote to Peter: 'I was v. highly honoured on Friday [10 June] and had a 33 min. interview with the Führer, which was most awfully interesting and at which he was most charming. He discussed particularly the fighting at Gheluvelt in 1914 where he had his baptism of fire.' It was clear from the conversation that the two men must have been close to each other on 29 October to 1 November 1914. As Andrew told a Norwegian journalist thirty-five years later: 'For a long time we stood over the map exchanging reminiscences over the area where the fighting had taken place, the road along which the Germans had attacked, the various fields and hills. Hitler was delighted and stressed that it was not the pale-faced Staff Officers but the ordinary front-line soldiers who could understand war. I tactfully refrained from telling him that I had actually been a Staff Officer at that time.' Hitler was notoriously able to turn on the charm when it suited him, but there is no reason to doubt that he respected Andrew as a fine soldier. Nor did this interview and subsequent meetings on diplomatic occasions, when Hitler reverted time and again to Gheluvelt, blind Andrew to the dangers likely to arise from what he was learning about German rearmament. Unfortunately he left no written account of his impressions of Hitler, but in September 1935, after he had left Germany, he lectured to the Imperial Defence College on Germany and included in his talk a lengthy analysis of Hitler's character.

The Nazis, he said, 'felt that their mission was to resurrect Germany, and the Party eventually selected Hitler as their leader because they were so impressed by his powers as a demagogue, a gift previously unknown in Germany. Hitler accepted the call because, saturated with the operas of the great revolutionary Wagner, he believed that he was the embodiment of "the guileless one", Wagner's *Parsifal.*' He went on to speak of Hitler's gift for playing on the emotions of Germans of every tribe and of how he took as his heroes Cromwell, Frederick the Great and Bismarck. 'His richest possessions are his instinct and his faith in it, while his enduring readiness to learn – his craving for sympathy – his passion for music and art go to complete this curiously feminine make-up; so that it is all the more surprising to find that hard streak in his nature which allows him to brook no opposition to his leadership.' At the end he returned to his earlier comparison of him with *Parsifal*, reminding his audience that '*Parsifal*'s *leitmotif* was to heal and to maintain the sanctity of the Holy Grail and not like others to war with the sword'.

This is an interesting and in some ways a flattering portrait of Hitler. Andrew was wrong in his belief that the early Nazis selected Hitler and in his suggestion that he was always ready to learn. Most modern historians believe that he was an outstanding example of a man with a closed mind, who combined rigid and unchangeable views with a genius for flexibility in tactics. On the other hand Andrew was very perceptive in spotting the combination of Hitler's artistic temperament with ruthlessness in ousting opposition. It may seem strange that as late as 1935, a year after the Night of the Long Knives, Andrew could have appeared less critical of Hitler than he afterwards became. While the events of June 1934 revealed the true nature of the man, many people at home and abroad were at first more impressed and pleased at Hitler's suppression of the SA than horrified at the widespread killings. That Hitler had come to terms with the Army, always popular in Germany, was what for the time mattered.

On 30 June 1934 Herr von Bieberstein and his wife had been invited to lunch in Andrew's house. He had been one of the first Germans from a good family to join the Nazis. It was clear that something serious was afoot. Andrew's two guests were obviously under considerable stress, judging by the number of cigarettes they smoked throughout the meal. It was impossible to ask any probing questions, and it was only afterwards that Andrew learned that von Bierberstein had received orders to go to Tempelhof airport after lunch in order to meet a plane from Munich and to conduct its occupants – many of whom had been his former SA companions-in-arms – to Lichterfelde Barracks. It was not difficult to guess their subsequent fate. During the preceding night Hitler had kept his promise to the Army. After personally arresting Röhm and ordering his execution and that of other leading SA officers he handed over the liquidation of all thought to be opposed to the Nazis to the SS. Between three and five thousand – accounts vary – were arrested all over Germany and usually murdered then and there, the SS finding it an invaluable opportunity to pay off old scores. Hitler admitted only to seventy-seven deaths and received Hindenburg's congratulations on his personal bravery in uncovering a dangerous plot.

When the weekend shooting had ended Andrew realised that it was wiser not to inquire after friends whom he had not recently seen. Some while later he attended a reception and was greeted by Herr von Arnim, who, having detected a momentary look of surprise on Andrew's face, said: 'Hullo! Thought I had been shot, didn't you?'

While the majority of the German people had no love for the SA, the extent of the murders, the number of people who suddenly disappeared never to be heard of again, came as a terrible shock. That the Army leaders were privy to what was planned is now certain, though probably not to the numbers to be liquidated. If Röhm and his senior officers really plotted to overthrow Hitler, unpleasant as he and many of them were, in a civilised society they would at least have been accorded some form of trial. For the moment the shootings weakened Hitler's position, until he was saved by a stroke of luck. In August Andrew and the family were on holiday at Heiligendam, near Lübeck, and the Crown Prince, also there, called up to Andrew who was on the balcony of their villa to say that he had just heard from East Prussia that Hindenburg had died. That was on 2 August, two days before the official announcement was made. The Army, as promised, rallied to support Hitler. The office of President was abolished, and a cowed people voted that Hitler should be both Führer and Reich Chancellor. His power was complete.

As Military Attaché Andrew was mainly concerned with the rapid development of the German Army, newly christened the Wehrmacht, and to pass on all that he had learned to the British authorities, whom he regarded as dangerously unreceptive to new ideas. In the course of his travels in 1934 he visited East Prussia as the guest of the Principal of the Charlottenburg Technical High School, a semi-military training college in Berlin. The Principal had inherited the family estates in East Prussia, which an ancestor had received from Frederick the Great on condition that he raised a private army to protect the lands from any danger coming from the East. During his visit Andrew was intrigued to discover that descendants of the original peasant soldiers were working on the estates and, like their forebears, were engaged in digging defences which would be stocked with arms, ammunition and food. The Principal explained that neither the peasants nor these elaborate defences could stop a modern invading army but that once an army had overrun the defences and advanced westward the peasants would be able to inflict considerable damage on the enemy's supply lines and could even hold up his supporting units. Andrew was greatly impressed by what he was shown, and when in 1940 he was Commander of XII Corps he included the same tactics among his plans to defeat an invasion.

On 4 July 1934 Andrew completed for Sir Eric Phipps a highly important paper on the state of the German Army. Much of his report had to be based on intelligent guess-work, supported by his own observations and private conversations, for it was a sign of increasing German secrecy that military attachés were no longer being given full information, and on visits to army schools and establishments they were now carefully 'bear-led'. He estimated that the German aim, well on the way to realisation, was to build up an army at least three times greater than was permitted by the Treaty of Versailles. That treaty had limited the size of the German Army to 100,000 men, recruited by voluntary enlistment, conscription being prohibited. Military aircraft, heavy artillery and tanks were forbidden, and the number of factories capable of producing war material was strictly limited. Some 2,000 Commissioners supervised the carrying out of these conditions and were not withdrawn until 1927. Despite attempts by Germany to evade these measures the nation was effectively disarmed until the end of the 1920s, though the secret agreement permitting Germans to train in Russia enabled future members of the German Army to gain experience of mechanised warfare impossible in their own country. It also had the unforeseen result of enabling diplomats stationed in Berlin to collect information about Stalin's Russia.

What interested Andrew greatly was the strong evidence of the steady mechanisation of the Army. Cavalry regiments all had 'motorised squadrons' attached to them, and every cadet was trained to ride a motor cycle and to drive a car. It was hoped that every civilian holding a driving licence would 'learn how to travel across and negotiate all types of terrain in a motor car or on a motor bicycle'. Whereas the war of 1914 had largely been a war of little movement, he realised that the Germans were planning for a future war of rapid mobility. To this end German car manufacturers were 'busily engaged in producing suitable types of engines, systems of suspension, wheels and tracks, which can be applied to the production of the new German tank'. He did not recount the current joke of the man anxious to construct a perambulator who found that, whichever way he assembled the parts provided in the kit, he had made a machine gun.

Turning to chemical warfare and new inventions, he admitted having no proof of his suspicions, but he believed that German chemists were making 'successful progress in manufacturing a lethal gas from cyanides'. 'From all sides come rumours of the installation of machines capable of producing a ray which can immobilise any machine capable of employing a magneto' and of a new form of 'flame-thrower' which is 'designed for use at a distance against armoured fighting vehicles, the armour of which it is supposed to cut like butter'. However, he felt bound to add that 'these rumours give me the impression that they have been circulated as a deterrent to any Power which might wish to take advantage of the present defenceless state of Germany'.

In Andrew's opinion Germany's most serious present weakness was the lack of trained reserves. Until the Treaty of Versailles was modified by Allied consent or openly flouted, it was necessary to conceal what was happening by seconding recruits to the SA, whose special uniform disguised the fact that such men were really soldiers. 'The events of 30 June . . . should not be allowed to obscure the military potentialities of the organisation.' For the moment Germany was not ready for war, but 'after some five years I believe that the Reichswehr of 21 infantry and 4 mobile divisions in peace will be capable of expansion into some 70 divisions on mobilisation, supported by a very strong air force and backed by a carefully organised industrial state'. This was the first recorded estimate of the likely long-term expansion of the Germany Army. There was little likelihood, he added in a postscript, of the Army turning against Hitler. 'The whole tradition of the Army is not to oppose the popular will and for the moment, and probably for some time, there will be no revulsion of feeling towards Hitler.'

This report earned Andrew a chorus of praise from Foreign Office and War Office alike. Sir Robert Vansittart minuted that Andrew's time as Military Attaché ought to be extended. 'He does his work so admirably that I should regard it as lamentable and most disadvantageous to the public service if there were any change of tenure in the coming critical years.' This view was endorsed by Sir John Simon and Anthony Eden: Eden minuted: 'Colonel Thorne's departure from Berlin would indeed be a loss. This remarkably well thought out despatch is characteristic of his balanced judgment.' So Vansittart drafted a letter to General Dill at the War Office suggesting that Andrew remained in Berlin for a while. The letter was never sent, as private soundings made clear that 'Colonel Thorne is highly thought of and in due course will get a much better job than that of M[ilitary] A[ttaché]. We must not stand in his way.'

Promotion was not long delayed. In mid-November Andrew was asked in confidence if he would accept the post of Commander 1st Infantry Brigade (Guards) at Aldershot. Across the letter he wrote in pencil 'Replied v. glad'. Official notification came on 5 December, informing him that he would hold the temporary rank of brigadier and that the appointment would start on 13 May 1935.

Before he left Berlin Andrew wrote two more reports which deserve notice. At the end of 1934 he wrote a long account of the year's events from the military standpoint. While to a great extent an expansion of his July report, Foreign Office officials noted the greater stress on German industrial mobilisation. 'It is understood that all the larger firms have already been issued with instructions and process specifications to enable them to turn to war production of armament and munitions . . . A definite policy has been adopted of locating, where possible, all large manufacturing works in the centre of Germany on the axis of Hamburg and Nuremberg with the object of removing them as far as possible away from hostile interference.' To judge by the absence of any official comment less notice seems to have been taken of one of his appendices. 'A long range rocket . . . has been taken up with the greatest interest by the Reichswehr and the Air Ministry. A factory and a proving ground in Pomerania have been put at the disposal of the firm which has been developing the idea and already the range has been increased from 30 to 45 km . . . Should it be possible to ensure accuracy of range and direction, the Germans will possess in this rocket a very valuable and inexpensive weapon.' His forecast was proved to be all too true when V1 and V2 rockets fell on Britain in 1944.

His final report was an account of his farewell conversation with General von Reichenau when presenting his successor, Colonel Hotblack, to the Reichswehr Ministry in May 1935. The General spoke to Andrew of German plans to evacuate part of the Russian population eastwards following a successful invasion of Russia and to replace them by another people, perhaps by Poles. The land thus left empty in Poland could be filled by Germans who needed more living space. Von Reichenau went on to hint that it would be wise for Britain to allow Germany a free hand to dominate Europe in return for German non-interference in British interests in the rest of the world. What was essential for Germany, he concluded, was to break 'the terrible encirclement of Germany' which would probably mean war, even in alliance with Russia if necessary.

The report of this conversation provoked conflicting comments from the Foreign Office and War Office. Vansittart, who had always been impressed by Andrew's reports, minuted that he fully upheld Andrew's analysis of German aims. 'Anyone who does not know them (e.g., the *Times* and the weaker-minded members of the House of Lords) is living in a fool's paradise.' A withering report by Lord Stanhope in his minute read: 'Colonel

Thorne is now to command the 4th (Guards) Brigade in the 2nd Division [actually the 1st Brigade in the 1st Division] at Aldershot and will view the German scene from the other end of the telescope. His views in 6 months' time will be much healthier and more suited to the House of Lords than this effusion.' With this Simon agreed, but Anthony Eden maintained his belief in Andrew: 'Colonel Thorne impressed me very much when I met him in Berlin. He will be difficult to replace.' In forwarding Andrew's final despatch to the Foreign Office Sir Eric Phipps added a personal note: 'I desire to take this opportunity of placing on record my warmest appreciation of Colonel Thorne's services as Military Attaché to this Embassy. He has been able to establish quite unusually good relations with Germans of every class and the information he has collected with excellent judgment on political as well as military matters has been of the greatest assistance to me. I view his departure with the utmost regret.'

Andrew returned home early in May, very conscious of the potential threat from a modernised German Army and the unreadiness of the War Office and of many senior British soldiers to entertain new ideas. Before leaving he had been presented with a photograph of Hitler with General von Blomberg which the latter had signed. He had sent the photograph to Dr Hans Thomsen, one of Hitler's staff, with a request that Hitler might also sign it. Shortly after his return he received two signed photographs, together with a note from Thomsen: 'I am returning to you the photograph which you sent me before leaving Berlin. The Chancellor was, of course, immediately willing to add his signature to Generaloberst von Blomberg's. And since you had got acquainted with him during your term of office, he thought you might like to have another portrait of himself as a token of remembrance of your mission to Berlin. This portrait, which I enclose and which I think is extremely good, is the work of young Wieland Wagner, Richard Wagner's grandson.' In his acknowledgment Andrew wrote: 'You know how very much I will value the portrait of the Chancellor as a souvenir. I am once more serving in the same Brigade against which the Chancellor went into action for the first time in the Great War.'

On 12 March 1935 General von Fritsch, Commander-in-Chief of the Army, wrote to Andrew to express on behalf of all Army officers who had met him their regret at his forthcoming departure from Germany. The letter ended: ‘Please accept my best wishes for your further military career.’ It was perhaps as well that von Fritsch could not know that in a little more than ten years’time Andrew would in Norway be in command of some 400,000 German troops, more than von Fritsch had ever commanded.

12

The Darkening Horizon: 1935 – 1939

On 13 May 1935, a week after King George V had celebrated the Silver Jubilee of his reign, Andrew took over command of the 1st Infantry Brigade (Guards). For a few months he and Margaret had to live at Frimley Hall Hotel while the official residence – The White House, Heath End, Aldershot – was being completely redecorated. It was pleasant enough to exchange courtesies with Thomsen about Hitler's photograph, but the invaluable evidence which he had collected about the state of the German Army only reinforced his belief in the urgent need to modernise the British Army before it was too late. In officer training, co-operation between the Services, weaponry, air warfare and defence against it, above all in forward thinking about new methods of mobile fighting, Britain lagged behind Germany. Complacency and excessive deference to tradition – what a colleague termed 'Boer War speed of change' – had to be challenged, and he took every opportunity to press his views both on the War Office and on those likely to hold posts of responsibility in a future war.

In September 1935 he lectured at the Imperial Defence College and in the following month to Aldershot Command on the growth of the German Army, telling his audiences about the men in charge of Nazi Germany and about their secret preparations for war. Yet despite his anxieties about German rearmament he maintained that the ultimate danger to Britain came from Soviet Russia. The concluding words of his lecture on 30 September were to be proved prophetic. 'Perhaps it may be possible to direct our policy so that we can co-operate with her [Germany] instead of opposing her; to guide her explosive force where it will hurt us least. Germany will undoubtedly make this as difficult as possible, owing to her blundering and blustering manners. But as, in my opinion, Soviet Russia is the greatest ultimate danger to the British Commonwealth and British ideas, I believe it would be sounder policy for us to fight alongside Germany against Russia than the opposite, which would complete the ruin of our Empire.' In voicing this personal opinion Andrew was nearer to the thinking of the War Office than of the Foreign Office. From March 1935 the views of the two began to diverge, with the War Office maintaining that the Foreign Office was painting too black a picture of Hitler and was wrong in its adherence to maintaining the terms of the Treaty of Versailles so strictly.

Whichever nation proved to be the next enemy, Andrew knew that the immediate task was to bring the British Army up to date. One of the lessons which he had learned in Germany was the importance of studying methods of concealing troops, weapons and buildings from ground and air attack by means of camouflage. Little or nothing had been done by the War Office in this important field. So, soon after taking command at Aldershot, he began to develop his ideas with much encouragement from Liddell Hart, the military historian. In the summer of 1936 various methods of camouflage were tested during two exercises around Aldershot. He received valuable co-operation from RAE Farnborough and from the RAF school of air photography. General Palmer of the Chemical Department experimented with colour designs in grey, ochre and green to conceal the shape of vehicles from the air, and air photography tested the effectiveness of netting and painted sheets in eliminating tell-tale shadows cast by armoured vehicles. Andrew raided Brigade funds to purchase sheets of netting, intended to protect garden peas from the birds, and he even bought garden parasols to hide his headquarters and to simulate a dummy one. Later in the year a report on the various forms of camouflage and on tests of their effectiveness was sent by him to the War Office, where it impressed General Wavell, a man long interested in methods of enemy deception. A committee under General Finlayson to study the whole subject was sitting at this time, and its formal thanks for Andrew's work was conveyed to him. Far more rewarding was the committee's decision to introduce camouflage on a large scale.

In the autumn of 1936 Andrew was somewhat unexpectedly

given the chance of testing his ideas on camouflage on active service. Rising tension between Arabs and Jews in Palestine led the British Government to reinforce the garrison there. The troubles in Palestine originated from British policy during the First World War. With a view to undermining Turkey's pro-German war effort and in the hope of strengthening British hold over the oil-producing areas in the Middle East, the British Government had encouraged the nationalist aspiration of the Arabs against Turkey, their suzerain power. Thus when the Arabs rose in revolt against the Turks during the war they believed that the British had promised to support their independence in certain not very precisely defined areas but of which Palestine was definitely one. In the dark days of 1917, in the hope that pressure from American Jews might bring the United States into the war, which might also have the effect of encouraging Russia not to withdraw from the war, Balfour, the Foreign Secretary, announced in November that Britain supported the Zionist movement. This aimed at establishing a 'national home for the Jewish people' in Palestine, though 'nothing shall be done which may prejudice the civil and religious rights of the existing non-Jewish communities in Palestine'. Despite the purposely vague wording of the Balfour Declaration it was quickly apparent that Britain could not fulfil rash wartime pledges of support for both Arabs and Jews in Palestine. Trouble was inevitable when in July 1922 Britain was charged by the League of Nations to accept the Mandate for Palestine, Iraq and Transjordan, with the express understanding that the Balfour Declaration should be put into effect.

Arab riots became serious from 1929 when the number of Jews entering Palestine increased dramatically as a result of the deteriorating situation in Europe. In October 1935 an attempt by Jews to smuggle a large consignment of arms into Palestine was discovered by the Arabs, who were encouraged by Italian money and propaganda to attack Jewish settlers and Jewish property. The Arab Higher Committee was formed to direct Arab agitation, and a general strike was proclaimed. The situation deteriorated during 1936 with the destruction of road and rail communications, sniping on military camps, attacks on Jewish fruit farms and damage to the oil pipe line. So far the Jews had shown restraint, but as they were known to be well armed civil war between Jews and Arabs could erupt at any moment. It was to strengthen the British military presence for maintaining the Mandate that Andrew and the 1st Guards Brigade were sent to Palestine.

On 16 September 1936 Andrew sailed from Southampton for Haifa, which he reached after a briefing in Malta on Mediterranean problems ten days later. For a month General Dill kept the 1st Guards Brigade in reserve in the area around Jerusalem. Andrew was responsible for security there and in Jaffa and Tel Aviv, with his troops protecting road and rail communications from sporadic attacks by armed bands of the Arab camel corps or by groups travelling in unarmoured cars. As far as it was possible to forecast events the immediate future appeared to be reasonably peaceful. A Royal Commission had been appointed to make recommendations on policy and the members were about to arrive. The Arab Higher Committee temporarily called off the general strike and, as Andrew explained in a letter to Margaret, it was a moment when Arabs needed to plough and sow their land and to gather the orange crop before the rainy season began, which would last until the next spring.

In a long letter to Peter Andrew analysed the political and military situation. On 18 October he wrote: 'We are in a state of suspense – which is always an uncomfortable position when the other side has the initiative.' There were, however, two factors which should assist the British in their well-nigh impossible task. 'Young Jews who served in the anti-Nazi bands . . . will have in their turn organised defensive and offensive bands which might relieve us of protecting the Jewish colonies.' More important would be 'the imposition of martial law which will free the soldiers' hands. (They have been shackled all through the present show) and this will enable really firm measures to be taken with the rebels under arms.' Martial law had been withheld pending the deliberations of the Royal Commission and Andrew admitted that it had been a temporary success. Everything turned upon the Royal Commission's recommendations, which he feared would give 'satisfaction to neither Jews nor Arabs and umbrage to both'. As he told Margaret: 'If they can persuade the Government to restrict Jewish immigration and limit their purely economic penetration in purely Arab sectors all may be well. Otherwise one feels there will be another strike when the crops are in, the rains are over and they [Arabs] have made some money.'

Towards the end of October the 1st Guards Brigade was gradually moved north and Andrew was given command of the 16th Infantry Brigade in an area with his headquarters at Nablus. At last he felt that he had a post in which he could really exercise command, and with the arrival of the Royal Commission he feared that his previous forecast had been too optimistic, for 'this is a country where political excitement and intrigue give more real pleasure than books, plays, operas, radios or anything one can think of'. In the event rioting did not recur, though it was deemed wiser for the Commission not to visit Samaria for the moment 'in case the small boys of Nablus should made rude faces at the elderly English gentlemen' as they passed through the town. Andrew was glad that among the Commission was his former chief, Sir Horace Rumbold, whom he saw frequently in the course of the next few weeks and who came to an Old Etonian Dinner on St Andrew's Day.

As a soldier it was Andrew's task to implement without question Government policy and to keep Jews and Arabs apart wherever his personal sympathies might lie. He confessed in a letter to Peter that he could understand Arab resentment. 'Even the large price they have received for their lands sold to the Jews is not recompense enough for the invasion of these alien people.' From the moment of his arrival in Jerusalem he had been struck by the similarity between the houses of the Jewish community and houses outside Berlin, an opinion confirmed by a visit to Tel Aviv. 'There one could see how the Jews have brought Europe (German Europe) to the Near East in no uncertain fashion. The town, its lay-out, its people and buildings have no relation to Palestine. They are simply a European Colony.'

At the start of December Andrew moved his headquarters from Nablus to Nazareth. During the second week of December he was temporarily in command of the 5th Division which consisted of all four battalions of the 1st Guards Brigade, together with elements drawn from the Lincolns and the Dorsets. By then the Government had felt able to bring back many of the troops sent to Palestine in September, and Andrew had high hopes of sailing for home on 19 December. Although he was only in Palestine for three months, as an expert in combining pleasure with business he had seized every opportunity of visiting archaeological and historical sites about which he had read on the outward voyage. British soldiers were forbidden to enter the Old City in Jerusalem but with American help he had managed to see all the places connected with the Gospel story. Herodian castles along the shores of the Dead Sea and remains of Crusader castles fascinated him. When Dill asked him to report on the problem of officer promotion in infantry regiments he not only worked very hard at the task (in addition to his normal duties) but skilfully arranged whenever possible to take evidence at military centres within easy distance of some site which he wished to visit. Nor were his travels confined to Palestine. The British Mandate gave him the chance of several visits to Jordan where he saw the ruins of Jerash and the marvel of Petra after meeting the Emir Abdullah in Amman. Before leaving Palestine he got leave for a short trip into Syria so as to see the beauty of Palmyra and the ostentatious grandeur of Baalbek.

Andrew's last fortnight in Palestine was saddened by the crisis of the uncrowned Edward VIII's abdication. A strong bond of mutual respect and affection had been forged during the First World War and the new King, who had succeeded his father just before midnight on 20 January 1936, continued to show his admiration for the Brigade of Guards. There had been a Royal Review at Aldershot on 13 July and two days later a presentation of new colours. On 14 August Andrew had been appointed an ADC to his Sovereign and friend. It is probable that away in Palestine he knew no more than the British public of what was happening, though he appears to have feared the worst. Not until 4 December did he refer in his letter to Margaret to 'the constitutional crisis which one had somehow always felt would never be allowed to arise thanks to the King's inherent good sense and instinct'. He added that the crisis was the sole topic of conversation, replacing even speculation about the date of sailing for home. On the same day Dill issued a directive urging the avoidance of 'all loose discussion of the subject, particularly before foreigners and waiters. The less the subject is discussed at all the better.'

Andrew heard of the Abdication from the Rumbolds shortly before the Paris edition of the *Daily Mail* arrived. On 12 December he wrote to Margaret: 'What a tragedy! but how much better that it should come now before the Coronation. I haven't seen the text of the whole message so it is difficult to judge but what I have read it is the message of a man who has used up all his resources of energy, physical and mental.' Undoubtedly Andrew felt a great sense of personal loss when as Duke of Windsor Edward passed into virtual exile. Coupled with that personal sadness was the knowledge that a Grenadier had failed to do his duty. 'I have to read the Proclamation to-morrow morning to the troops. The King is gone: Long live the King should be one's thought but it is so hard to say God save King George when one had so longed for a continuation of King Edward's reign.'

On 19 December Andrew embarked at Haifa, thankful that the cold weather had kept the Arabs quiet and that no sudden outbreak of violence had prevented him from leaving Palestine. There was nothing to be gained by vain regrets about the Abdication, and on 19 January 1937 he and Margaret, with Diana and Poppy, sailed on a cruise to the West Indies. They were back on 9 March. Two months later on 12 May they were in Westminster Abbey for the Coronation of King George VI and Queen Elizabeth.

The two and a half years between the Coronation and the outbreak of the Second World War were a period of rising importance and increasing responsibility for Andrew. In addition to his Aldershot command, he was ceaselessly involved in plans for the modernisation of the British Army. Early in 1938 he was invited to give evidence to Brigadier Massy's committee charged with commenting on the military education of a British officer. In reply to the first question in a lengthy questionnaire asking if he were satisfied with the present system his terse answer was 'No, I am not.' He went on in the evidence which he submitted to say: 'I have bored three successive Infantry Brigade Conferences at Hythe with my plea for the adoption of the German system of training young officers on entry and I have probably bored as many other officers with a plea for the adoption of the U.S. Army system of training officers after they have joined.'

Andrew maintained that the broader the education and the wider the experience of potential officers the better. For this reason he had sent his three sons to Oxford. Sandy and George had gone to Trinity College with a view to becoming university candidates for regular commissions, but Andrew felt that he could not then afford the £500 per annum private means for each of them which he judged necessary for peacetime Grenadiers. Presumably he did not consider other regiments. Peter followed their example in January 1934.

Powers of leadership could only be tested by entrusting a young man with responsibility early in his career. Andrew's proposed programme for a potential officer was the normal recruits course, followed by a period as an assistant squad instructor before going to Sandhurst. Thereafter he would serve for six months with a home unit and then go to a new creation – a staff school. By this time his worth had been thoroughly tested and a rigorous weeding out of less able men should take place. For those who survived there must be frequent courses to keep officers abreast of developments in tactics, weapons and organisation. With some hesitation he supported a suggestion of financial rewards following each acquisition of technical expertise, as in the case of foreign languages.

Ever since he returned from Germany he had urged the War Office to give greater responsibility to Warrant Officers and NCOs to test their readiness for a commission. For a long time he had tried, at first without success, to interest the War Office in the War Office Selection Board type of entry and thus ensure an initial scheme of very careful selection. At last he won his battle and the first WOSB was set up on lines which he had suggested.

On the last day of 1937 a letter from the War Office informed Andrew that he had been selected for promotion to the rank of major-general, to date from 14 February 1938. A month later he learned that he was to be General Officer Commanding, London District, from 1 December, a post which delighted him and which in fact he took over rather earlier – on 26 October. However, for the moment none of this mattered in comparison with the grave danger of war with Germany arising from Hitler's demands on Czechoslovakia.

Throughout the summer of 1938 tension had mounted in Europe. On 12 March Austria had been annexed by Germany and by mid-summer it became clear that Czechoslovakia's turn to be incorporated into the Reich had come. To Neville Chamberlain, the British Prime Minister, Czechoslovakia was 'a far-away country' with whom Britain had no treaty obligations. For the weak French Premier, Daladier, peace at almost any price was the main objective. So on 29 September, with no Czech representative consulted, a treaty was signed by Britain, Germany, France and Italy handing over the German-speaking Sudetenland to Hitler as the first stage in the country's destruction. An International Commission was to supervise the occupation of the ceded territories and would also organise a plebiscite in certain areas where the wishes of the inhabitants were to be consulted, as had occurred in the Saar in 1935.

Experience in the Saar led the War Office to set about the immediate formation of a small international force – known as C Force – to help in the maintenance of law and order in the plebiscite areas. General Brind, who had commanded a similar force in the Saar, was fully aware of the difficulties of commanding what was neither a military nor a police force. As he had said in a War Office paper, it was 'an armed force called out in aid of the civil power to which it is subordinate. It should not be used until the competent civil authority finds itself unable to cope with the situation within its own resources and calls upon the armed force to come to its assistance.' At this point it became the responsibility of the Force Commander to decide how far he could rely on the co-operation of the far from neutral local police force and the extent to which active armed support should be given at the risk of provoking invasion and a small-scale war. To the unenviable but highly responsible post of Force Commander Andrew was appointed.

He was a wise choice with his knowledge of Germany and of the language and with his skill in maintaining friendly diplomatic relations. A letter of good wishes from his brother-in-law Charles Howard-Smith, British Minister to Denmark and Iceland, might have been more encouraging: 'I am pretty sure that it will not be a military parade; on the contrary I should think it would be a distinctly difficult and unpleasant job.' The letter continues in a way which illustrates how well-informed Englishmen so often failed at this moment to realise the magnitude of Britain's and France's diplomatic defeat. 'As one looks back on this crisis it seems almost inconceivable that the Govt. could have got into such a mess and that we should have been within an ace of getting into one of the most wicked wars in all history and in my view quite definitely on the wrong side. However little we may like dictators, it is surely misguided to fight against them when they have got a good case and in a cause in which we have no interest.' Within eighteen months Denmark would be overrun and the British Mission temporarily interned.

It was intended that C Force should consist of the 1st Guards Brigade, a French brigade and a civilian body of 1200 members of the British Legion, chosen from the 17,000 who had volunteered. Their inclusion had been based on the hope that the friendly feeling, which had been steadily growing over the years between Legion members and their opposite numbers in Germany, would ensure by their presence as unarmed observers that there was no friction during the plebiscite. On arrival at Olympia each was issued with a blue serge suit, cap, armlet and a stout stick – 'the walking-stick warriors' as they were dubbed. Such was the force under Andrew's command, with Peter invited to come as his ADC.

Within a week it was clear that Hitler had no intention of submitting to the International Commission. Instead, Generals Keitel and von Brauchitz called the tune. It had been understood at Munich that the basis for the take-over of the Sudetenland areas of Czechoslovakia was to be the census of 1930. Hitler and his generals now insisted that the demarcation of population must be based on the situation in 1918 when Czechoslovakia had been part of the Austro-Hungarian Empire. The British and French members of the Commission yielded to force, and on 12 October the Commission decided that 'plebiscites may be dispensed with'. Two days earlier it had become obvious that C Force would never be permitted by Hitler to supervise anything and it was ordered to stand down forthwith. The British Legion volunteers, who had embarked at Tilbury, had reached Southend before being ordered home. As one of them later wrote: 'Never in history have returning warriors been so reluctant to return to the bosom of their families.'

With the immediate danger of a European war removed Andrew was free to take over command of London District on 26 October 1938. On that date he became a major-general but with seniority from 23 December 1937. 'I feel very proud', he wrote in answer to Peter's letter of congratulation, 'that I am now Major-General commanding the Brigade of Guards and I have almost forgotten how long I have had to wait but I do not regret it.' His office at the Horse Guards was over the central archway and was the room originally occupied by the Commander-in-Chief. The portraits of George III and Queen Charlotte, which had once looked down on Wellington, now watched Andrew as he sat at the circular desk.

London District consisted of the Metropolitan Police Area, together with that part of Essex from a point opposite the confluence of the River Darent and the Thames to Purfleet railway station and thence north-west along the railway line to the River Beam. It also included, though not for Movement purposes, the Guards Depots at Caterham, Pirbright and Windsor. Omitting the three depots, it is an area of about 750 square miles which for a military command is almost insignificant. Its size was of no importance compared with the fact that it is the most congested area in Great Britain, containing the seat of government, the headquarters of all the Services and ministries, the greatest port in the country and the principal termini of the four main-line railways.

It was an arduous command, very varied in its demands, with a great deal of ceremonial responsibility on top of the main task, which was overall command of the Brigade of Guards and ultimate jurisdiction over the Territorial Army force in London. All troop movements in the District were dealt with in Andrew's office, involving both those needed for ceremonial occasions and, far more important, the training of men likely before long to find themselves on active service. The Munich Treaty had gained a breathing space for British rearmament, but after the seizure of the whole of Czechoslovakia on 15 March 1939 even those who had most strongly defended Chamberlain's policy knew that sooner rather than later Europe would again be at war. For on 31 March a disillusioned Chamberlain told the House of Commons that he had given Poland a guarantee of British help if she were attacked.

During the ten months of peace that Andrew commanded London District he was concerned with two state visits – that of King Carol of Rumania and, of much greater significance, that of the French President Lebrun. For his share in the latter visit he was made a Commander of the Legion of Honour. He was officially on duty for the Opening of Parliament, the Armistice Day ceremony at the Cenotaph and two state banquets at Buckingham Palace at the time of the state visits, and on 2 June 1939 he took the salute at the final rehearsal of what for a while was to be the last Trooping the Colour. It was a hectic life, but interesting, and he was rewarded in the Birthday Honours by being appointed Commander of the Bath in the military division of that Order. Ceremonial mattered to him and must be performed to perfection. At the same time, although official records of his term as Commander of the London District unfortunately have not survived, it is a fair guess that his main preoccupation was with achieving the maximum amount of training before war came again and with preparing London for war in the midst of peacetime ceremonial.

Andrew could deal efficiently with ceremonial problems. What worried him was the serious unpreparedness of the War Office to fight a major war. Up to July 1939 no adequate movement control establishment had been authorised for London Area. Urgent arrangements for mobilisation were discussed at a series of monthly meetings, the first of which was not held until November 1938. By April 1939 there was authority for Reserve officers to be called up for training. Although HQ London District had made careful plans with the co-operation of the London station-masters for the movement of troops and had reported them to the War Office in May, no further steps had been taken when war broke out. Andrew's general overseeing of the Territorial Army in London District was no light task, for during 1939 the whole Territorial Army was being doubled in size and he was responsible for the formation of the 2nd London Division.

He was also responsible for the development of Civil Defence measures. Here he met with the usual frustrations. Those concerned with Air Raid Precautions still believed Baldwin's cry that the bomber will always get through and approached their task with little sense of urgency. Andrew did his utmost to remedy this by approaching the mayors of the London boroughs, most of whom at that time were Socialists and, more worrying, pacifists, to support a drive for an effective ARP organisation. Only Alderman Charles Key, of Stepney, was prepared to co-operate with him.

Although no records of the fact exist, it is certain that he must have been concerned with contingency plans for the safety of the King and Queen and other members of the Royal Family. While he would not have held sole responsibility for this, he would have taken part in discussions, as did his successor in June 1940 at the time when invasion was threatened.

In addition to all his official duties he and Margaret were moving house. Early in May 1938 they had seen an advertisement in *The Times* of the impending sale of the Lutyens-designed The Deanery at Sonning-on-Thames. It was a large house standing in half an acre of garden landscaped by Gertrude Jekyll. In addition there was a 6½-acre paddock some 300 yards away. The house, regarded as one of his most attractive buildings, needed redecorating, but the price was very reasonable as the owners were anxious to give up the house in view of the large number of London evacuees which it was scheduled to receive in the event of war. In mid-November they moved in.

By mid-summer the all too familiar territorial claims were being made on Poland by Hitler. Despite the impossibility of British troops being able to assist the Poles directly there was no doubt in anyone's mind that following an invasion of Poland Britain would be again at war with Germany. Towards the end of August a professional photographer had come to The Deanery to take a photograph of the Thorne family. All save Margaret are in uniform. Sandy, George and Peter were Grenadiers, Diana was in the ATS, Poppy in FANY uniform and Pansy a Red Cross nurse. With all the family at home for the moment but soon to go to their wartime posts, Margaret must have wondered whether they would all be together when the war ended. It must have seemed almost impossible to her that Andrew could again bear the charmed life of the First World War or that all her three sons would survive.

On 1 September as the *blitzkrieg* on Poland was launched

Andrew wrote to Margaret, knowing and fully sharing her thoughts:

> The situation does not look very good but it *had* to happen once we started to oppose Hitler and it is better that we should take this strong line. It is much more likely in the long run than a patched up peace without hope or prospect of endurance.
>
> We have much more to lose than most people and so it is ever so much harder for us to face the future but it is an opportunity to show that we are worthy of the Brats and that we can set them a good example of courage and endurance.
>
> You were marvellous in the last war; we must try and improve on our form because I believe we and the whole country will be put to a much harder test and if we fail our responsibility is so great. All my prayers for strength for us all.

13
The Second World War September 1939 – May 1941

SEPTEMBER 1939 – JUNE 1940: DUNKIRK

'They went with songs to the battle' – but that was in 1914. Britain went to war in 1939 in no mood of exultant patriotism but in a spirit of grim determination to finish a task which all had hoped had been completed in 1919. The entire Thorne family was soon actively involved in the war effort. Margaret, lamenting that she alone had no uniform to wear, was fully employed in voluntary work for the troops and in the Red Cross, reminded by Andrew that she was also 'the lodestone and sheet anchor of seven other individuals'. This family involvement enabled him to get The Deanery exempted from receiving its maximum quota of evacuees. Returning warriors needed somewhere to spend their leave. 'I don't know how you feel about it,' he wrote to Margaret a week after war was declared, 'but I am sure you agree with me that we can be very proud of the family – if we aren't intellectual giants we are certainly a nice, sensible, fairly capable lot of folk.'

On 18 October 1939 Andrew, whose professional star was in the ascendant, was ordered to take command of the 48th (South Midland) Division, which was to be ready 'for the front line in the not too distant future'. His reputation as the trainer of men stood high. The 48th Division, as an officer who had recently served in it told Andrew, needed what it had now got – 'a real leader'; for 'there is as yet no sign of a coherent whole. Units and bits of units are scattered all over the South and West of England, neither trained nor administered.' His headquarters were in Littlecote Manor, a lovely Elizabethan house some two miles south of the Swindon to Hungerford road. This was not the first occasion on which troops had disturbed its peace, for during the Civil War it had housed a regiment of Cromwell's Ironsides. On his first night at dinner in the Great Hall, with little but the light from the big log fire to illuminate the room, Andrew was momentarily startled to hear a croaking voice far off cry 'Good luck' from a dark corner. The good wishes came from a macaw. It was such a good omen that the macaw was made into the 48th Division's sign at once.

Andrew's sons preceded him to France. Sandy was a platoon commander in the 1st Battalion in Montgomery's 3rd Division. George was ADC to the GOC 1st Division, General Alexander, and able to give his father useful advice about the needs of a divisional mess in France – what must be brought from England. Peter was a platoon commander with the 3rd Battalion Grenadier Guards until March 1940 and later Intelligence Officer. Meanwhile Andrew was doing his utmost to train the 48th Division for active service. The BEF under Gort as Commander-in-Chief had begun to cross into France on 10 September, using western ports to minimise the danger of air attack. In contrast to a similar operation twenty-five years earlier, mechanical vehicles now totally replaced animals. Andrew was in France for the first ten days of December to meet Dill and Brooke, following a family dinner party in Lille arranged by George. He was back in England on 10 December. Part of 48th Division crossed at the end of the month when Andrew once again slept on French soil at the start of a campaign. With the arrival of the remainder of 48th Division early in January the first contingent of the BEF – some 222,000 men – was complete.

The determination of the Belgian and Dutch Governments to maintain a strict neutrality prevented the construction of adequate defences in those countries. All that was politically possible during the so-called 'phoney war' was to strengthen the inadequately protected French frontier between the end of the Maginot Line and the sea. Absence of fighting at least gave opportunities to continue weapon training, artillery practice and troop exercises involving movement over a large area in co-operation with the RAF. Trench digging through soil either frozen hard or waterlogged was no joy for the troops. 'The clay is very stiff and sticks beautifully to the shovels', as Andrew reported to Margaret. Sandy and Peter were more forthright in their comments on inadequacies. Peter, who admitted having 'a civilian approach' to his work, told his father that '60% of the boots in the Company are so rotten that they could not survive 15 miles over the pavé, while in arctic weather the troops have twice been issued with two pairs of winter pants but no vests.' Andrew, as an old campaigner, was more philosophical. 'It looks as if the memories of the last war are sufficiently vivid to ensure that the round chaps are put into round holes . . . Comparative efficiency reigns.'

At this stage of the war it was possible for his sons to visit him, dine in the mess and occasionally stay overnight, which enabled all of them to keep Margaret informed of their doings. In February Andrew had succumbed to a severe bout of the prevalent influenza. His doctor had dealt with him firmly, reminding him that he was not as young as he was, but had given him a clean bill of health provided that 'thereafter he did not take quite so much unnecessary exercise'. Among those who came to see him in bed was the Duke of Windsor, who had been attached to the British Military Mission at Vincennes and was visiting units of the BEF. 'E.P. came upstairs and was in admirable form – he sat without fidgeting for well over half an hour and talked away easily and happily without touching any raw spots.'

In their letters home to Margaret Andrew arranged with her to lease Dunconusg to the RAF for the duration of the war; Peter wickedly suggested to her that his father's staff 'must be getting a little tired of the 1st Guards by now'; George, with brotherly devotion, gleefully reported to her that Andrew had told him that Peter's name had been taken by his Brigadier 'for (1)Arguing, (2)Lying (3)Disobeying (4) Impertinence and general lack of discipline'. The story had clearly lost little in the telling. In return Margaret could keep them all abreast of family news. Diana was at the school of Military Engineering; Poppy in addition to her service in the FANYs was in process of becoming engaged; while Pansy, working in a hospital, wished her brothers to know that they were no longer to treat her as a child.

As in the First World War Andrew wrote almost daily to Margaret, dwelling on the achievements or otherwise of his French cook, who had tried to cook 'à la Littlecote (which in any case was rather indifferent)'; surprised that 'there should be no parlour maids available'; and showing his characteristic love of countryside and flowers. Living close to the coal-mining area of north-eastern France made gardening unrewarding and 'the French do not seem to waste their time or money on planting anything which cannot be eaten or utilized somehow!' Once away from the coal pits he delighted in finding cowslips in a wood and cottage gardens in which the flowers were beginning to bloom. Probably unconsciously he followed Walter de la Mare's advice: 'Look your last on all things lovely every hour.' Many of his letters contained passages of encouragement to Margaret, who was depressed in a large house like The Deanery without her family at home. Mrs Manning, whose husband was a sergeant in the Grenadier Guards band, and her two children, evacuees from London, could not provide the company which she wanted. They were, in fact, a very pleasant family, and Mrs Manning in the first months of the war knitted a sweater for George which did not have to be discarded until 1984. 'Please do not think of moving out of the house until Mr Bate [the solicitor] recommends you to do so. It is impossible at present to say if it is likely that we can [afford to] live in The Deanery after the war or not.'

Margaret had been seriously ill in Berlin with cancer of the breast which had necessitated a major operation. Although she had made an excellent recovery she continued to suffer from minor ailments, which now included influenza and German measles, made harder to bear in loneliness. In February 1940 her mother died, over ninety years old. Andrew, who as a young man found her forbidding, had come to feel affection as well as respect for her and it is clear that his family were genuinely fond of her. Understandably Margaret was fearful of what must lie ahead and she worried at Churchill's warnings of grim times to come. It was virtually impossible for Andrew to provide adequate comfort, for she never fully shared his untroubled Christian faith.

On 9 April 1940 the 'phoney war' ended as Hitler's armies overran Norway and Denmark. Andrew could not prevent his old professional admiration for German military skill from coming out in his letters. 'One cannot help admiring the old Boche for the extraordinary skill with which they mounted and delivered the seizure of two countries. Whether it was strategically sound remains to be seen but tactically it was beautifully done. Curse them!' He was certain that the BEF would soon be heavily engaged and would be at a grave disadvantage with the continued neutrality of the Dutch and Belgians and the already apparent lack of the will to win among the French troops. On 10 May, while Andrew was enjoying a short spell of leave at home, Hitler invaded Holland and Belgium. Having done little or nothing to defend themselves, both countries appealed to Britain and France for help. He at once returned to his division and on 12 May wrote a little too optimistically to Margaret: 'The Dutchmen seem to be doing remarkably well in spite of the appalling difficulties inherent in the German tactics with their parachutes.' This was the last letter to reach Margaret until after Dunkirk.

Until the British and French forces were permitted to enter Belgium all that Gort could do was to make detailed plans for a future advance. It had been agreed with Gamelin – described by Margaret after a lunch meeting in 1939 as 'a very dull and second-rate little man' – under whose orders, or lack of them, Gort laboured, that the River Dyle offered the most promising defensive line and that I Corps under General Barker should hold the sector from Wavre to Louvain. The 48th Division would form the reserve of I Corps a little south of Brussels. When Andrew returned from his broken leave he rejoined his division where it had taken up its new position.

Up to 15 May, the day on which the Dutch Army laid down its arms, I Corps was not seriously engaged, since the Germans restricted their activities to heavy bombing of the rearward areas on that part of the front. This led to a pitiful flight of refugees, choking the road, hampering troop movements and providing a perfect target for the bombers. On that day Gort was asked to take over part of the front held by a French division on the right, and Andrew was ordered to detach one of his brigades for the purpose. However, by next day it became clear that the French could not hold their ground, and defence of the Dyle line became impossible. Accordingly Gort received orders to withdraw his forces that night to the Senne Canal and on the subsequent two nights to the River Dendre and then to the River Escaut.

Despite a deteriorating situation to the south, I and II Corps were on the Senne Canal by the afternoon of 17 May with 48th Division covering their right flank from Enghien to Lembecq. Two days later the division had completed its withdrawal to the

Escaut and was preparing to defend the river line, only to discover that the level of the water was dangerously low, being in places less than three feet deep. This was partly due to unusually dry weather, but more to the closing of the sluices near Valenciennes in order to inundate the countryside – at the expense of the BEF. Furthermore, by now it was apparent that Allied forces in the north-eastern area – the French force nearest to the sea, the Belgian Army, the BEF and the bulk of the French 1st Army – were in serious danger of being cut off from the main French forces in the south by the German encircling movement.

On 21 May the CIGS, General Ironside, arrived at Gort's headquarters with Cabinet orders that the BEF should move south-westward and attack Amiens so as to prevent this loss of contact with the main French forces. Gort pointed out the impossibility of obeying these orders when most of his troops were holding back the enemy on the Escaut and when contradictory orders were reaching him from the French Higher Command. Not until 23 May did Weygand see fit to inform Gort that he had superseded Gamelin as Allied Commander-in-Chief and that he must have time to study the situation before announcing new plans. Such a delay was fatal and confirmed Gort's belief that a withdrawal north-westward to the Channel ports would soon become inevitable.

On 24 May 48th Division was fighting on the Escaut near Maulde. Some enemy had managed to cross the river disguised as refugees, but they had been discovered and were driven out by bayonet. Nevertheless, the Corps Commanders warned Gort that they could not hold the line for more than twenty-four hours and that it was essential to withdraw their troops behind the defence works along the Franco-Belgian border. On that day the Germans cut the rail links with Abbeville, and plans were hastily made to move stores and supplies back to Boulogne, Calais and Dunkirk. It was too late. Boulogne and Calais were being heavily attacked: Boulogne surrendered on 25 May and Calais, despite the heroic sacrifice of the Rifle Brigade, was lost next day. It was this sacrifice of brave men which Churchill was to justify as winning an invaluable three days during which supplies could still be landed at Dunkirk for troops, short of ammunition, who had been fighting since 23 May on half rations. The safety of the

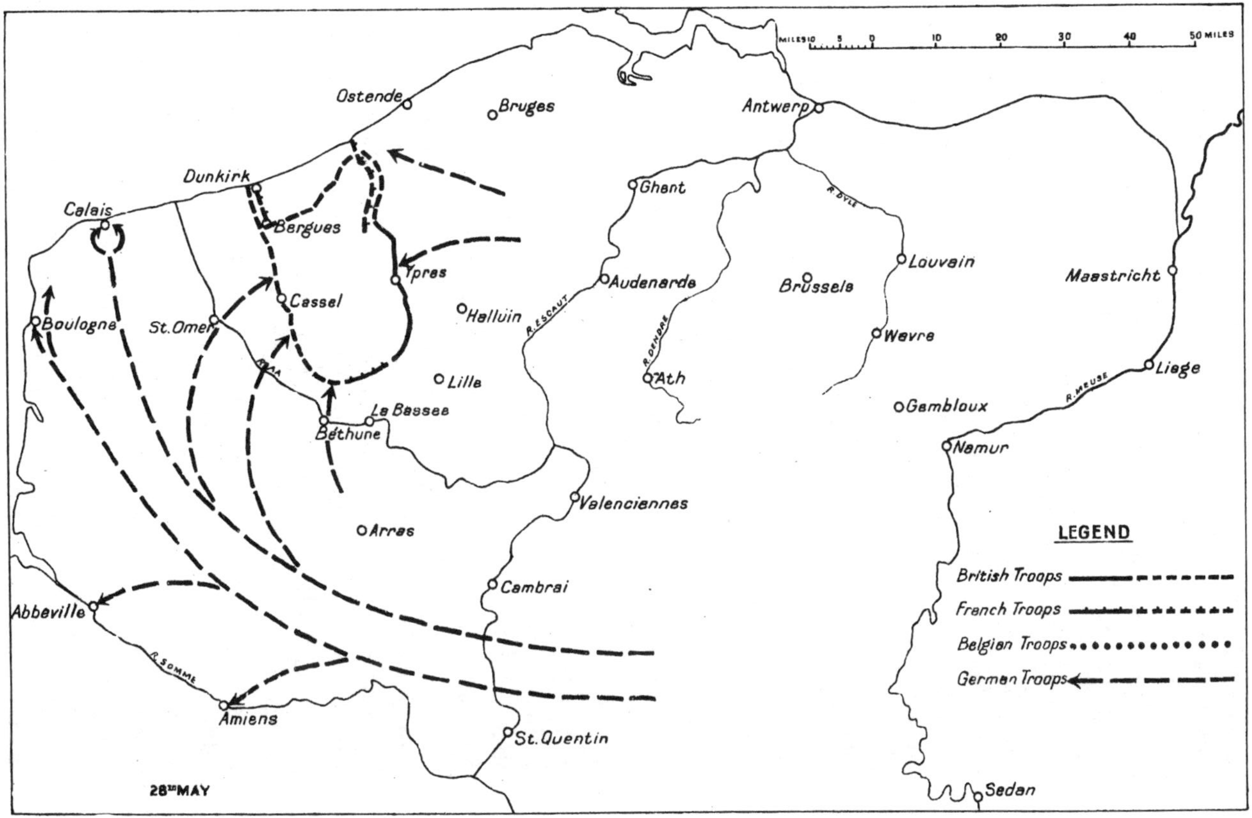
MILES 10 5 0 10 20 30 40 50 MILES
Ostende
Bruges
Antwerp
Dunkirk
Ghant
Calais
Bergues
R. DYLE
Louvain
Ypres
Audenarde
Brussels
Maastricht
Cassel
Halluin
Boulogne
St. Omer
R. ESCAUT
R. DENDRE
Wevre
R. AA
Ath
Liege
Lille
R. MEUSE
La Bassee
Gembloux
Bethune
Namur
Valenciennes
Arras
LEGEND
British Troops
Cambrai
French Troops
Abbeville
Belgian Troops
R. SOMME
German Troops
Amiens
St. Quentin
28TH MAY
Sedan

greater part of the BEF now turned on how long the defensive perimeter around Dunkirk could be held. In that rearguard action Andrew and the 48th Division played a crucial part.

The British sector on the perimeter ran from Bergues on the right flank and thence along the lines of canals to Furnes and Nieuport. Andrew was ordered to send one infantry brigade into Dunkirk and one to Cassel and Hazebrouck. Finding that the French had made adequate troop dispositions in the town itself, he sent the 144th Infantry Brigade to Wormhoudt and Bergues, where to Gort's satisfaction he set up his headquarters. 48th Division held a dangerously responsible position, and from the high ground at Cassel, the most southerly point of the line, he could see the threatened panzer onslaught developing. On 28 May Belgium capitulated, and Gort received Cabinet orders to withdraw as many of the BEF as possible and an equal number of French troops through Dunkirk. 48th Division were now in continuous contact with the enemy along a front of more than twenty-six miles from Bergues to Cassel and on to Vieux Berquin. The Division was ordered to hold its positions at Bergues and Wormhoudt for a few hours longer while I and II Corps were moving to the beaches. During the night of 28/29 May the garrisons at these two places were extricated with great difficulty and survivors made their way back to Dunkirk. On 31 May their embarkation began.

Such in outline were the movements of the 48th Division under Andrew's command during the twenty-two day campaign. Of his personal part more needs to be said.

Andrew was a superb military tactician, and his skill was never better demonstrated than by his brilliant handling of the 48th Division on the long retreat from the River Dyle to Dunkirk. It was very much a personal achievement, for in spite of a trusted staff and some wholly reliable units he knew that there had been insufficient time to train the division to face a *blitzkrieg*. In addition, like other divisional commanders, he suffered from the incompetence and virtual breakdown of General Barker, who had recently taken over I Corps from Dill and who was not relieved of his command until 30 May. During a chance meeting with a friend inside the perimeter he said that as Divisional Commander he was finding it necessary personally to site almost every section as he tried to deploy the division in a defensive position. 'They are quite untrained. They dig in the middle of fields in full view of any approaching enemy.' In a letter to Anthony Eden after the war he described the final stages at Bergues where 'I had to improvise an ad hoc force of British and French administrative troops, some gunless French Territorial gunners, stiffened by one company of the Glosters'. With personal achievement went a continuous sense of personal responsibility for the safety of those under his command. As he told Eden, 'The defence of Cassel seemed vital to the safe withdrawal of the BEF and in the end it was turned by German infantry breaking through the gap between 145 and 144 Brigades. But I cannot ever forgive myself for not getting back 145 Brigade in time to avoid losing Nigel Somerset and too many of his Brigade as P.O.W.s.'

This sense of personal responsibility did not imply that Andrew expected little from his men. His greatest admiration was always accorded to those who put their duty first at whatever personal risk. Sensitive to other people's problems and weaknesses, he was never sentimental about them. Sentiment was a luxury which could not be afforded in wartime. Yet he knew that a man whose nerve was in danger of breaking under the strain would not be given fresh courage by abuse. At one moment during the retreat as his men were passing through a French town they were attacked by German aircraft. A young private soldier lost his head and rushed down the street shouting and firing his Bren gun wildly at the aircraft overhead. He almost ran into Andrew, who was walking in the opposite direction. Andrew stopped him with a sharp tap on the shoulder. The man was aghast at being stopped by an officer with red tabs. 'You have a flybutton undone,' said Andrew and moved on.

Andrew, deeply distressed at having to leave behind 145 Brigade to fight with gallantry to the end of their ammunition before being forced to surrender, was now free to move towards the beaches and the waiting ships himself. At about the same time George had been ordered by General Alexander to act 'as a one man information centre on the road junction with my back to the sea, telling all and sundry that I Corps should go west towards Dunkirk, II Corps east towards Furnes . . . It was amazing the number of friends and familiar faces I met . . . An hour or so and several thousand troops later I spotted a group of three with arms linked making slow progress towards me. My heart missed a beat when I recognised Papa, apparently being supported by his aged ADC, Alan Perrins, and his Orderly, Guardsman Pearce. However, on closer inspection it was clear that the 55-year-old A.F.A.N.T. was dragging his exhausted ADC and Orderly along. I was able to divert this 48 Division HQ party to our "A" Mess, one ruined cottage, and produce a cup of cocoa, biscuit, slice of bully beef and blanket and "bed space" in the sand dune. This ration was repeated for breakfast. I feel all dutiful sons should like to be able to offer this sort of support to parents in what might pass as an emergency!'

Once on the beaches Andrew steadied his men by his own example, wading deep into the sea up to his armpits as he tried to teach them how to row the many ship's boats floating off the beach until they were picked up. Sir John Nicholson, then a company commander in the machine gun battalion of 48th Division, has a vivid recollection of Andrew at Dunkirk. 'We were tired and I expect scared by almost unopposed German aircraft: beach embarkation into a trickle of ships lying offshore was excruciatingly slow: some weapons had already been discarded and discipline was probably getting ragged. On the second morning the General stood on a sand dune accompanied by a signaller to whom he declaimed this message: 'To His Majesty the King, Buckingham Palace. Sir, with humble duty, unless more ships are sent quickly, the gallant soldiers of your 48th Division will not reach home.' This, as he doubtless intended, had an electrifying effect on several hundreds in hearing and on the rest among whom it soon spread . . . By a seeming miracle enough ships arrived on the afternoon tide to lift morale.' When Andrew's own turn came he scrambled up the nets hung on the side of the destroyer, furious with himself for inefficiently dropping his briefcase into the sea as he climbed to safety. On 1 June he was in England.

As has been said, Andrew possessed an almost childlike faith in the power of prayer. Just before the final retreat into Dunkirk, having had little or no sleep for several nights, he found time for two hours' rest. Instead of sleeping he washed and shaved before finding a small wayside church in which to say his prayers. It is not hard to guess that those prayers were offered for the safety of his men and for his own worthiness to lead them. It is certain that they must have been offered for the safety of his family and equally certain that they were answered.

Sandy, thankful that the Battalion HQ signallers had not jettisoned their equipment and could signal their presence to nearby vessels, returned in an Isle of Man ferry, which narrowly escaped being dive-bombed by a Stuka. Peter had been wounded in the neck by a mortar bomb, which had exploded between him and another officer. 'Five men from the 3rd Battalion, including two men from my Intelligence Section, by an extraordinary coincidence had arrived at that particular section of the perimeter just after we had. They got me along to the beach – it must have been very laborious as I kept on "blacking-out" – and we joined the somewhat ragged column making their way to the embarkation points.'

He returned by hospital ship to make a good recovery. George, happy to be aboard a comparatively comfortable fishing smack tied up to the Mole while awaiting the tide, had to abandon ship when a shell smashed its stern but boarded a nearby destroyer alongside the Mole, in time to play cricket for the Eton Ramblers at Eton on the Fourth of June. To complete the story of the almost miraculous survival of the Thorne family, Neville Wigram, soon to be Poppy's husband, also a Grenadier, returned unscathed. Andrew's orderly, Guardsman Pearce, also returned safely though wounded, and was conveyed to Colchester Military Hospital in Poppy's ambulance, deeply depressed at the thought that few of the family were likely to survive.

JUNE 1940 – MAY 1941: XII CORPS

On 8 June 1940, a week after returning from Dunkirk, Andrew was appointed to take command of XII Corps, a post which carried with it the rank of lieutenant-general. On the same day General Ironside, Commander-in-Chief Home Forces, who had been Commandant at the Staff College when Andrew was there in 1923, wrote to him: 'You will find plenty to do down in your Sector. There is no time to keep weaklings or men who cannot work a full twenty-four hours. I want you to be absolutely brutal in turning people out and getting better in.' L.D.V.s [later the Home Guard] should be of great use to you for the static defence – shot guns and bombs and these Molotoff Cocktails. Press on with these things and the mobile columns . . . Glad you and your boys are out. God bless you, Bulgy. Keep going.'

Andrew had no illusions about the magnitude of his task. He was responsible for the defence of Kent, Sussex, and parts of Hampshire and Surrey, while the coastline to be defended ran from Greenwich to Hayling Island, the most invasion-prone strip of coastline in the British Isles. To repel a threatened invasion his forces consisted of the 3rd Division, trained and ready for service in France but earmarked to be sent to Northern Ireland; one theoretically motorised brigade; 5,000 stevedores, only later armed with rifles, for whom no dock work existed; a miscellany of minor units; and a district headquarters at Tunbridge Wells. Except for the 3rd Division the standard of training was either very low or, among the stevedores, non-existent. The Corps possessed little artillery, no tanks and almost no ammunition. The deliverance of so many of the BEF from the Dunkirk beaches had only been accomplished by leaving the greater part of the Army's equipment behind.

The plan which Ironside presented to the Chiefs of Staff on 25 June for the defence of Britain provided for a 'crust' of troops along the coast to meet the first invaders; behind them in great depth were mobile columns and static strong points intended to delay the enemy until the mobile columns were brought into action; and, finally, covering London and the industrial areas there was to be a 'GHQ Line' in the form of a continuous ditch running from Yorkshire to the Blackwall Tunnel and on to Maidstone and south of London. Andrew expected if pushed back from the coast to stand and fight on this line after the enemy advance had been delayed as long as possible by mobile columns. Ironside's plan met with much criticism, especially from Churchill, who approved of the mobile columns and defence in depth but saw the 'crust' as another doomed Maginot Line. The debate on the various forms of strategy to be employed was largely academic, for had the German invasion been launched immediately after the French armistice was granted on 25 June the Home Forces would have been totally inadequate to repel it.

As we now know, not until 16 July did Hitler issue the directive for Operation Sea Lion, the code name for the invasion of Britain.

On 29 June Anthony Eden, as Secretary of State for War, visited XII Corps and reported to Churchill that 'there is no anti-tank regiment nor anti-tank gun in the whole of the Corps area'. He added that its commander had no tanks at his disposal nor any means of repelling a *blitzkrieg* attack by infantry and dive bombers. Churchill had in fact on the previous day sent a minute to General Ismay asking him to get hold of the General commanding the southern side of the Thames estuary 'whoever he is' and bring him to lunch at Chequers on 30 June. When they met, Churchill was more optimistic than Andrew about the failure of an invasion, believing that the Navy would make such an operation extremely hazardous. At the same time he appreciated Andrew's anxiety that with his present divisions 'scarcely equipped and only partly trained' he could ill afford to lose the 3rd Division to Northern Ireland. He might hold the left flank of a German advance in Ashdown Forest but not the right flank attacking from Canterbury to London. Churchill was convinced by Andrew and ordered the division to remain in Sussex.

The possibilities of guerilla warfare inevitably occur to those in command of manifestly weaker forces than the enemy enjoys. At once Andrew's mind had gone back to his years in Berlin and the visit to East Prussia where he had witnessed the value of 'stay-behind' guerilla bands, who in hiding allowed the enemy to advance over them and then attacked their lines of communication from the rear. He was the first officer to appreciate at this moment what came to be called 'auxiliary units', and he applied to the War Office for and obtained the services of Peter Fleming, the well-known explorer and writer. Picked members of the Home Guard, led by one or two Army officers, were expected to emerge from hiding and to inflict as much damage as possible on the enemy before being captured or killed. Fleming disapproved of such wasted effort and substituted a longer-term plan. Elaborate underground hideouts, stocked with rations, cooking materials, wireless sets and explosives were constructed. Each unit would consist of some dozen men and a subaltern, able to operate behind the enemy lines for a few weeks or even months. About twenty of these auxiliary units were formed and to them were attached small 'cells' of Home Guard members, trained at weekends in sabotage and the use of high explosives. Fleming even toyed with the idea of their using bows and arrows with an attached detonator, so that individual Germans could be shot without disclosing the position of the archer.

The idea of auxiliary units interested Churchill, who in a minute of 25 September to Eden said: 'I have been following with much interest the growth and development of the new guerilla formations . . . known as 'auxiliary units'. From what I hear these units are being organised with thoroughness and imagination and should in the event of invasion prove a useful addition to the regular forces.' While Peter Fleming organised the whole scheme in its early stages, the idea, as he recognised, was Andrew's. Fleming's admiration for him is clear from a letter which he wrote at the end of 1940 before being reluctantly transferred to other work. 'It made all the difference to owe allegiance to a sympathetic and accessible Commander on the spot.' He compared Andrew's commonsense understanding of what could and could not be achieved with the 'romanticism' of his next commanding officer and his staff 'for whom an enemy is hardly worth killing unless he can be killed by a tarantula fired from an airgun by a Bessarabian undertaker on Walpurgis Night'. After the war Fleming admitted to serious doubts about what the auxiliary units would have achieved if put to the test, but he had no doubts about what Andrew was achieving. In an obituary notice in *The Times* in 1970 he wrote: 'As the summer wore on XII Corps' strength and skill at arms increased, as did that of its auxiliaries in the Home Guard; but the situation remained ominous and it was in great part due to Thorne's tireless energy, his powers of leadership and his imaginative use of scanty resources that, if Operation Sea Lion had been launched in September 1940, Hitler's Wehrmacht would (with any luck) have suffered its first defeat.'

While in command of XII Corps Andrew's day usually began at 6 a.m. in order to get through the mass of paperwork before breakfast and thus leave the day free for touring his large area, holding conferences or meeting the seemingly endless stream of distinguished visitors from London intent on seeing 'the front line'. Churchill and members of his Cabinet, leading British and foreign generals, American and other neutral observers, all had to be shown what XII Corps was doing. It was a time-consuming business and is said at one moment to have caused Andrew to wish that the Prime Minister would not so often interrupt vital work in his delight at visiting the coastal defences around Dover – a remark which Andrew believed to have been unwisely passed on to Churchill and which would not have endeared him to the Prime Minister. A letter to Andrew from General Dill shows that at least some visits were rewarding. He wrote congratulating him on 'a wonderful show for the American observers on 26 August . . . the primary object of this visit has been achieved, namely to convince our visitors that we have the will and the power to see the war through to a successful termination – a fact about which they seem to have had some misgivings.'

With vivid memories of the tragic plight of refugees in France and Belgium and of their uncontrolled obstruction of roads urgently needed for the Army, Andrew was insistent on fully preparing the civilian population in his area for what might lie ahead. To this end a fortnight after taking command he formed a committee of local Members of Parliament and at the same time began forging close links with the police force, often a rare alliance in the past. Military planning had to be his top priority, and as the days went by he watched with satisfaction the growing strength of the coastal defences – the miles of barbed wire, the gun emplacements and the impeding blocks of concrete on the beaches. Inland anti-tank obstacles and concrete pill-boxes at crossroads to be manned by the Home Guard until mobile forces arrived had to be hastily constructed. Deep ditches had to be dug across golf courses or even through private gardens. Every kind of obstacle to hamper airborne troops had to be devised. In this heavy work, between periods of drill armed with axes, his stevedores were invaluable. He must have gained much private amusement from some of the early efforts of the Home Guard, but he gave them his wholehearted support and encouragement, admiring their patriotic dedication and determination, well aware that they might soon be playing an important delaying role if an enemy force landed.

In that fine summer of 1940 Andrew enjoyed driving through Kent and Sussex, meeting the officers and men under his command, instilling into them his own confidence in ultimate victory and encouraging them to even greater efforts. All the while he was working to overcome the dangerous shortage of weapons for the military units, who were also desperately in need of much basic training. He even at the start commandeered obsolete rifles and guns from local museums. Ralph Arnold, his new ADC, who became a close friend of the family, later wrote that to serve Andrew might appear to be a 'cushy job' with good food and a comfortable bed but in reality it was hard going, especially on tour. 'If General Thorne saw a hill he had a compulsion to climb to the top of it. If there were no hills, and if he had time to spare, he would get out of the car and indulge in a curious Boy Scout's progress – so many paces walking, so many paces running slow, so many paces running *hard*, so many paces walking. Then back to the car again. We covered a lot of the flatter parts of Kent and Sussex in this healthy but tiring way.'

One very small part of his work gave Andrew particular pleasure. XII Corps needed its own distinguishing sign, and he hit on the idea of a design which would incorporate 'the three great indigenous trees of England, the oak, the ash and the thorn'. Apart from the nice play on his name, as a lover of Kipling he knew that these three trees formed the basis of a poem in *Puck of Pook's Hill*, an appropriate choice as Pook's Hill was on the Sussex and Kent border.

> Sing oak, and ash, and thorn, good sirs
> (All of a midsummer morn),
> England shall bide till judgment tide,
> By oak and ash and thorn.

He was put in touch with an artist, Kenneth Hobson, who completed a design in mid-August.

On 12 October Hitler issued a directive postponing Operation Sea Lion until the following spring. From September 1940 the Battle of Britain was being fought out in the Kentish skies, and Hitler knew that without air superiority his invasion was doomed. Furthermore, by the time that spring came Hitler's mind was occupied with plans for the invasion of Russia. Operation Barbarossa had killed Operation Sea Lion as effectively as British pilots had defeated Goering's Luftwaffe. This change of plan was not at first known in Britain, but with the passing of the early months of 1941 the danger from invasion slowly receded as British power of resistance daily increased.

On 19 April 1941 Andrew learned to his dismay that from 1 May he was to leave XII Corps and become General Officer Commanding-in-Chief, Scottish Command. On the same day he received by personal delivery a letter from Montgomery in his own handwriting, written from his V Corps Headquarters. 'I was rung up yesterday by M.S. at G.H.Q. who informed me that I was to be moved from here to take over command of XII Corps. What does it all mean? And where are you going to? I asked if I was to regard it as a compliment and he said "Yes"!! I suppose one has to do what one is told but I cannot see why one should be moved from one Corps to another . . . Perhaps you could send me a line as to what it all means.' Two days later at the end of a conference Andrew briefly announced to a stunned audience his imminent departure from XII Corps and his replacement by Montgomery. As the Conference broke up Charles Britten, a fellow Grenadier, went up to Andrew and asked what was happening to him. He received the terse reply: 'I have been banished to Scotland.' When it became known that he had been promoted to command an army the letters of congratulation expressed what one writer described as 'the utmost gloom and despondency' at the loss of an outstanding corps commander who had become a personal friend to so many. Andrew spent the morning of Sunday 27 April saying his goodbyes before Montgomery arrived for lunch. He handed over his command at 3.30 p.m. and then drove home to The Deanery.

The Scottish Command might rank as command of an army, but it was not the kind of promotion which pleased Andrew. He had been in the thick of the Dunkirk fighting and had then been given command of the most dangerous sector in the defence of Britain, winning golden opinions in both of these assignments. To be sent to the safety of Scotland felt very much like being kicked upstairs. He was the last man to parade his grievances, and in his later years his family hesitated to probe an old wound. Somewhat naturally they believed that their father had been the victim of a military power struggle in high places. The Scottish appointment was such an important turning point in Andrew's military career, an apparent check to his steady progress towards the top, that it deserves closer examination, a task made very difficult by the lack of written evidence.

It is beyond dispute that the decision to move Andrew from XII Corps was made by Brooke, acting on behalf of Dill, then CIGS, who was on a prolonged visit to Greece and the Middle East with Eden, and that it was officially approved by Margesson, the Secretary of State for War, on 24 March. Brooke, who had replaced Ironside as Commander of the Home Forces in the previous July, was entirely within his rights to act in this way, and it is impossible to tell whether Dill, who always had a high opinion of Andrew, would have agreed to Brooke's suggestion had he been in England. What must remain forever uncertain are the reasons which prompted Brooke's suggestion.

In *Notes on My Life* Brooke wrote: 'In Scotland it had become necessary to replace Freddy Carrington and I decided on Bulgy Thorne for this Command.' A 'painful' interview with Carrington, who bitterly resented his removal, was followed by the announcement of Andrew's appointment. It would appear that Brooke, who had been a friend of Andrew ever since they were Staff College instructors together, regarded the move to Scotland as advancement for Andrew, as indeed it was. Brooke's biographer, General Fraser, believed that Brooke's letter of congratulation to Andrew was a genuine expression of his feelings, whatever its recipient felt. However, the removal of Andrew from a key post in the defence of Britain to the comparative safety of Scotland and his replacement by Montgomery does not seem to be fully explained by the need to make a change in the Scottish Command.

The handwritten letter from Montgomery to Andrew purported to express surprise at the telephone message that he was to move from V to XII Corps. Brooke certainly rated Montgomery's dynamism highly and knew that he was one of the very few men whose control Montgomery accepted. There is no overt proof that Montgomery in any way prompted Brooke's decision, but he was an intensely ambitious man who may have seen a potential rival in Andrew, a man only two years his senior and a far more highly decorated officer with a far longer experience of commanding troops in war. It is arguable that Montgomery may have privately envied Andrew's unforced popularity when he himself was always at pains to project his personality on his troops. He was never a close personal friend of Andrew, although like Brooke they had been colleagues at the Staff College. Temperamentally the two men were poles apart, and Andrew once described Montgomery as a difficult person and his own worst enemy. Most of this can only be guesswork. What is not conjecture is Montgomery's opinion of Andrew's work as Commander of XII Corps, criticism reminiscent of his opinion of Auchinleck whom he had succeeded as Commander of V Corps.

With characteristic lack of modesty he wrote on 7 May to Oliver Dawnay: 'I have been very busy since my arrival here. I rather fancy I burst on Kent like a 15-inch shell and it was needed!! Wives are being evacuated by train loads; it is just a matter as to whether the railways will stand the traffic. A number of heads are being chopped off – the bag to date is 3 Brigadiers and 6 C.O.s. The standard here was very low.' In this letter Montgomery made no mention of the fact that the area under his command was smaller than that originally guarded by XII Corps; nor that by May 1941 the situation as regards armament and equipment had been transformed since Andrew took command; nor did he suggest that serious danger of invasion was daily more unlikely, although this was now his belief. He intended to make an impact as a new broom so as to be respected.

It is difficult to escape the conclusion that Montgomery's criticisms of Andrew, as they had been of Auchinleck, were largely orchestrated to build himself up and were thus often unfair. The main target of his attack was Andrew's disposition of his meagre forces, together with what he despised as 'beach defence mentality'.

On 10 December 1940 Brooke had held a conference of all army commanders, which neither Andrew nor Montgomery as corps commanders were eligible to attend. Its purpose was to formulate a general policy to defeat the threatened invasion. The East and South Coasts of Britain presented a formidable task for the defenders since, as the minutes of the conference stated, 'the length of beaches suitable for the landing of all arms slightly exceeds that of the Western Front [in the First World War] from the sea to Switzerland'. It was decided that, as the entire coastline could not be adequately defended, the highest priority must go to holding the beaches in the most vulnerable areas, that is in Kent and Sussex. In July 1940 Montgomery, then in command of 3rd Division, had troops on the beaches – some detailed to defend Brighton pier – in the same way as Andrew; for this was the policy laid down, and while any possibility of invasion existed there were always troops along the southern coast. Only as more forces became available was it possible to leave coastal defence to static 'beach' divisions and to withdraw 'mobile' divisions to reserve for counter-attacks. Montgomery's biographer expresses surprise that there is no hint in Brooke's diaries or letters that he disapproved of Andrew's dispositions. He could hardly have done so when Andrew was carrying out the plan laid down at the December conference.

Montgomery's criticism of Andrew's dispositions must refer to 1941 and not to the dangerous months after Dunkirk. By the spring of 1941 the invasion threat had steadily receded until it was almost non-existent. From his actions in command of V Corps, it would seem that Montgomery believed that the time was ripe for a different policy. In April 1941 he had abolished the use of the term 'beach defence' in his corps so as to avoid having two classes of troops in the Army – one static and one mobile. At the same time he had stopped all work on coastal defences in his area, except for maintenance of existing construction, so as to free troops for more mobile training. He had also ordered the ban on wives in his area before he did the same in Kent. Montgomery's aim was to build up expeditionary forces against the day when they would return to France, and he planned to get all Army formations trained to a single standard of professionalism. Being in command of a less vulnerable area than Andrew, he could more easily afford to think of future needs. Andrew, in command of the area of England most directly threatened in 1940/41, could never forget that invasion remained a possibility which it was his prime duty to repel. Did Brooke believe that by May 1941 it would be safe to extend Montgomery's policy in V Corps to XII Corps in Kent? If so, would this not best be done by Montgomery himself, whose ability to be ruthless when he considered it necessary came less naturally to Andrew? All that can be said is that this is a possible explanation for Andrew's move to Scotland.

A much later conjecture about the working of Brooke's mind at this moment can be easily rebutted. It has been suggested that Brooke feared that Andrew's mind was too conditioned by his experiences in the First World War and that, despite his recent campaign which ended at Dunkirk, he was insufficiently aware of modern German forms of warfare. If there was one man who really knew the German Army and, of greater importance, understood the German mind, it was Andrew. He had long established himself as a forward-thinking soldier, and he had carefully kept abreast since his years in Berlin of developments in the German Army. It had long worried him that the War Office semeed to lag dangerously behind the leaders of the Reichswehr. If his mind had been too dominated by the First World War ideas it is odd that he should have been given the key post of commanding XII Corps and that he should have been left in command for a year before anyone discovered that he was out of date.

One other explanation of Andrew's move to Scotland which has been suggested is that Churchill may have resented Andrew's reported criticism of his frequent visits to coastal defences as interfering with vital preparations against invasion and so may have been in some way responsible. This is unlikely; however impressed he may have been by Montgomery when he visited 3rd Division late in June 1940, Churchill's interest in army commanders was mainly restricted to those in charge of large-scale operations abroad. Furthermore, there is no evidence to support this theory.

The decision to move Andrew from XII Corps remains as Brooke's alone. Whatever prompted the decision, other than the need to find a new army commander for Scotland, or whatever influences affected his decision can only remain a matter of pure conjecture.

Andrew very properly longed to crown his career with an active service command, and there were some who believed him to be the right man to command the 8th Army in North Africa, though such an appointment does not seem to have been seriously considered. But 'sudden the worst turns the best to the brave'. In his well-concealed disappointment Andrew could not foresee that his greatest achievement lay ahead.

14
The Second World War 'Scotco': May 1941 – April 1945

THE DEFENCE OF SCOTLAND

During 1941 Andrew said to Peter that the Scottish Command ('Scotco') was the command he would have most wanted in peacetime but was the least wanted during a war. Two years later when Peter was in India a letter from his father shows how much he still longed for a more active command. 'I have ceased to be a soldier and do such things as inspecting the Boys Brigade in the interval at the International match this Saturday at Hampden Park, Glasgow! But I do wish I could be a soldier before I get cast for old age!' It was galling to have in his command a number of prestigious units whose training he must supervise but whom he would never lead in battle. Needless to say, this sense of 'banishment' was never openly expressed and only rarely shown to those closest to him. Before leaving XII Corps he had been approached by General Haking inviting him to be his successor as Colonel of the Hampshire Regiment. It was a great compliment and doubtless some comfort in his 'banishment'. Many letters passed between him and Haking, but by 1943 he decided to refuse the honour.

'As G.O.C.-in-C. Scottish Command my chief responsibility is the defence of Scotland against possible invasion.' Scotland might seem comfortably out of danger in comparison with the area defended by XII Corps, and in the more remote areas a sense of realistic commitment was often lacking. Yet in 1941 an invasion was still a possibility and, although hardly an invasion, it was near Glasgow, shortly after Andrew took over, that Rudolf Hess landed in the belief that he could negotiate with the British Government with the help of the Duke of Hamilton. Andrew based his plan of defence on the assumption that a German invasion of Scotland would take the form of an airborne landing, probably in Fife, as an area well protected by the Forth and the Tay. Having effected a successful lodgement, he expected that panzer columns would drive westward in order to cut the country in half. To meet this danger he put Canadian Army tunnellers, who were then stationed in Scotland, to work in carving out a large operational base in one of the Lomond Hills across the Firth of Forth from Edinburgh.

It was essential to ensure the closest possible co-operation with the other two Services so that joint schemes of defence of Scapa Flow, Rosyth, Loch Ewe and the East Coast ports could be worked out. Emergency harbours had to be constructed at Gairloch and Port Ryan, which meant co-operation between Scotco and the Transportation Directorates. The Regional Commissioners were responsible for making certain that intimate co-operation existed between the military and civil defence at all levels. Andrew's ability to get others to work willingly for him and his gift of encouragement to all in his command were invaluable at this time.

Compared with the closely linked defences of South-East England, Andrew now had to deal with great distances between strong points, which he termed 'hideous gaps in a magnificent landscape'. To defend an area of this size put a great strain on the available manpower, which necessitated relying on the Home Guard even more heavily than in Kent and Sussex, making them an essential part of Scotco. An article in *The Times* in August 1941 by its Military Correspondent, Cyril Falls, showed great faith in the Scottish Home Guard. 'Most of the Home Guard are crofters, stalkers, keepers and ghillies, who know every inch of the ground. If parachute troops landed unseen their presence would be known from such things as the movement of deer or grouse seen with a stalker's eye.' Communication between isolated groups could be maintained by means of a specially devised code of notes on the bagpipes, whose sound carried ten miles down the glen if the wind were right.

Inevitably much of Andrew's time was spent travelling all over Scotland to inspect troops in training; to keep isolated units in places like the Orkneys up to the mark; to give advice and encouragement to small detachments of the Home Guard; and often to placate powerful landowners for damage and inconvenience to their properties by troop training. As Ralph Arnold, his ADC who came with him to Scotland, later wrote: 'The grouse had to be preserved even though the Dieppe raid was a failure.' To make this constant travelling possible Andrew had at his disposal two small aircraft – a D.H.Rapide and a Dove. Since flying conditions in Scotland were normally so unreliable, most of his journeys were made in a grey-painted Rolls Royce, lent to the Command by a patriotic shipping magnate, Lord Craigmyle.

Constant travelling had its enjoyable aspects, for Andrew had inherited a deep love of the Scottish countryside, and there were hills in plenty for him to climb during a break in the day's work. He needed exercise more than ever in a land with an exhilarating climate where, as he travelled north, rationing ceased to exist. He used to allow himself and the ADC on duty what he called 'little treats' when he would stop to visit some place of historic interest or of outstanding beauty. If he shook hands with the guardian of a site, it was a sign to the ADC that a tip was not required; if he merely thanked him, the ADC had to produce half-a-crown. He always sat well forward in the tip-up seat so as to be easily seen, and because of the blindness in his right eye, on the left-hand side of the car; the ADC acknowledged any salutes coming from the right. Failure to recognise him or the car's distinctive flag led to many embarrassing interviews for the ADCs with officers senior to themselves. By contrast, he would give a lift to service men, learning much from their conversation and constantly amazed by their ignorance about the course of the war.

Ralph Arnold recalled how in 'a burst of typical originality' Andrew appointed a woman as his second ADC. He and another general had agreed to take this hitherto unheard-of step; the other general lost his nerve, but Andrew invited Mary MacDonald, a junior commander in the ATS, to join his staff. She herself believed that he did this after learning of Russian criticism that the British and Americans failed to make full use of women. Whatever prompted Andrew, the appointment was a success. Mary MacDonald, a clever woman who later became a tutor in history and politics at Somerville, was highly efficient in the office, drafted many of Andrew's innumerable speeches and took her turn on tour. The appointment was eventually ended when, according to her, Higher Authority hinted that it was not proper for the Army Commander to travel around his command with an unmarried woman. The driver was insufficient chaperone.

To command Scotco diplomatic skill was essential; it was a sensitive appointment. Apart from endless tactful juggling with GHQ Home Forces and the War Office to get his way, it was his task to maintain harmonious relations between the three Services and to handle, often with extreme care, the Commanders of the Canadian, American, Norwegian, Indian and Polish forces who were all part of Scotco. He was on the best of terms with the Canadian lumberjacks and the Norwegians, with whom his relations were soon to be very close. He had always liked Americans, and he admired the dexterity of the Indian mule columns. On the other hand the Polish Corps was a law unto itself. Their code of discipline was very different from that in the British Army, and disturbing news of soldiers tied to trees or found suspended from the branches caused him concern. The escapades of their parachute brigade under their colourful leader 'Sas', Colonel Sasiebuski, were a constant source of anxiety. The Poles were commanded at first by General Kukiel, a former professor of history, who became War Minister in the Polish Government-in-exile. He was replaced by General Sprekovich, a tall dark man of peasant stock, who had been a prisoner of the Russians and who took a disenchanted view of the Russians as allies and of all who had not shared his first-hand experience of them. He spoke no language but his own.

Andrew chiefly enjoyed and took pride in the training of the Highland and Lowland Divisions. 'It was remarkable', he noted, 'how the terrain in Scotland helped to improve the capacity for leadership amongst junior officers and NCOs. They were thrown by the nature of the country much more on to their own.' Scotland proved an ideal training-ground – for Commandos and saboteurs in the Highlands, for Combined Operations on the south-west coast and in the Moray Firth, and for secret naval experiments. All had to be carefully concealed from enemy reconnaissance, and there were areas in Scotland from which it was necessary to debar civilians for a time.

Andrew's immense knowledge of all things military made a

visit from the Army Commander an awesome occasion. His standards and his integrity were of the highest order, and he expected the same from his subordinates. At the same time experience of commanding Territorial formations in both World Wars had taught him that it was pointless to expect the same standards as he would demand from Guardsmen; but he did expect all units to achieve the best results of which they were capable. He did not always find it easy to cultivate an outgoing personality, nor did he, rather surprisingly, possess a natural sense of humour, which made those who did not know him and who had to meet him on formal occasions think that he was very serious-minded. In a way they would have been right; but all those who were close to him enjoyed his great sense of fun. He was much less happy when forced to address a large body of men than when he could watch them on an exercise. He was not a natural speaker and much preferred the chance to talk to men individually. In December 1942 he described in a letter to Margaret his visit to troops who had just completed an extensive exercise in pouring rain. 'I left them, having been to see as many of them as possible to see how they were. They were all very cheerful, all soaking wet, some tired, some very sleepless, but all in the best of form after 15 days in the open air in Invernesshire in December! Aren't human beings wonderful and adaptable creatures!' These were words of one whose experiences in the First World War had given him a deep and lasting concern for the welfare of the rank and file, to whom in Scotland, much to the surprise of their commanders, he often alluded as 'poor darlings'.

Although in the middle of a World War, Andrew was expected also to fulfil the peacetime functions of his position. Civic life in Scotland was a minefield through which he had to pick his way with the delicacy of Agag. Correct precedence at functions was, as one ADC noted, more important than Air Raid Precautions. The flamboyant Provost of Edinburgh, Sir William Darling, with his sheriffs and baillies, Members of Parliament, holders of high offices of State and a crowd of civil servants, the Regional Commissioner, Lord Rosebery, and his staff, all had to have their positions duly recognised. The hierarchy of the two Churches, whose relationship was not always marked by Christian brotherhood, leaders of the professions and of trade and commerce could easily be slighted if some were apparently more favoured than others. Despite his heavy military responsibilities Andrew took great pains with this side of his command, knowing the necessity of civilian co-operation if a united front against the enemy were to be maintained.

In the belief that civilians should understand what the fighting forces were enduring and achieving, he established cordial relations with the press and took care to have an efficient press officer on his staff. Editors were supplied with all the information which could safely be divulged, and their comments on the impact of the Army on civilian life were sympathetically heard. He had the habit, not uncommon to generals of an older generation, of invoking, and even appearing to demand, aid from the Almighty in the war effort. He astonished one press conference by concluding his talk with the assertion that the ultimate aim of all involved in the war was to be better able to serve Him whose service is perfect freedom – a simple statement of a deeply held faith.

Andrew never had the slightest doubt that the soldier needed more than ever to be sustained by a religious faith. As he told the General Assembly of the Church of Scotland in May 1943, the nature of modern warfare was a stern test for each man. 'To the weight of concentration of fire from weapons on land – guns, howitzers, mortars and small arms – is added the weight of aerial bombardment, screaming bombs, incendiary bombs, the blast and shock of high explosive bombs. There is the attack by tanks. There is the peril of the minefield. There is also the insidious unceasing and, thank God, the hitherto unsuccessful attack by propaganda. There is also at the same time much more loneliness of action in the field. Think in particular of the parachutist, the sniper in his post, the two men in a slit trench, the crew of an A.F.V., the small team of men probing for mines.' Hence his appeal in this Address for at least fifty Army chaplains a year from the Church of Scotland alone, men able 'without the protection of their pulpits . . . to justify their faith'.

Early in his time in Scotland he had written to all officers in Scotco stressing the importance, for them and for those under them, of religious faith. Characteristically, at the request of the Moderator of the Church of Scotland he had written to General

Paget protesting against attempts in battle schools to inculcate blood-lust and hatred. This was not the way for a man to conquer his natural fear. 'When a person is prepared to risk his own life to prevent the death of someone he loves, fear leaves him and courage takes its place.' In this speech to an Edinburgh cadet corps he was perhaps giving a glimpse of the secret of his own courage. However, he never believed that religious faith alone was sufficient to uphold a soldier's morale. The modern soldier needed to be more broadly educated than had been the custom, and some study of history and current affairs should be compulsory. In addition to the usual games all soldiers should undergo courses in arduous training, both to keep them fit and to foster initiative.

Physical fitness, his own and for those under his command, had always mattered greatly to Andrew. Apart from his personal need for exercise, his preoccupation with keeping fit came from his experience of unfit comrades in the First World War. He used to tell of two brigadier-generals who were so physically exhausted by the retreat of March 1918 that they were incapable of taking any rational action in a constantly changing situation which needed the most resolute of mental processes. On most days he ran in the grounds of Gogar Bank, his official residence, wearing a mackintosh if time were short so as to perspire more freely. He had many theories about health, one of which was that to sit long hours at a desk impaired the circulation. He therefore had a special sloping table constructed at which he could work standing up on the vast mass of documents which he had to read and master. Montgomery had dealt with sedentary and out-of-condition officers by ordering them to go on runs, in which it has been noted he did not himself join. Andrew's method was to force all of his staff to attend lessons in Scottish dancing. He himself was a natural dancer: many of his staff were not. He employed two elderly Scottish schoolteachers as instructors, who were no respecters of rank and dignity as all ranks became inextricably mixed up in reels and strathspeys. Many senior officers disliked this and resented being made to look slightly ridiculous in front of their juniors. A more strenuous proof of Andrew's own fitness came in August 1943 when, with only a modest start, he won the Handicap Race in the Scotco Headquarters sports.

When he first arrived in Scotland, he lived with Ralph Arnold for a brief period at Dalmahoy, a handsome but decaying mansion outside Edinburgh which had become a golf club. This suited one who, when the day's work was done, could play eighteen holes in the long summer evenings. He stayed here until his predecessor, General Carrington, moved out of Gogar Bank, a beautiful house in the Colinton area of Edinburgh. Carrington had been bitterly hurt at being deprived of the Scottish Command, and Andrew was sensitive enough not to appear anxious to speed his departure. Margaret was able to join him here and, having found a soldier cook who had been a chef at a Highland hotel, was able to end the previous cook's nightly offering of soup, boiled haddock and caramel custard. More important was her value to Andrew as an accomplished hostess, coping with an endless stream of visitors ranging from King Haakon of Norway and the Crown Prince to local Home Guard commanders, whose worries or imagined slights were forgotten in the friendly atmosphere. Gogar Bank also became a family home where leave periods could be spent in comfort. All visitors were expected to take part in organised games which, according to an ADC, were 'pursued with some earnestness' – Grenadiers v. Others.

The years in Scotco were years when the family increased in numbers. Sandy led the way in April 1941 when he married Joscelyne, daughter of Sir Ralph and Lady Verney, in the Guards Chapel. Three months later Poppy and Neville Wigram, son of Lord Wigram who had been Private Secretary to King George V, were married at Sonning. George followed his twin's example a year later, being married to Juliet, only daughter of the Hon. George and Lady Agnes Peel, in the Guards Chapel. The first grandchild, Sandy's son Nicholas, was born in January 1942 and the first granddaughter, Cherry Wigram, appeared in the following April. Andrew managed to be present at all three weddings, and whenever possible he travelled south for the baptisms. Family affairs meant that Margaret travelled frequently between Gogar Bank and The Deanery until at the end of 1942 the C-in-C Home Forces issued an order compelling all officers to live either in barracks or the equivalent and forbidding wives to live within seven miles of their husbands. This order for a time brought to an end the happy home life at Gogar Bank, which became the mess for Andrew, his five senior staff officers and his two ADCs. Margaret felt the separation deeply, and a combination of loneliness, servant problems, evacuees, and the enervating climate of the Thames Valley led to her growing dislike of The Deanery. In her loneliness she worried about the inevitable changing relationship with her children, all now grown up and three of them married. Andrew did his best to comfort her. 'Pray for them and be cheerful: that will help them most of all.'

From the moment that Andrew took command in Scotland his days were filled with military and civic duties. During 1942 he began to be involved in a new problem which came to be all-important: the liberation of Norway from the Germans. It was in the Birthday Honours of this year that he was appointed KCB – an honour described in a host of congratulatory letters as long overdue and hailed in the Scottish press as a deserved tribute to 'the most popular GOC Scotland for years'.

NORWAY AND SCOTCO

On 9 April 1940 after 125 years of peaceful history Norway was invaded by Hitler's forces. The same day Vidkun Quisling, formerly Norwegian Minister of War and a Nazi sympathiser, proclaimed himself Prime Minister and tried in an unsuccessful coup d'état to overthrow the Government. A neutral nation, unaccustomed to war, with a comparatively small population, could be no match for the Wehrmacht, but sixty days of fighting were needed by the Germans before Norway was overrun. King Haakon VII and the Government escaped to London, where they were to remain for the next five years, solely concerned with the ultimate liberation of their country. For the moment the Germans ignored Quisling, and Josef Terboven, a Nazi gauleiter from the Ruhr, controlled the country, which Hitler fondly hoped would remain calm and quiet in submission to Nazi force.

Norwegians now faced a painful dilemma in deciding how far to obey their new rulers. Should they accept the inevitability of Nazi rule and keep the economic system of the country going, thus saving themselves from probable destitution, or should they resist? The summer of 1940 was a difficult and confused time for them. After their own defeat had come the fall of France and the evacuation from Dunkirk. The Germans seemed to be invincible, and despite the traditional belief in Britain they felt deserted and morale was understandably low. The Norwegian Government in London was tainted by defeat and much criticised both for its failure to maintain neutrality and for inadequate leadership once the fighting had started. Negotiations began between the remaining members of the Norwegian Parliament and the German Reichskommissar on a new form of government more suited to the circumstances. As a result an appeal was sent to the King in exile to abdicate for the duration of the war and to his Government to resign. Taking his stand as the guardian of the Norwegian Constitution and on the advice of his ministers, King Haakon stoutly refused to yield. It was the first ray of hope.

However, it was the German attempt deliberately to nazify Norway, their backing of the Norwegian 'Quislings', their contempt for the rule of law and their clear intention to incorporate Norway in a greater German Reich that enraged the Norwegians, leading them to organise civil and semi-military resistance. An attack was launched by Terboven on Norway's democratic institutions in turn: local government, farming co-operatives, sporting and athletic bodies, the medical profession and the trade unions. When in December 1940 the members of the Supreme Court resigned in a body in defence of the Constitution it was a powerful encouragement to further resistance. If anything more were needed to strengthen Norwegian resolve it was the appointment in February 1942 of Quisling to the grandiose but empty role of Minister-President. His attacks on the Norwegian way of life and the accompanying cruelties led to a determined fight by bishops and pastors and by teachers against his attempt to nazify the churches and their schools.

Once the brave decision to resist the imposition of the Fuehrer Prinzip had been made, communication between London and Norway to co-ordinate resistance became essential. Fortunately the great length and rugged nature of the Norwegian coastline made it impossible for the Germans to patrol it adequately. So in September 1940 the first courier from the Norwegian authorities in London landed in Norway. Two months earlier the Special Operations Executive (SOE) had been set up to assist and direct resistance movements in Nazi-occupied countries, and a Scandinavian branch was soon added. During the late spring of 1941 secret Resistance units – collectively known until 1944 as Milorg – were gradually formed.

Andrew's initial involvement in Norway's struggle came in September 1941, when as Army Commander in Scotland he received orders to build up an Intelligence service on the German dispositions in Norway. There was at this time no question of offensive action but it was considered important to encourage Norwegians, and at a future date the collected information might well prove invaluable. At battle headquarters a 'Norway room' was assigned for the purpose, staffed by a small team containing two Norwegian officers, and by April 1943 much battle and topographical information had been amassed, which became essential as the liberation of Norway was planned. Furthermore, there were a considerable number of Norwegians in Scotland at this time. The Norwegian Brigade was part of Scotco; the Norwegian ordnance depot was at Dumfries; a reception camp for refugees crossing the North Sea was set up in Shetland, where there was also a base for craft operating under SOE orders. This latter organisation was also responsible for strengthening wireless communication between Britain and Norway.

Contact with Sweden was important. From April 1940 until 1945 the Swedes had always been aware of the possibility of a German attack from Norway, Denmark or Finland. While maintaining its neutrality Sweden had built up a strong defence force, and the border with Norway was heavily fortified. At the same time Swedish sympathies were increasingly on the side of the Norwegians, and standards of strict neutrality were not maintained. In order to help fellow Scandinavians, Norwegian health camps and subsequently police camps began to be established from 1942 onwards, the first being Gottora, near Gothenberg. As the war developed these camps became more and more military camps for training the large number of Norwegian young men who had escaped to Sweden. The assistance of Swedish police and Swedish military was barely concealed. By 1945 more than 10,000 Norwegians formed a military force on Swedish soil, as well trained and equipped as was possible in the circumstances.

The Swedes were also aware of their danger if, after a German defeat in Europe, the German forces in Norway continued the fight. Had this happened Sweden could not have maintained her neutrality; but in the closing stages of the war, with her diplomatic relations with Germany unbroken, pressure was exerted to prevent the establishment of what became known as *Festung Norwegen*, strongly fortified and garrisoned areas with munition dumps from which to prolong German resistance.

Relations with Milorg were more important. Men prepared to face the dangers and hardships of Resistance were usually fiercely independent characters, eager to receive directions from London and to be part of the Allies' plans but having some very definite ideas of their own. Yet co-ordination of effort was essential, and by the end of 1941 Milorg had agreed to be placed under the Norwegian High Command in London. By 1942 the 20,000 members of Milorg desperately needed the arms and ammunition which SOE supplied and which also directed training in underground activities and sabotage. While the courage of Milorg members was beyond question, a century-old tradition of peace and a strong commitment to the rule of law had resulted in an undue faith that all their compatriots were equally loyal. This resulted in a serious lack of a proper sense of security – and consequently avoidable deaths in their ranks. While prepared unhesitatingly to give their own lives for their country, assassination proved to be deeply repugnant to their nature. Only very late in the war did they reluctantly consent to liquidate fifty-nine of the worst 'Quislings', proved traitors and informers.

Milorg alone could not defeat the Wehrmacht: its essential purpose was to give vital help from within Norway once an Allied invasion began. Hopes that such an invasion was imminent ran high when a series of raids, organised by Combined Operations, took place. At the same time during 1941/42 SOE sent into Norway some twenty groups of instructors and radio operators as well as valuable weapons, and daring acts of sabotage were carried out. Plans for a direct invasion of Norway, known as Operation Jupiter, were drawn up, as Churchill believed that this would be a way of relieving pressure on the Russians. But early in 1943 he reluctantly accepted the advice of his naval and military experts that Operation Jupiter would be doomed to failure if attempted. Combined Operations also abandoned plans for further attacks on the Norwegian coast, attacks which had led Hitler to increase the number of his troops in Norway but which could never affect the outcome of the war. When the Allied invasion of North Africa took place, the Norwegian people were forced to realise that a long struggle still lay ahead – Milorg units which had been organised and equipped rather hastily in the hope of an Allied invasion were vulnerable to the Gestapo, and the loss to Milorg in killed and imprisoned was considerable. Milorg accepted that it must undertake an important but very different role – to prepare for the potentially dangerous situation which might arise if German forces in Norway continued the war on their own.

So far Andrew had had no major part in the Norwegian operations, but from the summer of 1943 the problems posed by Norway demanded an increasing share of his time and soon became his major concern in Scotland. He had probably hoped that Operation Jupiter would have given him the chance to prove himself as a commander of an army in action, but plans for the operation had never reached a point at which command appointments were made. With the abandonment of Jupiter Allied planners at SHAEF had made the important decision that while an invasion of Norway which led to that country's liberation would have been welcome, it could only have been a peripheral achievement, which by itself could not have brought about Germany's unconditional surrender. This was to be the task of Operation Neptune – later rechristened Overlord – with the Second Front assault on France across the Normandy beaches, which was to take priority over all other schemes. This decision meant that Andrew became fully involved in two quite distinct operations, although both concerned Norway.

The ultimate liberation of Norway was the task of SHAEF in conjunction with the Norwegian Government. At first it was purely a joint Anglo-American undertaking with Britain the prodominant partner but with both countries sharing all responsibilities – political, legal and financial – equally between them. When in the summer of 1943 it seemed possible that the weight of the Allied air bombardment might force a sudden German surrender Andrew received orders from SHAEF to start planning a force for the liberation of Norway. This complex assignment was given the code name Operation Rankin Case C Norway.

Two virtually insoluble problems forced the planners at Scotco to rely heavily on guesswork. First, it was impossible to forecast with certainty the likely response of the Wehrmacht formations in Norway to the defeat and surrender of the main German armies in Central Europe following the success of Overlord. Rankin C assumed that strong German forces would still be in Norway and might either agree to the general surrender or stand and fight, which would in a country like Norway lead to a hard and costly operation for Allied troops. A further directive from SHAEF followed before long – Rankin B – in which the planners were asked to make additional plans for a situation in which Germany withdrew her troops from Norway to meet the challenge of Overlord. In January 1944 the Scotco planners were joined by Norwegian representatives whose more intimate knowledge of the country led to considerable changes in Rankin C and another SHAEF directive to rewrite the whole plan under the new code name Operation Apostle. When in August 1944 a German collapse seemed increasingly possible SHAEF decided that the time was ripe to bring into existence the force planned on paper for the liberation of Norway to be known as Force 134. Of this Force Andrew was now appointed Commander-designate.

The leading figures in Andrew's team were Rear-Admiral Ritchie and Air Vice Marshal Boret as the other two Service chiefs. Colonel Charles Wilson of the US Army was Andrew's deputy and Brigadier Hansen, VC, was in charge of the military planning for the rapid importation into Norway of food, medical supplies, and everything needed for the restoration of civilian life. To achieve the needed saving in manpower Andrew used Scotco as much as possible. He set up two new staff divisions, one for civil affairs and one for disarmament, both of which were active in Edinburgh by the early summer of 1944.

In August 1944 Civil Affairs held a staff exercise which was attended by SHAEF representatives, leading Norwegian Army officers and by the five Norwegian ministers nominated to return to Norway with Force 134 – as well as by the then Crown Prince Olav. The understandable wish of those Norwegians present that the Allied occupation of their country should be as brief as possible was clearly stated by the Crown Prince, who said: 'You are expecting to go in and re-establish an old government . . . a government that has been developed by the people themselves to suit their own needs and which, if it is not perfect, has the advantage of being their own. It may be necessary to guide and direct in some cases but you will get much further in every stage with co-operation than with command.' The Norwegian people would not wish for long to feel that they had only exchanged one form of military rule for another, however benevolent.

The decision by SHAEF to 'activate' Force 134 served to highlight the second insoluble problem with which the Scotco planners and Andrew in particular had to grapple. With the liberation of Norway low on the list of SHAEF priorities, it was going to be impossible until the very last moment to know with absolute certainty the order of battle of Allied units which would comprise Force 134. There could be equally little reliance upon what shipping, aircraft, and material would be available. As Andrew wrote in his report to the War Office after the liberation: 'One by one units and formations, British and U.S., originally trained and allotted to Norway were swallowed up by operations in Germany.' This was especially true of American troops, who were moved to Western Europe directly their training in Scotland was finished. The greatest loss was the removal of the British 52nd Division in September 1944 to fight under Montgomery, for so much of the planning had assumed its assignment to Norway. Only the comparatively small Norwegian Brigade was certain to remain under Andrew's command; the remainder of Force 134 was unknown.

In October 1944 Soviet forces, with no prior warning to the Allies or to the Norwegian Government, invaded Northern Norway and captured Kirknes. This was the first stage towards the liberation of Norway, and Andrew wanted to send an Allied force to Finnmark to join the Russians. This was refused by the Russians, but they agreed to accept a small contingent of the Norwegian Brigade from Scotland. Units of the Norwegian police force in Northern Sweden were also admitted by the Russians, and they reached Kirknes by aircraft or on foot. Andrew eagerly supported a quickly extemporised plan to send a mountain company of the Norwegian Brigade to Kirknes where, despite difficult communications, contact was maintained with Scotco. Before long the Soviet force was withdrawn to take part in the assault on Berlin, but the Norwegian troops and police held the area so far liberated.

As the Germans retreated through Finnmark they pursued a scorched earth policy, destroying communications and laying waste the countryside. Would this happen all over Norway in a final act of desperate resistance after a general surrender in Germany? Communications were difficult enough in normal times in Norway: the destruction of roads, bridges, railways, telephones and power stations would gravely hamper and prolong the Allied task. In these circumstances the safety of thousands of Norwegians in prison camp would be at risk and it would be difficult to forecast the behaviour of the civilian population with no central or local government to take charge. Moreover, the force available to Andrew to defeat or disarm some 340,000 German troops was totally inadequate. In face of all these imponderables Andrew's report makes clear that two factors dominated the planning of Apostle: the overriding need of reducing to a minimum the time-lag between VE Day and the arrival of all available Allied troops; and the necessity of reliance upon Milorg as the only friendly armed force on the spot.

Fortunately Milorg was rapidly becoming less of an uncertain quantity, thanks in no small measure to the support of SOE. A degree of unity had been achieved at a conference held in Sweden in May 1943 when a young Norwegian lawyer, Jens Christian Hauge, was in reality recognised as its official leader. Under SHAEF directive, early in 1944 SOE started the serious equipping and arming of Milorg. During the last year of the war 1,200 sorties were made from British airfields to remote wooded and mountainous areas controlled by Milorg, in the course of which 35 British and American aircraft and 250 men were lost.

During 1944 Milorg affirmed its allegiance to SHAEF and to the Norwegian High Command in London. Allied confidence was still further enhanced by the two visits which Hauge made to Britain that year. Sir Laurence Collier, who was Minister to the Norwegian Government and Ambassador between 1942 and 1951, described Hauge as a man whose 'manner is self-confident and superficially genial but there is reason to believe that he is really wary and suspicious of foreigners'. Andrew would not have endorsed this opinion. Between him and Hauge a lifelong friendship was forged in the war years, a friendship invaluable in smoothing or removing many potentially serious differences both before and after liberation.

As a result of Hauge's visits it was agreed that Milorg's main role must be the prevention of the scorched earth policy suffered in Finnmark. Hauge urged that his members should also pursue an active campaign of sabotage against the railways. This was agreed, subject to overall control from Britain. Milorg undertook the important task of ensuring the capture of all Gestapo documents when Germany surrendered, but only within very narrow limits did Hauge accept the necessity for Milorg to undertake the liquidation of dangerous Quislings and informers. Meanwhile the detailed planning for Apostle went steadily ahead.

From 28 June 1943 Andrew had become involved in a totally separate operation, though one indirectly concerning Norway. On that day he had attended a conference, code-named Rattle, at the Holywood Hotel in Largs, presided over by Mountbatten and including so much 'top brass' from all three Services that it was nicknamed the 'Field of the Cloth of Gold'. The purpose of the conference was to devise ways in which the destination and date of Overlord could be concealed from the Germans. By seeming threats against other parts of Europe it was hoped to cause the Wehrmacht to make faulty strategic dispositions in North-Western Europe and to induce mistaken tactical dispositions by threats against the Pas de Calais once Overlord had been launched.

Operation Fortitude North, as the plans were named, was aimed specifically against Norway and the Scandinavian countries. Its purpose was to compel Hitler to keep his twenty-seven divisions, then stationed in Norway, Finland and Denmark, idle on D Day but expecting to face a joint Anglo-American-Russian assault on Norway. Its counterpart, Fortitude South, was theoretically on a much larger scale and was intended to persuade the Germans that the Normandy landings were only a diversion and that the real invasion would be near Calais. It was with the planning of Fortitude North that Andrew was much more closely concerned.

This operation was designed to play upon Hitler's known obsession about Scandinavia. From the autumn of 1941 he had displayed a growing conviction that an invasion of Norway was being planned in which the Russians would probably join. Lack of any evidence did not prevent him from insisting that 'Norway is the zone of destiny in this war'. He had been deeply impressed by an essay written in 1928 on German naval strategy in the First World War. The author, Admiral Wegener, had argued that the war had been lost because the German High Seas Fleet had been pinned in the German Bight. To avoid a repetition of this in another war Germany would have to seize Norway's ice-free ports. This Hitler had done in April 1940. Scandinavia was also vital to the German steel industry, for 73% of its iron ore requirements were imported from Sweden – a great proportion through Norway. There has been speculation that Andrew's appointment to Scotco strengthened Hitler's fixation about Norway. Hitler and many of his senior officers had known him and had respected his military abilities in Berlin. It is conceivable, but beyond proof, that Hitler could have thought it improbable that a soldier of Andrew's calibre would have been posted to Scotland unless a Second Front were to be launched from there against Norway. Whatever the influences working on Hitler's strange mind, it is certain that the 150,000 German troops stationed in Norway in June 1941 had been increased to well over 400,000 three years later. It was the task of Fortitude North to keep them all in Norway on D Day.

As Andrew knew all too well in planning Apostle, the troops which he commanded in Scotland, together with associated Norwegian and American units, were never sufficient to invade any country, let alone one so easily defensible as Norway. Therefore for the purposes of Fortitude North's deception plans a mythical army had to be created – the non-existent Fourth Army. From the beginning of 1944 the planning of a fake assault on Norway had received top priority among SHAEF's deception experts, and Eisenhower delegated the task of executing the deception to Andrew. He, in turn, appointed Colonel Roderick Macleod to take charge of the detailed work on Operation Skye, and on 5 March, when the two men met in Edinburgh Castle, about twenty officers were assigned to Macleod from a recently disbanded corps headquarters.

Details as for a genuine invasion of Norway were worked out, based on a two-prong attack. In the North the primary objective was the iron port of Narvik, thence on to Gallivore in Sweden and a link-up with a Russian force from Petsamo. In the South a commando raid would seize Stavanger and the airfield, followed by a southern force with Oslo as its ultimate aim and a consequent threat to North Germany. Of the mythical Fourth Army entrusted with this invasion Andrew was the obvious choice as commander, for this is what those Germans who had known him would expect. His movements were kept sufficiently secret so as to appear genuine but could be noted by the prying eyes of German agents. Visits by King Haakon and by the Crown Prince to the 52nd Division, to which the Norwegian Brigade was attached, were all part of the scheme, and on 8 April 1944 the King broadcast a promise that the 'hour of liberation will soon strike in Norway'.

Daring commando raids against German garrisons and industrial installations were carefully designed to have all the marks of pre-invasion tactics, as well as causing useful damage to Norwegian supplies destined for the Reich. Naval sorties and British and American reconnaissance flights, ostensibly for photographic purposes, were frequent. Another move in the game was to declare the Firth of Forth a protected area, which could only be entered or left with a special pass and subject to strict security checks. Any German agent was likely to assume that the areas would be used for the embarkation of troops whose obvious destination was Norway. The danger from enemy reconaissance planes was luckily averted by shooting them down very successfully.

From 22 March operational and routine radio messages such as would be normal within a large army began to be transmitted. Macleod insisted that all messages must be militarily plausible and must be sent in the most secret cipher. Since most ciphers could ultimately be broken or cipher books captured, meaingless groups of letters or deciphered information that Mary had a little lamb would at once arouse suspicion. Furthermore, messages had to have a reasonable link with the type of activity being simulated. Questions on behalf of the 87th Field Cash Office must deal with pay and allowances, those from the 55th Field

Dressing Station must concern something akin to the building up of adequate supplies of drugs and medicines. In this way the Fourth Army held artillery exercises and possessed its own artillery practice camp – all by wireless!

The fiction was wonderfully successful. SHAEF Intelligence reported that three more divisions had been sent to Norway, making a total of twelve divisions, all of which remained in Norway over D Day, and only one was removed from the country on 16 June, too late to affect the Normandy landings. By 20 May the Fourth Army was no longer needed to threaten Norway and was moved to the South of England, there to take part in the attack which the Germans expected on the Pas de Calais. The German forces in Norway, with U-boats and strong air support, remained on the alert awaiting the invasion which a year later took the form of accepting their unconditional surrender.

On 18 July 1944 General Eisenhower wrote to the US Secretary of State for War saying that 'the threat to Norway which had been maintained by Scottish Command had greatly assisted the Normandy landings' and that he was most appreciative of the whole-hearted support which General Thorne and his Staff had given SHAEF.

As the Allied forces, following the success of Overlord, fought their way towards Germany, preparations for the liberation of Norway became Andrew's main concern. On 31 January 1945 a SHAEF directive formally defined his position. A Supreme Headquarters Allied Expeditionary Force Mission to Norway was set up under his command, and on 2 February he was promoted to the rank of full general. A secret memorandum from Eisenhower to the Combined Chiefs of Staff on 10 February made clear that the Mission was 'accredited to the King of Norway' and would act as the channel through which communication between SHAEF and the Norwegian Government was to be maintained. The Mission was firmly instructed to 'rely on SHAEF political advisers for political advice', with a marginal note 'It had better!' making crystal clear that SHAEF alone was in ultimate control of the operation.

Operation Apostle had been meticulously planned to meet

every known difficulty, but the most perfect planning could not remove the two imponderables which continued to trouble Andrew. His task would have been greatly eased had General Boehme, commanding the Wehrmacht in Norway, been instructed to withdraw his troops to Germany. However, this was highly unlikely and the alternatives of surrender or continued resistance remained. Andrew believed that surrender was the more likely outcome following a German unconditional surrender in Western Europe. Yet surrender, however preferable to a slow war of attrition, did not remove the problem of controlling and disarming the Germans with a force at best only one tenth of the German strength. The other related imponderable was the dangerous time-lag between surrender and the arrival of the main Allied forces.

It was at this point that Andrew's insight into the German mind proved supremely important and contributed to the seemingly miraculous ease by which the actual liberation of Norway from the German army was achieved. The policy which SHAEF had decided to adopt following a German surrender was to destroy the cohesion of the German forces and to belittle as much as possible the prestige and authority of the German commanding officers. At all costs German military might must be destroyed. Andrew obtained permission from SHAEF to adopt a diametrically opposite policy in Norway. His plan was that the German forces in Norway should be left as a kind of military organisation under their own system of command. The Wehrmacht, under the shock of capitulation, was to leave all its military installations and positions and move to certain defined reservations, there disarming itself, its men becoming prisoners of war. He himself, as supreme military authority on behalf of SHAEF, would issue the orders to Boehme and his staff, who would then be responsible for implementing them in the usual way. He believed that the German sense of discipline was so deeply rooted that obedience to orders from their own officers would be unquestioning. It was a risk, but he insisted that with inadequate forces under his command no other course was possible. In the event he was to be proved triumphantly right though, as he quickly came to realise, it was a policy likely to be unpopular with many Norwegians who 'naturally would expect to see every German behind barbed wire at once'. However, the Norwegian Government accepted the plan, and there would be 40,000 Milorg men on whom he could rely.

This plan also got round the difficulty of the dangerous time-lag between surrender and the arrival of the main Allied forces. It could be implemented the moment that the German commander-in-chief surrendered. So special control and disarmament parties, known as Herald parties, were organised and trained to deal with the main German headquarters. The Herald party earmarked to deal with General Boehme's headquarters, to be led by Brigadier Hilton, and two senior officers for Bergen and Trondheim, would be flown in at once: the other parties would be transported by destroyers to the main ports a day or two later.

Everything was now ready to put Operation Apostle into action and to see whether the long months of detailed planning would succeed. On 30 April Hitler and his mistress, whom he had married on the previous day, killed themselves in the Berlin bunker. On 4 May the German forces in north-western Germany, including Denmark but not Norway, surrendered unconditionally to Montgomery, who characteristically received the Germans alone without any staff officers being present. Admiral Doenitz, whom Hitler had nominated as his successor, hoped Norway might be a pawn in his hands, and he wanted to continue the fighting against the Russians in order to avoid large numbers of his troops becoming prisoners of the Russians, but this was totally unacceptable to Eisenhower. So at 2.41 a.m. on 7 May the Germans signed an instrument of unconditional surrender on all fronts at Eisenhower's headquarters. Eisenhower, unlike his subordinate, left his staff to meet the Germans and accept their surrender.

There was a strange postscript to the story of Hitler's final days in the bunker. Only later did Andrew learn that among Hitler's papers found in the bunker was a German translation of an article which he had written in 1932 for the *Household Brigade Magazine* on the battle of Gheluvelt. Did Hitler realise before he died that the man against whom he had fought in 1914, and whose qualities as a soldier he had admired in Berlin, would soon be in supreme command of the Wehrmacht in Norway? Or does the existence of this article in the Bunker strengthen belief in the possibility that from the moment of Andrew's appointment to Scotco Hitler expected him to have been already designated as the Commander-in-Chief of the Second Front, which would take the form of an invasion of Norway rather than of France?

15

The Liberation of Norway: May to October 1945

On 7 May 1945 the remnants of the German Government in Flensburg announced the German capitulation. From 7 May until 9 May 40,000 Milorg men quickly appeared and occupied all the vulnerable points. All Quislings were rounded up and the gates of the concentration camps thrown open. Notices appeared in the streets instructing the Norwegian people at a moment of relief and joy to behave with dignity, calmness and discipline. For the next two days they were the only armed force actually on the spot and so well did they fulfil their task that all sabotage was prevented, a complete haul of Gestapo documents was made and by the time that Allied forces arrived they were able to concentrate on disarming the Wehrmacht. Thanks to a late telegram the Norwegian 'police' force awaiting the order in Sweden did not join the Home Forces until late on 10 May.

Meanwhile at Scotco there was uncertainty. By means of a clandestine telegram SHAEF had already on 5 May directed the leader of Milorg to communicate to General Boehme, whom Doenitz had appointed Supreme Commander in Norway over all German forces, including the Navy and the Air Force, that if he wished to contact SHAEF he could do so on certain stated frequencies. This message Boehme ignored.

Shortly before midnight on 7 May Doenitz's orders to Boehme reached him at his headquarters in Lillehammer. His forces in Norway were to be surrendered. Fighting was to cease at midnight on 8 May and all orders from the Allies were to be obeyed. Further orders would be sent to him from Scottish Command by means of a commission arriving on 7 or 8 May by aircraft flying up the Oslo Fjord at 300 metres, firing red signals. Confirmatory orders in writing only reached Boehme on 8 May.

He was to capitulate to Scottish Command. Not until noon on 8 May did Boehme's acceptance of these terms reach Scotco. Andrew's prediction was right: the will to continue resistance did not exist.

The first Herald party – Brigadier Hilton, Colonel Hay, the Norwegian Commander Askim and others – at once flew to Oslo. After a brief conference with the Home Front leadership they were driven to Boehme's headquarters, where at 10 p.m. Eisenhower's terms of surrender were formally presented to him. It was made clear that every German soldier, save for a few essential guards on stores and establishments, must at very short notice be cleared out of towns and villages and moved into about 180 previously selected camps outside urban areas, known as reservations, where they should disarm themselves. To avoid the possibility of isolated bodies of fanatical Nazis trying to ignore the general surrender all weapons of 20mm and under were to be dumped under Allied supervision. Officers were allowed to retain their pistols, as were those guarding the reservations. All Allied ex-prisoners of war were to be set free at once and provided with thirty days' full scale of rations. Boehme might insist that he commanded an undefeated army but he had no option save to accept in full Eisenhower's terms of surrender and the plans which Andrew and his team in Scotland had devised to deal with the immediate aftermath of liberation.

Once Boehme had surrendered events moved quickly. Between 9 and 11 May the 1st Airborne Division, including the SAS Brigade and the Norwegian Parachute Company, were flown into Norway. The remaining Herald parties left Rosyth on 13 and 18 May and were landed at the chief Norwegian ports. On 11 May Andrew and his fellow Allied Joint Commanders, together with Crown Prince Olav and the Norwegian Ministers, embarked at Rosyth and reached Oslo two days later. In glorious weather HMS *Ariadne* steamed slowly up Oslo Fjord where, as Andrew described the scene in a letter to Margaret, 'everyone who had a boat or who could get into someone else's did so and came out to cheer him and the squadron. The only one who didn't appreciate it was the German officer naval pilot who came on board off Lista lighthouse. It must have been very humiliating for his feelings to see the real joy and gladness in the faces of the people.' Even at such a moment Andrew could feel for the humiliation of a beaten foe.

Looking back over his six months in Norway as Head of the Allied Mission, Andrew in his Final Report ascribed the success of the operation to four main causes. First, it was due to the long months of continuous planning and practical training in Scotland, which had been additionally valuable in fostering mutual confidence among potentially rival interests. Second, as he had expected, the morale of the Wehrmacht in Norway had been gradually destroyed by the steady opposition of the Norwegian people, by what he termed 'Arctic melancholia', heightened by the insidious effect of grave news from home and finally by the Allied victory in Europe. Third, 'the almost magical appearance of Milorg on 7/8 May' ended all chance of German resistance. Fourth, the survival of the German tradition of discipline in the Wehrmacht, on which he had banked, had enabled the disarmament and repatriation of the German forces to be undertaken swiftly and without serious trouble.

This summary disguised the extreme complexity of Andrew's task and omitted one factor of great importance – the personal contribution of Andrew himself as Commander, Allied Liberation Forces in Norway, as Force 134 had been renamed. If ever the right man was in the right place at the right time it was Andrew in Norway between May and the end of October 1945. Laurence Collier, who had not at first greatly taken to him, a reservation probably accentuated by finding himself as a professional diplomat subordinate to a soldier in the early phases of liberation, nevertheless recognised Andrew's difficulties in a despatch to the Foreign Office. 'He is, as you have said, not one of the world's greatest intellects and he is not always as tactful as he means to be; but a man who has to cope with Americans, Russians and Swedes, as well as Norwegian Home Fronters [Milorg] and the British War Office has no easy life.' A warmer and more just tribute came from General Brownrigg, who after visiting Andrew in Oslo in August 1945 wrote: 'In all my life I have never seen a man so thoroughly on top of a complicated and difficult job.' During Andrew's six months in Norway his own abilities were tested to the full. His skill in enthusing others and eliciting their support in a common enterprise was one secret of his success.

On 17 May – almost the only wet day in a golden summer – Norway's Constitution Day was celebrated with parades of the Home Forces and of children. Allied troops were present only as spectators. Andrew watched the parades with the Crown Prince from the balcony of the Palace. In the evening he attended a ball at which it was his duty to open the dancing. 'In the middle of the dance', he told Margaret, 'Nansen (nephew of the explorer) asked if I would let his Committee buy some German wine from the cellar. After much consultation I found myself having to produce as a present from myself eight dozen bottles of champagne which will cost me some £24. However, it was their National Day and the first Ball since 1939!' He later decided that the two million bottles of champagne and countless cases of brandy which had fallen into Allied hands could be issued to units at a cost of one shilling a bottle and the proceeds given to the Red Cross, which eventually benefited to the tune of several hundred thousand pounds. For the Norwegians he knew the need was for colour and gaiety after being starved of them for five years and he encouraged every kind of festivity. In more sober vein the National Theatre was opened with a gala performance of Ibsen's *Peer Gynt*, an inordinately long work which he witnessed on a later occasion. By contrast he ordered his garrison commander at Oslo to pick four attractive Norwegian girls and with the aid of a pipe major to instruct them in the intricacies of an eightsome reel, to be performed by them with himself and three other officers when the Crown Prince came to dinner.

The necessity for rapid and good communications was vital, especially while Germans were being moved into their reservations. A Signals staff officer had been included in each disarmament party but until more signals experts reached Norway it was necessary to rely on German operators. Andrew had always known the value of disseminating accurate information to people at home, and so as early as 13 May broadcasts to the Norwegian people began. Two days later an Allied press servicing office was set up with the help of Norwegian journalists. Allied films were distributed to cinemas where crowded audiences gathered despite the heat. Mobile cinema units were sent to remote areas. Pamphlets and all forms of Allied literature were widely read. For liberated Soviet citizens there was a daily broadcast in Russian. Nor was the enemy forgotten: a twice-daily news service was broadcast to the German forces. This needed special permission from SHAEF, for Andrew's policy was the direct opposite of that being pursued in Western Europe, where the aim of broadcasts was to weaken the respect of soldiers for their officers. In Norway the success of the Mission depended entirely on the maintenance of German discipline.

The prime purpose of the Mission was the disarmament and eventual repatriation of the Wehrmacht. In the first of his weekly reports to SHAEF Andrew was able to claim that by 25 May about seventy-eight percent of German personnel had reached their reservations and had been disarmed without serious trouble. Everything depended upon the forces at his disposal, and at Bergen, where no troops were available, there had been some unrest. He had hoped that the 52nd Division, which had been trained in Scotland and then posted to Germany, would have been now sent to Norway, but this plan was cancelled. Not until 10 June after the arrival of the US Task Force and of 303 and 304 Brigades could Andrew safely report that Allied control of the Wehrmacht was complete and that the long process of screening, in order to unearth wanted war criminals and SS and Gestapo men, who tried to hide among their compatriots, could begin.

For geographical reasons and the proximity to Russia, North Norway proved the most difficult area. Before the liberation began SHAEF had decided that control in this part of Norway should be entrusted to the Norwegian Brigade which reached Tromso on 26 May. Here a far greater concentration of German troops and Allied ex-prisoners of war than had been expected was found, and the task proved too demanding for each unit alone. This gave the Soviet press the chance to assert that there was a serious lack of control by the British and Americans. On 30 May Andrew was dismayed to learn that a party of Russian officers had arrived at Trömso, apparently without leave. His second weekly report to SHAEF tells of his reaction: 'My suspicious mind . . . saw this recce party returning to Murmansk to report the exceeding lightness of Allied control at present exercised in North Norway and thus giving the Soviet government the happy thought that they ought to assist us in the disarmament of the German forces in this area and that they would immediately dispatch Soviet forces for this kindly purpose.' He at once asked Flag Officer Norway to send a warship to Trömso to remain in harbour until the situation was clarified. It transpired that the Russian officers had in fact requested permission to enter Norway from the Norwegian High Command, which had failed to inform Andrew.

In the meantime on 31 May an official Russian delegation under General Ratov reached Oslo, where they were firmly told that the Allied Mission was in control and that their sole purpose would be to assist in the repatriation of Russian ex-prisoners of war and other Soviet citizens. Andrew had little doubt that trouble with the Russians was not at an end but for the moment he could tell Margaret: 'I am really glad of his [Ratov's] arrival as there were at one moment lots of Russians all trying to help!'

As Andrew wrote in his weekly report to SHAEF, on the same day that General Ratov arrived in Oslo the rest of the Norwegian Government also returned 'terrified that a further absence from Norway might prejudice their chances of re-election'. According to him he was having the greatest difficulty in persuading Norwegian politicians and also the Home Forces that despite the comparative smoothness of the liberation it was not yet safe for the King and the Royal Family to have returned with the Government. He found the Norwegian Government unable to understand the dangers posed by the continued existence of 400,000 Germans on Norwegian soil, preferring to believe that the Allied 'army of occupation' could now be safely withdrawn. It required considerable persuasion to get Ministers to agree to the publication and display of two proclamations, one by the King and the other by Eisenhower, explaining the military reasons why military rule must be retained for a while. This step was essential because the Norwegian Constitution did not permit any outside control on any grounds. Once this was agreed it was possible to end the purely military phase of the liberation and to arrange for the King's return. On 7 June, five years to the day since he left Norway, King Haakon with the Crown Princess and her three children stepped ashore at Oslo to be greeted by Andrew with the all sufficient welcome: 'Sir, I return to you your kingdom.'

When he first arrived in Oslo Andrew, as a temporary measure, took over the German headquarters at Storgate 33. As soon as possible he moved to Gimle, four miles outside Oslo, which became his home and the senior officers' mess. The house had been partially built by a Norwegian shipping magnate who went bankrupt before completing it. The shell had stood for twenty years before Quisling completed the house at a cost of a quarter of a million pounds. He wanted everything to be on the grand scale and he filled the house with furniture and art treasures looted from Norwegian and West European homes and galleries. The result was vulgarly ostentatious. There was a large library – Quisling as a young man had been an intellectual – on which Andrew commented: 'It is very interesting to see how widely he read and yet how little his reading has helped to make him a sane man.' He had turned the house into a fortress with bullet-proof shutters on each window and deep bomb-proof shelters. Andrew, after stripping the room of most of its elaborate furniture, took over Quisling's bedroom for himself. One feature met with his approval – the free-standing bath in the adjoining room. Its ease of cleaning appealed to him, and some years later he had a similar bath installed at Knowl Hill House. The large garden needed as much time as he could spare on it, and his need for exercise was partly met by cleaning away brushwood and old accumulations of rubbish. His staff were expected to share his enjoyment. Despite the time involved he enjoyed showing off the house to the large number of people interested in it. These included the Royal Family and a steady flow of Norwegians intent on regaining their family possessions. It made a pleasant end to the evening when, after a dinner party, guests were invited to identify and label their own or the national treasures. Nothing could be removed until proof of possession had been accepted by the police. Journalists welcomed any chance of seeing the house, especially at the time of Quisling's trial. On one occasion Andrew welcomed 120 of them and to his amusement his ADC 'caught some of them examining my much darned winter pants in the belief that they were Quisling's'. At the conclusion of the trial Mrs Quisling came back to Gimle in a forlorn attempt to persuade Andrew to quash the death sentence passed on her husband. It was a painful interview.

As Andrew had foreseen, his Mission had to deal with a number of conflicting requirements. Norway had to be relieved of more than half a million foreigners at a moment when the war against Japan had not yet been won and when, as a result, troops, aircraft and shipping were difficult to obtain. At the same time food, fuel and many necessities of life had to be brought into a country always heavily dependent upon imports and whose resources the enemy had stolen over four years. Nor was it helpful, when Andrew was striving to restore Norwegian sovereignty in full, to have to answer persistent criticism, based on national prejudice and a lack of realistic sense, from a Government only enabled to return, in his opinion, by an Allied victory. He could understand the very natural wish of Norwegians to see every German immediately behind barbed wire, but he hoped that at least the Government could realise that – to put it no higher – sufficient barbed wire for such a task did not exist in Norway and could only be imported in place of food.

The political situation was, as yet, unstable. A new caretaker Government took office in June, led by Einar Gerhardsen. He was the leading personality in the Labour Party and had been a prominent member of Resistance during 1940 and 1941, before being captured and sent to a German concentration camp. Other Home Front members joined the Cabinet as did Trygve Lie, the future UN Secretary-General, who became Foreign Minister, and Oscar Torp, a man whom Andrew knew well and with whom he could work easily, in the important post of Defence Minister. As time went by Andrew found that the complaints and criticisms came more from the military leaders than from the chief Ministers. Those Norwegian soldiers with whom he had planned the liberation in Scotco and with whom he had established a close relationship were being swiftly replaced by officers who had spent the war years as prisoners in Germany and who, in consequence, were less able to appreciate post-war problems and needs. This shift of military leadership was undoubtedly a setback to Allied co-operation and was keenly felt by Andrew. More than once he had to meet the Prime Minister and Torp in order to have his point of view fully understood and accepted.

Almost less forgivable in his eyes was the constant pressure exerted on him by the British War Office from mid-June onwards to release some of his none too numerous troops, seemingly oblivious to the ever-present danger of a breakdown in German discipline. Very slow progress had been made in raising and equipping the eighteen Norwegian Light Infantry battalions to which SHAEF had agreed. They might at least have filled the gaps left by the withdrawal of Allied troops had they existed. With his American deputy, Colonel Wilson, Andrew worked in close accord; the Russians continued to be the most awkward of allies. For the sake of clarity it is simplest to deal with each of Andrew's problems separately, but to appreciate the complexity of his task, the fact that he was dealing with them all at much the same time must not be forgotten.

The Home Forces had done a magnificent job at the moment of liberation, but Andrew needed assurance of their ability to deal with any serious trouble from the Germans. So in his first two months he visited and inspected a great many units all over Norway, seeing, it was said, more of the country even than the King, and returning from each tour greatly impressed and relieved. Despite the number of speeches demanded and the functions to be attended, the tours were highly enjoyable. It was a little embarrassing to know what to do with the flowers pressed on him by grateful Norwegians as he walked along the ranks of a Home Forces parade but his welcome was very moving. He found the scenery breathtakingly beautiful as he travelled by motor launch – sometimes with a German pilot – up and down the fjords to remote villages. Although 400 fathoms deep the water on top was very warm and afforded excellent bathing. Salmon and strawberries galore were described to poor Margaret, then languishing at The Deanery with strict rationing still in force. However, by mid-July with all Germans disarmed and in their reservations it was possible to allow the Home Forces to stand down. They were in a true sense of the word the People's Army. Farmers and labourers, office-workers, fishermen and civil servants had left home during mobilisation in the early days of May and they were now anxious to return to their jobs and the country needed them there.

To Andrew's disappointment very few wished to enlist in the Norwegian Army, but the Light battalions, recruited from volunteers, contained a hard core of Milorg men and Milorg also contributed greatly to the new Home Guard, created as a permanent part of Norway's military establishment. From Milorg's collaboration with the British grew a deep-rooted spirit of friendship and alliance of no little importance in the years ahead.

In August 1945 Cyril Falls, the Military Correspondent of *The Times*, had visited Norway to report on the progress of disarmament and repatriation of the Wehrmacht. In an article he described how impossible it would have been 'to administer, disarm, feed and repatriate them unless they were made to help themselves. They do their own staff work (which is excellent), draw their own food from their own reserve stocks, repair roads, rebuild bridges, sweep the coast clear of mines, collect their own armaments and equipment into dumps and pack the proportion which is to be sent away; and finally sail home in their own ships as fast as they can be "screened" and the transport can be found . . . Only in the final stages before repatriation are soldiers who pass the screening taken in hand, segregated in pens and sent home in crowded ships. Up till then the German hierarchy under General Boehme does the work . . . The German Armies in Norway are thus treated as a piece of machinery which is activated by control from outside and is scrapped section by section as it ceases to be required.' As Falls later wrote in the *Illustrated London News*, it was a plan which had 'a touch of audacious genius in its originality'.

Nothing hampered the work of rehabilitation more than the existence of about 1,250 minefields, and it was right that the dangerous task of removing over a quarter of a million anti-tank and anti-personnel mines should be undertaken by German soldiers under the supervision of the Royal Engineers. At the time of capitulation Andrew had written to General Boehme saying that it was not his intention to violate the honour of German soldiers, but that they must restore the damage which they had created. German casualties in mine-clearing were not heavy, yet when it was learned that a subordinate officer had ordered a body of Germans to run over a minefield to prove that the ground had been cleared, the order was cancelled and an apology made.

In Andrew's opinion, Germans were to realise that they had been totally defeated but not in any way to be degraded or treated with cruelty. Any suggestion that the Wehrmacht be permitted any sort of honourable marching-out from Norway, for which the Germans hoped, was unthinkable. Boehme continued to boast that he commanded an undefeated army in Norway, conveniently overlooking the destruction of the 20th Mountain Army in Finland and Northern Norway while under his leadership. Once within the reservations and disarmed, they were prisoners of war. This was realised by Boehme when he cabled to Keitel in mid-May that the Wehrmacht had been turned into an unarmed and unorganised mass. Andrew's methods of disarming the Germans had attracted the attention of Stalin. At the Potsdam Conference on 24 June Stalin suggested to Churchill, who had spoken of British lack of manpower, that some of the 40,000 unarmed German troops in Norway might well be used to dig coal in British mines – as he intended to use some of them in Russia. Fortunately Andrew was not ordered to implement this scheme. Following this exchange between Churchill and Stalin the telephone lines between Oslo and Potsdam were, according to him, red hot.

Andrew's method of treating the Wehrmacht in Norway had tended to create in international law an entirely new class of persons defined as 'disarmed military personnel operating under a military organisation and military law of a foreign country, with only the top command and control changed by the act of surrender'. The category of 'disarmed military personnel' was his brainchild, which required and received SHAEF's formal approval.

The repatriation of German soldiers presented far greater problems than their disarming. Not until the end of July was enough shipping available, and at first conditions obtaining in the area controlled by 21st Army Group and in the American sector were so chaotic after the devastation wrought by Allied bombing and with acute food shortages that Andrew had the utmost difficulty in arranging for the majority of Germans to return home. Teams of experts in screening had to be brought over from Scotco to unearth and arrest counter-intelligence personnel and to identify wanted Nazi criminals, and about 2,700 were kept in captivity. A further hundred senior German officers whom he had found 'a nuisance' were flown to Britain as prisoners of war. Of the vast majority of Germans passed for repatriation, each man carried a walking stick in place of his weapons and was permitted only forty pounds weight of personal kit, no item of which could be of Norwegian origin. Andrew was anxious to get them out of Norway as soon as possible, for until the takeover of German food stores had been organised it had been impossible to prevent the Wehrmacht from living on better rations than the Norwegians, an understandable cause of friction between the Norwegian populace and their liberators.

Meanwhile, the repatriation of Soviet ex-prisoners of war, given first priority by SHAEF's orders, led to awkward demands by General Ratov on behalf of his Government and some plain speaking by Andrew. About 87,000 Russians, chiefly soldiers, were discovered in stalags or on work detachments along the Norwegian coast and on isolated islands. Having been imprisoned in horror camps and used as slave labour, most of them were in a shocking condition, though less affected by typhus than Andrew had feared but Ratov denied. Initial control was hampered by the vast distances to be covered and by lack of communications. Most of the men were in rags and to their disgust had to be clothed in German uniforms. There were some disciplinary troubles but nothing more serious than incidents caused by the effects of wood alcohol and raids on German wine stores. 'The opportunity was taken of giving some Germans an experience of living in the camps where they had previously held their prisoners of war.'

On 30 June a great Allied parade was held in Oslo, which Air Chief Marshal Harris and General Bradley, representing Britain and the United States, attended. Some Russian generals arrived at the last moment. Jens Hauge recalls that on this occasion the Russian troops appeared in American uniforms, doubtless to the annoyance of General Ratov. Hauge maintains that Andrew deserves great credit for insisting on including his Russian allies in the parade and that this had to be arranged at the last moment solely on Andrew's authority. He had no dislike for the ordinary Russian soldier, of whom he saw much during an extended tour of Northern Norway during repatriation. 'I lost my heart to the very delightful childish people which they were at the moment. They are so well behaved, and it is only when they get their hands on alcohol that they become a damn nuisance.'

Augustus Thorne

Mary Frances Thorne, with Mollie and Andrew

Mulgrave: Andrew on extreme right

Andrew and Margaret, about the time of their marriage

The 'Old Funk Hole' on the Aisne, 1914: Andrew on the left

General von Schleicher, then German Defence Minister, with Andrew on manoeuvres in 1932

Diana *Peter* *George* *Poppy*
Sandy *Margaret* *Andrew* *Pansy*
Before mobilisation, 1939

Andrew with Scottish Home Guard, 1943

King Haakon with Andrew: Scotland, 1942

Quisling's house, Andrew's residence in Oslo

General Eisenhower shaking hands with Andrew, 1945; Lieutenant-General Sir Edward Grasett in background

The injured Andrew making his farewells: Oslo, 1945

Andrew and Margaret greeted by General Hansteen on Andrew's recall to Norway, 1950

Jens Chr. Hauge with Andrew, 1950

The repatriation of these Russians was complicated by two factors: the changing attitude of the Swedish Government and conflicting definitions of Soviet territory. In a neighbourly contribution towards ridding Norwegian soil of unwanted foreigners, the Swedish Government had at first rather surprisingly offered to accept 300,000 Germans and Russians and to keep them until they could be sent home. Towards the end of the war, the Swedes had told Boehme that they would accept German troops, but not Terboven or Quisling. No mention was then made of Russians. Second thoughts led to a withdrawal of the original promise, but not before the end of June.

More serious was the problem of defining who was and who was not a Soviet citizen. SHAEF had ruled that only those who had lived in the USSR prior to 3 September 1939 should automatically be repatriated. Ratov on behalf of his Government claimed all Balts and Poles who had lived east of the Curzon Line. Regardless of Soviet protests all Russians were screened. Those who lived west of the pre-war frontier were asked if they wished to go to the USSR. If they replied 'No', they were termed 'disputed persons' and housed in special camps to await a decision. With the arrival in Oslo of a Polish Commission, Ratov dropped all claims to the Poles, and the remaining 1,500 disputed persons were divided between the British and American zones. Once the dispute was settled the evacuation of Russians proceeded rapidly and was complete by the end of July. Despite endless complaints by Ratov, 'the arrangements made worked smoothly and though we were barely satisfied that the provision of rations and comforts for the journey were adequate, they were all that the Soviet Delegation would allow the Swedes and ourselves to provide. The degree of discomfort is likely to increase sharply as the Soviet citizens near their home and the Soviet authorities are evidently determined not to give any opportunity for unfavourable comparison.'

The planners at Scotco could not have given any preliminary consideration to one problem, because they were unaware of its existence. Some 37,000 'displaced persons', that is those who were neither German nor Austrian, had been unexpectedly uncovered. French, Belgians and Dutch could be repatriated without too much difficulty once transport became available. A

War Office directive that ninety percent of the transport must come from ex-enemy stocks added to Andrew's worries. In view of the world shortage of transport he felt that he could only accept the order, but delays were inevitable, aggravated by the lack of proper maintenance, which had rendered a large proportion of German vehicles useless. The Czechs proved unexpectedly difficult to repatriate, as Czech liaison officers refused to accept more than 3,000 on the grounds that the remaining 11,000 were Sudeten Germans! These were later settled in the American zone. Of the 15,000 Poles in Norway about 10,000 had served in the Wehrmacht, and except for 1,000 or so who did not wish to return to Poland all were repatriated. The dissidents found a new home in France. Although given the best camps, the Yugoslavs created the most trouble as there was nobody in authority among them whom they were willing to obey. Gradually they returned home through Sweden. Some 'displaced persons', such as those who had lived in Baltic countries, proved impossible to repatriate, and for the time being were cared for by the Norwegian Ministry of Social Welfare. In the end Andrew calculated that his Mission had dealt with over forty different nationalities and that betwen May and December 132,000 of the 133,000 non-German or Austrian nationals had been evacuated from Norway. It was a remarkable achievement, demanding infinite tact and patience from all concerned, together with an ability on Andrew's part to issue clear directives and to enforce them with firmness.

Close relationship between the Civil Affairs staff and the Norwegian Government had begun in England long before liberation. The task had been made easier by the Home Forces' prevention of last-minute sabotage. Once supplies had been landed they became the responsibility of the Norwegian Ministry of Supply and Reconstruction, which took over full responsibility for distribution. This avoided one potential source of friction, for it was a Norwegian and not an Allied decision to refrain from distributing badly needed food, coffee, coal and medical supplies until sufficient stocks had been accumulated to ensure that those living in outlying districts received equal treatment with those in or near the big towns. By the end of 1945 669,000 tons of supplies had been brought into Norway, a figure far in excess of the most optimistic hopes. Once the military phase of the liberation had ended the task of supplying Norwegian civilians became exclusively the responsibility of the Norwegian Government.

Civil Affairs staff had also to deal with a variety of problems ranging from domestic issues arising from marriages contracted between Norwegians and Germans or with Allied troops to the legal difficulties raised in the Allied military courts, which Andrew had set up for the trial of Germans charged with offences committed since their surrender. Questions of military discipline and serious breaches of Norwegian law caused him much anxiety, which he should have been spared, and often subjected him to personal criticism and abuse in the Norwegian press and in that of many countries.

Fearing that the SS and units of the police in the Wehrmacht might well cause trouble, it had been part of the Allied capitulation terms that General Boehme should arrest some of these men as a precautionary measure. Boehme appealed to SHAEF to rescind this order, asking not to have to arrest any of his men against whom no personal charge had been made. SHAEF instructed Andrew to 'discuss the matter further with the Germans', which, in effect, forced him to suspend his order. Collier, now Ambassador in Norway, told the Foreign Office that SHAEF had thereby weakened Andrew's hand in future dealings with the Germans.

Far more serious was the case of Captain Blell, a German officer who had shot a Russian shortly after the German surrender. The case was tried in one of Andrew's military courts, and Blell was found guilty and condemned to death, a sentence approved and confirmed by Andrew. Then a legal battle started. Andrew had confirmed the sentence on the advice of one of his legal advisers in G5 at a moment when the Senior Adviser happened to be in Stockholm. On his return to Oslo this man disagreed with his junior's opinion, believing that there was insufficient evidence of premeditated intention to commit murder. The case was referred to the Deputy Judge Advocate General, who disagreed with both advisers, and the three experts argued the fate of Blell for two hours. The upshot was that Andrew confirmed the sentence but commuted it to life imprisonment. 'The reprieve came on the evening before the execution, and except for the condemned everyone seems unhappy at my action,' he told the CIGS.

Then the storm broke. Some accused him of culpable weakness; others, especially the Russians, accused him of continued sympathy with the German military caste. The War Office at first doubted whether he had ever possessed the authority to set up the military courts. However, a meeting in London ended by supporting him, ordering him to 'notify the German Commander that for the avoidance of all doubt the German Forces have since 23.01 hours 8th May 1945 and will in future be subject to the Allied Military Court for military disobedience and for offences against Norwegian Law'. Throughout the Blell case Collier had strongly supported Andrew in two long despatches to the Foreign Office. 'In this, as in his other troubles here, General Thorne has shown himself honest, conscientious and . . . desperately anxious to be just and do right . . . I do not see how he can be blamed for listening to the strong – indeed in Blell's case, violent –representations of his highest legal advisers.' A little later he defended Andrew from the charge of excessive caution. 'In general, Thorne seems to have been very patient and reasonable both with the Germans and with the Norwegians. The latter undoubtedly feel that he sometimes errs through excess of caution – a sentiment which, I gather, is shared by some of his Staff – but then he is by nature a cautious Scot who is always determined to "mak sikker" like Robert Bruce when he made a thorough job of the Red Comyn!'

Norwegians might be critical of Andrew's handling of the comparatively unimportant Blell case, but their real anger with him was reserved for the way in which the stores of German military equipment were disposed of. One of the ways in which the aim of the United Nations to secure a lasting peace was to be achieved was by preventing any revival of German military might. Hence Eisenhower's order that every piece of German war material not required for the war against Japan or of no use for civil purposes must be destroyed. All German property and war material had been declared to be the property of the Allied cause and not of each liberated country.

In pursuing the policy of destroying German military equipment as laid down by SHAEF criticism of Andrew came partly from articles in the Norwegian press, partly from within Parliament, but mostly from the leading soldiers. Press attacks could be answered and there was never serious conflict between him and the chief Ministers in the Government. The Norwegian military leaders like Major-General Hansteen and even Crown Prince Olav himself, with whom Andrew had worked closely in Scotland, had been quickly replaced by senior Norwegian officers headed by General Otto Ruge, who had returned from prisoner-of-war camps in Germany unaware of the spirit of co-operation fostered at Scotco. More than once Andrew had to ask for Government help to meet the criticisms and outdated attitudes of the new military leadership. These changes were political decisions of the Norwegian Government which he was powerless to prevent.

Andrew had some sympathy for the Norwegians, who had sustained such heavy losses in materials during the German occupation. Moreover, after VJ Day (15 August) it became even harder to pacify Norwegian feelings 'outraged by the sight of Allied personnel wantonly – as they felt it – destroying priceless weapons, equipment and machines. They refused to take into consideration that they would be unable to man or maintain them and that their retention would necessitate replacements and spares being continued to be manufactured in German war factories.' Andrew persuaded SHAEF to allow him some discretion in implementing the order, but he remained relieved that much valuable material had been destroyed at the start of his time in Norway when Allied forces were so thin on the ground.

One aspect of Andrew's policy was fortunately unknown to the Norwegian press. The financial subdivision of Civil Affairs impounded 138 million krone from German nationals and also impounded all foreign currency. For a moment there was a danger of devaluing the Norwegian currency, and over one weekend, while the necessary arrangements to prevent this were being made, the whole sum was placed to the credit of Andrew's personal account in his bank. It was the only time in his life when he was rich beyond the dreams of avarice.

By early September Andrew was convinced that there was a Communist attempt to whip up anti-British and anti-American feeling. Significantly there was no corresponding criticism of the

Soviet Union. He believed that it was important to prevent any possible danger that a new left-wing Norwegian Government might look to Russia for help rather than to the West. He was wrong in this assessment but was able to increase the amount of German war material allocated to the Norwegian Government. At the same time he issued a long explanation of the Allied policy to the Norwegian press which most, though not all, papers printed. With hindsight he later admitted that there had been insufficient explanation of SHAEF's orders under which the Allied commanders acted.

If Norwegians were critical of some of Andrew's actions, he was extremely critical of their slowness in rebuilding their army. The Norwegian commander, General Ruge, with whom his relations became increasingly strained, maintained that he could do little while German war material was destroyed or withheld and that while this Allied policy continued the Storting, the Norwegian Parliament, was refusing to vote money for defence. Whether there was some truth in this or not, the trouble lay much deeper. In a long letter to Ruge, dated 9 September, Andrew set out his criticisms and offered suggestions for improvement. The senior officers, in his opinion, were far too old for their work and too bound to their office chairs. Administration at top level was hopeless, resulting in an army of isolated units insufficiently directed and lacking any combined sense of purpose. This had largely been due to the mistaken belief that tactical studies were all-important, regardless of any supporting administration. From his own study in Scotland of the problems facing an invader of Norway he was certain that the geographical difficulties made three divisions, adequately supported and maintained, a far better defence of the country than the six divisions for which Ruge was clamouring and which would be equally inefficiently administered. Andrew had the highest praise for the young Norwegian soldier, admirable for a parachute regiment or for the guerilla forces essential in Norway. What these young men at present lacked was proper leadership. Since any future attack on Norway was bound to start from the air, decentralisation was essential. Finally, he suggested that each year there should be a prolonged staff exercise to monitor progress and to weed out incompetents.

The importance of this letter in Andrew's career is that failure to implement these suggestions was to lead to his recall to Norway in 1950 to advise on the reform of the Norwegian Army. For the moment, as he told Alanbrooke, he had failed. All that had happened was that before he left Norway six divisional generals had been appointed of whom two were over sixty years old and the other four over fifty. Their task was unlikely to be onerous as no divisions existed for them to command.

On 4 June Andrew wrote to Margaret telling her that he had just heard officially from the CIGS that his Scottish command was at an end and that when his work in Norway was finished he would be placed on the retired list. 'It is as interesting a finish to a professional career as anyone could wish for.' Although constantly 'swamped with interviews and problems . . . I will certainly never be able to say that I was bored with the job.' At midnight on 13/14 July SHAEF officially ceased to exist. On its final day Andrew was summoned to Headquarters where Eisenhower invested him with the United States Legion of Merit for 'exceptionally meritorious conduct' and congratulated him on his skilful and diplomatic handling of all the intricate problems which arose from Allied agreements with the Norwegian Government. The Allied Mission was broken up into its two main parts, but Andrew remained as Commander-in-Chief Allied Land Forces, Norway, with ultimate responsibility to the Joint Chiefs of Staff in Washington. A time limit, however, was imposed. Permission for ALFN to remain an integrated headquarters was conditional upon its work being completed by the end of November 1945. This necessitated the acceptance into a shattered Germany of all repatriated Germans and a share of the displaced and disputed persons. Only in this way could the pledge of the Allied commanders that Norway would be free of foreigners by the end of six months be fulfilled.

To be Head of the Allied Mission in Norway made exceptionally heavy demands upon Andrew's wisdom, his diplomatic and social skills and his stamina, and in no respect had he been found wanting. It was not all hard work, for there were attractive compensations. It was only a short run before dinner from his bedroom to the fjord for a swim; sailing in that wonderful summer when the temperature in Oslo reached 90 degrees was a particular delight; even official tours were infinitely preferable to pacifying General Ratov or trying to explain Allied policy to suspicious Norwegian journalists. Early in July he had the interesting experience of a visit to Germany where, as he told Margaret, he spent a long time 'interviewing Ribbentrop and Hermann [Goering]! Wasn't it a bit of luck! I was more than interested. Our cross-examination of Ribbentrop was in English, the Fat Boy's was in German – equally thrilling!'

On 20 September Andrew celebrated his sixtieth birthday. Among messages of congratulation were telegrams from King Haakon and from Eisenhower. Before attending a performance of *Peer Gynt* at the theatre there was a big party at Gimle when 'I managed to blow out all 60 candles at one puff – not too bad for 60!' Three weeks later he subjected his wind to a much more severe test by taking part in the ten kilometres 'Peace March'. 'Having reached the age of 60 I should have done 5 km. only but felt I must compete against all the others. Thanks to a good hot bath and Mr Quisling's sunlight lamp I had no cramp at all in the night.' He had covered the course in seventy minutes.

Throughout August and September the work of repatriation went steadily ahead, and thanks to the efforts of Civil Affairs life in Norway began to return to normal. This did not mean the end of Andrew's worries, for as the country was cleared of foreigners and food became more plentiful the necessity for the Mission remaining in Norway was less and less clear to Norwegians. 'I think that we will just about miss outstaying our welcome if we can get the remaining Germans and ourselves out quickly,' Andrew informed the CIGS on 13 September. There had been some indisciplined behaviour by members of the SAS units, and Collier was particularly anxious that they should return to Britain as soon as possible. 'They ought, of course, to have left long ago, but Thorne is said to have had a certain weakness for them at the beginning because they were commanded by his own nephew.' No such criticism was levelled at the composite battalion of Foot Guards, commanded by Colonel Thomas Butler. Each day the battalion provided the guard at the Hotel Bristol, the Allied Forces Headquarters in Oslo, and Andrew hoped that the daily ceremony, complete with corps of drums and pipes, would set a standard to be emulated by the very slovenly Norwegian Army. The ceremony was watched each day by crowds, who began to assemble at least an hour before the guard was mounted. This did not please Andrew. 'It is a matter for regret that so large a number of people have so much time on their hands.' Idleness was always to him inexplicable and largely unforgivable. Nevertheless, there was every reason for the Mission to end its work. The SAS trouble had been appropriately punished and good relations restored, but there was urgent need for more accommodation in Oslo as 2,500 students would soon be arriving for the opening of the university, and the university authorities had apparently forgotten to make adequate provision for housing them.

As the time for his departure from Norway – fixed as 1 November – drew nearer, Andrew in such moments as he could spare was forced to consider possible future employment and a move from The Deanery. During July Margaret had been having further antrum trouble and had always found the Thames Valley climate enervating. Andrew at once wrote to her: 'We must certainly try and find some more suitable home. I am sure we can do so and in any case with my big fall in income (I miss the extra General's pension) I doubt very much if we could afford to live at The Deanery.' He had vague ideas of building a wooden house somewhere with surrounding bungalows for visiting families, but nothing came of it. It is clear from a letter written in January 1946 declining to become chairman of a Battles Nomenclature Committee at the War Office that he hankered after settling finally in Morayshire, as this was the reason given for declining the offer. A far more interesting proposal had been made to him in September 1945: 'I have just been asked if I would like my name considered for the job of running UNRRA in Shanghai!! It would bring me £2500 a year and living expenses. It would be almost an historic event for the Thorne family as my Father went to Canton in 1845. Augustus Thorne (Jun:) should almost certainly go in 1945 to make the circle join completely. I am wondering what to do but imagine I must refuse as I want a job at home. Still, it is interesting.' A telephone call to Margaret before the letter was posted abruptly ended any plans which he might have had for accepting. Late that night he completed the letter: 'I do so agree that Shanghai is not the place for a couple such as we are with all our many family ties.' A trifle wistfully he ended the letter: 'But it would have been attractive in some ways.' A month later he told Margaret that he expected to return in a cruiser. He had decided not to stay for a time in Scotland but to travel back home where he would 'spend some time divesting myself of all my responsibilities'.

From mid-October a series of farewell lunches and dinners were given in Andrew's honour, which, he confessed to Margaret, 'are getting me down'. On 10 October he was personally invested by King Haakon with the Grand Cross of St Olav. There had been some criticism of the King's wish to do this but he made it clear that if he did not get his way no honours of any kind would be awarded to any member of the Allied Mission. That evening Andrew wrote to Margaret: 'I have been given the best Order they possess, so that it, together with what the King said about my work here and in Scotland, is a complete recompense, thoroughly appreciated by me . . . It is a very handsome decoration and will cover any dirty marks on my white shirt if ever I have the opportunity to wear it.'

Two days later Andrew forwarded to Jens Hauge copies of a 'top secret' appreciation of the problem of the defence of Norway which the new Labour Government Prime Minister, Einar Gerharlsen, had been glad to accept. No man knew more about the subject than Andrew. He had studied the ways of attacking Norway ever since 1941, and had things gone less smoothly in 1945 he might well have been at the last moment in command of a very dangerous operation. Much of his time during his last few days in Norway was spent in preparation for a final press conference to be held on 30 October, but he managed to fit in a flying visit to Stockholm to thank the Swedish Crown Prince and the Swedish Government for training the police battalions during the war, thereby having helped to remove the dangerous time-lag between the Wehrmacht surrender and the arrival of sufficient Allied forces to disarm the German troops.

The press conference went very smoothly as Andrew reviewed the task of the Allied Mission, its difficulties and its achievements. He explained the impossibility of harsher treatment of the Germans, which the Norwegian people naturally desired. At the same time he gently reminded Norwegians that the British also 'have some cause to dislike Germans . . . The population killed to the total population is higher than that of any other Allied nation. Over a million homes in Great Britain have been destroyed. Our overseas investments have been spent on the war effort', but we were spared the terrible experience of an enemy occupation. He ended by saying that the completion of the military task in Norway would be under the command of Major-General Graham but that all British troops would have left Norway by Christmas. 'I could not have had', he said, 'a more interesting appointment with which to finish up my forty-two years of military service.'

From the Conference Andrew went to the Palace for a farewell luncheon with King Haakon, who, at the end of the meal, 'suddenly stood up and said that he had never seen Norwegian troops drill and march so well as the [Norwegian Mountain] Brigade yesterday and that as I had trained them [in Scotland] I had evidently learned how to manage his independent-minded subjects extremely successfully; so that he had decided to present me with the Freedom Medal . . . the one that all his soldiers would share with me the honour of wearing.' Later, in England, Jens Hauge had the pleasure of presenting the medal to Andrew, together with a superbly bound volume of photographs as a memento of Milorg.

Personal letters of gratitude followed from the Prime Minister, the Foreign Minister, Trygve Lie and General Ruge. Even the often acerbic pen of the British Ambassador when writing to Ernest Bevin, then Foreign Secretary, was devoid of anything but praise. He recalled the length of time which it took the Norwegian people to recognise the value of Andrew's work, but he maintained that the organised opposition to Andrew had been the work of the Communists. All Norwegians now recognised their debt to him. 'He has even maintained good personal relations with General Ratov!' With all past differences between Andrew and the Norwegian Government forgotten, everything was now planned to give him a worthy send-off when he embarked in HMS *Diadem* on the afternoon of 1 November. There were to be three guards of honour on the quay from the Army, the RAF and the Norwegian Army. A further guard of honour of Royal Marines was to greet him on board. The Crown Prince would head the body of leading Norwegian figures assembled to bid him a personal farewell.

Before any of this ceremony took place, fate dealt the accident-prone Andrew a particularly cruel blow. On the morning of 1 November he left his Headquarters at the Hotel Bristol to pay a final courtesy call on the British Ambassador. Across the street stood his large official car, once the property of Terboven, who had committed suicide when the Wehrmacht surrendered. As he began to cross the street to his car he was suddenly struck by a civilian car travelling at a dangerously high speed and thrown about ten yards along the road. As he told a body of journalists who later interviewed him in Edinburgh: 'I did not see who was driving it. I turned a somersault and a half and at that moment lost interest in finer points. I did not bother about "who done it". I was rather dazed but I remembered to pick up my beret . . . I knew that I had not been seriously damaged because I could move all my limbs.' He was, however, in agonising pain, yet insisted on going through the ceremony on the quayside. 'Inspecting four guards of honour was rather a trial,' he told the Edinburgh journalists, 'and I'm afraid I had to do it in a most unsoldierly-like fashion [leaning on a stick] because it was impossible to stand erect.' Andrew had always conquered pain when he felt it necessary but never had he put on so brave a face as on the afternoon of 1 November. In a very moving scene HMS *Diadem*, dressed overall, with a band playing the haunting Skye Boat Song, slipped her moorings and carried Andrew across the sea to Edinburgh and to a bed in the hospital inside the Castle of which he had been so proud a Governor for four years.

In hospital an X-ray revealed a seriously displaced vertebra, almost certainly weakened by his riding accident in Berlin. After ten days he was allowed to return to The Deanery on condition that he remained in bed for a prolonged period. In a kindly gesture King George had commanded Sir Alan Lascelles to send Andrew a copy of the message which he had received from King Haakon as Andrew left Oslo, expressing 'my acknowledgement of the remarkable manner in which General Thorne has fulfilled his difficult mission in this country' and his admiration of the way in which 'this gallant officer's tact and great effort' had contributed so greatly to the liberation of Norway. Perhaps even more pleasing to Andrew was to learn as time went by that he had earned the proud title in Norway of 'Our Thorne'. As he lay in bed contemplating the problems of retirement he could not know that in five years' time Norway would need him once again.

16
On Active Retirement: 1946 – 1970

For a man like Andrew, to whom inactivity was intolerable and almost a sin, the prospect of retirement, when fit and alert, must have seemed daunting. He had made an excellent recovery from his serious accident in Oslo and by February 1946 was recuperating in Brighton. At the end of January he had been officially notified by the War Office that after sixty-seven days on full pay he would on 8 May be placed on the Regular Army Reserve of Officers with a pension of £1,500 a year. On his sixty-second birthday, 20 September 1947, his name was removed from the Reserve as no longer liable to be recalled to Army service. His distinguished military career was apparently at an end.

However, there was no danger that Andrew would be left to spend his days gardening at The Deanery, much as he enjoyed this, especially when working in the paddock where he was in no danger of attracting criticism for harming Gertrude Jekyll's original layout and where he could safely clear away undergrowth to his heart's content. Over the next few years invitations to undertake voluntary work of many kinds were frequent. He was glad to be involved in the Regimental Comrades Association and with the British Legion. In May 1946 he became Chairman of the Guards Club, a task which he took very seriously, making himself unpopular with those members of the Committee who infrequently attended meetings and whose resignation he suggested. As one who had always believed in the importance of continued education for his soldiers he took an interest in the Workers Educational Association, and in a very different educational sphere he was proud to be elected President of the Old Etonian Association for 1949/50. Despite his interest in the welfare of young people he resisted pressure from the Chief Scout, Lord Rowallan, to become Deputy Chief Commissioner at

Imperial Headquarters. With memories of the Poles in Scotco he had less difficulty in declining an invitation from the Duchess of Atholl to become Chairman of the Joint Committee of Welcome for the Polish Forces in Britain. Nor was he tempted by a suggestion that he should allow his name to be considered as Governor and Commander-in-Chief of Gibraltar. Although this was a position of importance, he feared that three or four years in Gibraltar would be cramping and claustrophobic.

Early in 1947 he was approached by the Home Office to fill a vacancy on the Council of Supervision of Broadmoor Hospital, to which he agreed. When two years later a change in the hospital's constitution occurred, he became chairman of a newly formed committee of visitors, and he continued with this work until 1964. That he had thrown himself into the life of Berkshire was recognised in 1949 when he was appointed a deputy lieutenant for the county. If he needed assurance that his life as a soldier had not been forgotten – despite his short-lived attempt to drop the 'General' and to be known simply as Sir Andrew – he found it on Christmas Eve 1948 in *The Times*. In the 'Who or what were . . .' section of the seasonal quiz was the name 'Bulgy'.

Ties with Norway remained strong. On 9 April 1946, the anniversary of the German invasion, he broadcast a five-minute message of good wishes. Thanks to the kind efforts of Jens Hauge and General Rolstad, he and Margaret with some of the family enjoyed a summer holiday in Norway and there were thoughts of repeating the holiday in 1947, but another invitation had been received. Neville Wigram, Poppy's husband, had been appointed Military Secretary to the Governor-General of New Zealand, General Sir Bernard Freyberg, VC, and Andrew and Margaret were invited to stay at Government House before touring the country. After arranging for Peter to look after his affairs during his absence, he made copious lists of his and Margaret's belongings. They did not travel light. Ten pieces of luggage consisting of cabin trunks, suitcases, deck chairs, golf clubs and fishing rods accompanied them. He felt that he needed to take seven suits for what was intended to be a two months' visit. It was a wonderful holiday and only had to be shorter than planned when news reached them of Pansy's engagement to John, the Master of Erskine, a Captain in the Scots Guards and son of Lord

Erskine and Lady Marjorie. They returned home in time for the wedding in April 1948.

Perhaps because Andrew's career had necessitated frequent moves from one house to the next he was a great home lover and also a home maker. The Deanery was a most hospitable house where children and grandchildren, relations and friends were warmly welcomed. Rather surprisingly, after a life of following him around, Margaret did not put down roots easily when he retired. She never appeared to want to live in one place for very long: the grass always seemed greener elsewhere. She disliked the climate of the Thames Valley, and The Deanery was an expensive house to run. Andrew's earlier thoughts of retiring to Lossiemouth were soon abandoned. Margaret loved Morayshire in summer but could never have borne the winter months, and Andrew realised that his growing commitments made it impossible to live so far from the London area. In July 1949 he was invited to become Governor of the Royal Hospital, Chelsea, where a flat was provided. He refused, partly because Margaret was becoming arthritic and access would have been difficult for her. It is true that there was a lift to the flat, but, as he told Peter, when he learned that the lift was maintained by the Office of Works, he had no hesitation about his refusal.

By midsummer 1949 Andrew had decided that they must leave The Deanery. Both he and Margaret had always longed to own a 'modern' house with big windows and a flat roof. They were both interested in architecture and had a large number of books about modern building. To satisfy this wish Andrew bought Land's End House at Twyford, and they moved there from 1 November. It was an unwise choice, for the nearest bus stop was forty minutes' walk away, which made it very difficult to attract servants; but it remained the family home until October 1956. While looking for a more suitable house Andrew sounded out the Church Commissioners about renting a flat in Lambeth Palace, but this was not possible. Eventually he settled on Knowl Hill House in the Reading area, which he bought in 1955 and into which, after extensive alterations, he and Margaret and Diana moved in October 1956. This became their final home.

In his various homes Andrew tried to be a do-it-yourself pioneer without conspicuous success. He was a fairly competent carpenter, but trouble came with his love of buying innumerable labour-saving gadgets which he believed could be rendered even more efficient if he turned certain knobs. He installed an oil-fired burner to warm The Deanery which worked entirely satisfactorily but which, he felt, could be still further improved by some fine adjustments to its mechanism. In no time a black oily soot began to fall all over Sonning. On another occasion he installed a dish-washing machine, then quite a novelty. He filled it with beautifully clean glasses and set it in motion to test its efficiency. After a while he could not resist lifting the lid to see if all was going well, with the result that he and the kitchen were drenched with hot soapy water. He was safer in the garden.

Andrew's legacy to Norway at the conclusion of his Mission in 1945 had been his suggestions for the modernisation of the Norwegian Army. He knew that traditionally-minded generals like Ruge would not take kindly to his advice, but he had hoped that men like Jens Hauge would be in a sufficiently powerful position to bring about some of the changes which he had advocated. In fact, progress was painfully slow. Some two months after he had left Norway a letter from Colonel Garner-Smith, who had become Military Attaché in Oslo, told him that Hauge greatly missed Andrew's presence in Norway and also that Trygve Lie's appointment as Secretary-General of the United Naitons meant the loss of a forward-looking ally. Resistance by the old guard prevented defence from being regarded as a matter of urgency and 'the general attitude is to say "il faut cultiver notre jardin"'. By 1949 letters from Norway suggested that the Government, although a member of NATO, might have difficulty in resisting Russian pressure, and it was clear that little was being done to ensure the country's defence.

In March 1950 Montgomery, now a field-marshal and chairman of the Western Europe Commanders-in-Chief Committee, had visited Norway and had advised the British War Office to send a small Mission to Norway to help with the modernisation of the Norwegian Army. Hauge, who had become Minister of Defence, and General Hansteen, the Chief of the Army, had welcomed the idea and, as ardent supporters of Andrew's views, had insisted that he was the right man to head such a Mission. In a letter to the War Office Montgomery opposed this. 'I doubt whether General Thorne is up to this sort of thing any more. We should send a younger man.' This wildly wrong opinion throws some added light on Montgomery's officially friendly relations with Andrew. Andrew was only two years older than Montgomery.

The War Office disregarded Montgomery's advice, and on 9 November 1950 the Military Secretary, General McLean, wrote to Andrew: 'The Norwegian Government have asked H.M.G. to send to Norway a senior British officer to report on the organisation and efficiency of the Norwegian Armed Forces and to recommend whether or not an inter-Service Mission should be sent to assist the Norwegians to re-organise their Armed Forces on a more efficient basis. The visit might last about three weeks or so and would have to take place in the fairly near future . . . The War Office have been invited by the Chiefs of Staff to approach you to ascertain whether you would be prepared to accept this temporary appointment.' Andrew accepted with alacrity. A formal letter of invitation from Hauge was sent on 22 November. In it he suggested that Andrew might like the assistance of a United States officer and added: 'Needless to say, the Ministry of Defence is looking forward with pleasure to the time when the Chief of the Allied Liberation Forces of 1945, who rendered such great services to Norway, will return to give advice to the Norwegian Authorities.' In a postscript Hauge hoped that Margaret would come with him.

Two days later Andrew attended a meeting of the Chiefs of Staff Committee at the War Office when the terms of reference of his visit to Norway were decided. He told the Committee that Hauge had made it clear that his primary task in Norway would be to strengthen the Government's hand in dealings with the Storting. Nothing, Andrew had long been convinced, could be achieved until the post of Commander-in-Chief was abolished and a Chiefs of Staff system on British and American lines substituted. Furthermore, he doubted whether subsequent to his visit a formal Mission was the best way to help the Norwegians. He thought it infinitely preferable for facilities to be offered by Britain for visits from Norwegian officers of all three Services. 'The Norwegians are a proud race and they would much prefer to have opportunities to train their own officers in this country than to accept a British Mission in their country.' To this the Committee agreed. They gave him full discretion to discuss any problem which Hauge raised, while bearing in mind that officially he was only concerned with the Norwegian Army.

Andrew wasted no time in getting to grips with this welcome but unexpected assignment, and by 4 December he was attending his first meeting in Oslo under Hauge's chairmanship. Four Norwegian officers were present: General Hansteen as Chief of the Army, Colonel Pran and Colonel Brodin, Chiefs of the Army Staff and of Administrative Staff (Finance) respectively, and a close friend, Lieutenant-Colonel (as he then was) Leif Rolstad, who was appointed Andrew's adjutant. Andrew was glad to work once again with the American, Colonel Ford Trimble; and Major Vincent Budge, his staff officer and a Grenadier, completed the committee. Prior to the meeting General Hansteen had submitted to Andrew a list of the questions which he hoped would be studied. While accepting this list, Andrew asked leave to alter the order in which he studied them. He explained that he would prefer to start at the top with the organisation for command and control in war and then work down to the organisation of individual units. This was agreed and a tightly packed timetable of talks and conferences, with a week of travel in the middle, was planned to start next day and conclude on about 21 December, after which, his Mission completed, he and Margaret would return home and in due course he would submit his formal report.

Meanwhile the War Office had decided to restore him to the Active List while undertaking this Mission. With effect from 14 November 1950 his status was to be that of 'a re-employed retired officer, re-employed for Military Service' with full pay and allowances, replacing his retired pay. The letter telling him of this was written on 21 December, with a note that the appointment would be gazetted on 9 January 1951.

Before this letter reached Andrew ill luck had again struck him. This time it was not an accident, but after only ten days on the task he succumbed to a severe attack of pneumonia. Fortunately Margaret could help to look after him, and in a remarkably short time he appeared to have recovered and was well enough to return to England. As Hauge wrote: 'I understand your body is just as strong as your spirit.' He did not know that shortly after reaching Land's End House Andrew suffered a serious relapse with a severe attack of pleurisy on top of recurring pneumonia, necessitating immediate removal to hospital. Although before leaving Norway he had been able to submit an Interim Report to the Norwegian Ministry of Defence, his task had not been completed and he intended to return to Norway directly he received his doctor's permission.

Without at first being aware how ill Andrew had been, Hauge was pressing him to return and complete his Mission by mid-January. There were two reasons for this. Nothing could be done to improve Norway's Armed Forces without the approval of the Storting, and this would not be given without a reasonably accurate forecast of the cost involved. Hauge's more serious anxiety concerned the international scene. During the Cold War there had been some talk of a defence pact with Sweden, but this had been abandoned when it was realised that such a pact would entail the loss to Norway of arms supplies from the West. Instead, Norway in April 1949 had become an original member of the North Atlantic Treaty Organisation, which inevitably limited her full freedom of action since membership of NATO involved sharing in the joint defence of Northern Europe, and in 1951 NATO North set up its headquarters in a suburb of Oslo.

Much now depended on those in charge of the Organisation, and it was a relief to Hauge to learn at the end of 1950 that President Truman had agreed to permit Eisenhower to become Supreme Commander of NATO Forces in Europe with headquarters in Paris, now designated as SHAPE, or Supreme Headquarters Allied Powers, Europe. With the choice of Montgomery as Deputy Supreme Commander, charged with training, equipping and integrating the national forces allotted to NATO, Hauge rightly foresaw that if Andrew were to continue to lead an independent Mission in Norway the possibilities of friction with SHAPE were considerable, unless Andrew completed his task and submitted his recommendations before SHAPE became fully active.

For the moment there was no question of Andrew's doctors allowing him to return to Norway, so he gladly assented to a proposal that Colonel Trimble should continue with preparatory work in ways suggested by Andrew, to whom Trimble would report regularly. By 6 February he could tell Hauge that he was going to Worthing to convalesce and that he expected to return to Norway by about 18 March. At the beginning of March he was delighted to welcome four senior Norwegian officers, including Rolstad, who, following his suggestion, formed the first party to study British military organisation for themselves in England.

In the meantime all was not going ahead as smoothly in Norway as Andrew had hoped. A long letter of 23 February from Colonel Jackson in Oslo gave him an account of Hauge's difficulties. He was meeting with considerable opposition even from within his own Labour Party, and only by a narrow majority was the cost of his defence plans accepted for the forthcoming budget. The Finance Minister opposed him and intended to resign after the Storting had debated the complete budget. The real opposition to Andrew's proposals came to Hauge from the most senior officers, who felt that they were too far-reaching for a small country like Norway, and that because of close ties with Sweden the two countries should adopt similar command structures. Fear of losing their jobs, Jackson hinted, influenced their views. Despite all opposition Hauge's support of Andrew's plans remained firm.

The Easter holiday made it advisable for Andrew to wait until 1 April before returning, but on 7 March he wrote to Hauge about future procedure, hoping to be allowed to bring one or two experts with him as after nearly five years in retirement he was 'not sufficiently up-to-date to give an opinion without seeking advice from those who are in daily contact with the problems involved'. On the vexed question of the reorganisation of the Norwegian High Command he conceded that any revision 'would be premature until it is clear what the set-up under General Eisenhower is going to be'. Then on 14 March came an unexpected message from the War Office telling Andrew that the Norwegian Military Attaché in London had telephoned. 'Please inform General Thorne that the Norwegian Ministry of Defence suggests his visit be postponed for about two months owing to unforeseen circumstances.' The reason for the postponement was partly Hansteen's wish that Andrew should inspect troops in the field during June but was much more due to uncertainty about

SHAPE's plans. On grounds of health Andrew welcomed the delay, preferring to return in June rather than in April. It would also give him a chance of discussing his proposals with Eisenhower.

Andrew welcomed the delay for another reason which he did not at that moment divulge to Hauge: he was now having doubts about the advisability of completing his Mission. On 16 March he had characteristically informed the Military Secretary that in view of Hauge's postponement of his return he did not feel it right to remain on full pay. This letter was probably the result of a meeting which he had had on the previous day with Montgomery when they discussed his future plans for Norway and which led him to write to Hauge on 21 March: 'A new situation has arisen and I feel I must put this important factor before you. SHAPE has had an unusually speedy gestation and has begun to function fully at the top. Under these circumstances I wonder if I am the correct person to offer advice on military re-organisation? Will not SHAPE resent what to them would appear as the interference of an interloper? . . . I now feel that I would be still more helpful to Norwegian defence if I were to drop out and leave the provision of military adavice to SHAPE.'

At the same time he wrote in similar terms to the Chiefs of Staff, and on 25 March Field-Marshal Slim, the CIGS, replied, expressing 'our very real appreciation of your unselfish and public-spirited action in asking to be relieved of the rest of your Mission to Norway . . . This generous act has avoided a situation which, due to the recent rapid assumption of responsibility by SHAPE, might well have become a most difficult one.' Andrew had done what he felt was right but he was naturally disappointed at being unable to complete his work.

His decision caused dismay in Norway where Hauge and Hansteen and others did not conceal their belief that Montgomery was the real cause of Andrew's withdrawal. This prompted the British Foreign Office, apparently urged on by Collier, who had shed his early reservations about Andrew's ability, to intervene and to make clear to the Ministry of Defence how deeply the Norwegians regretted what had occurred. 'General Thorne's long-standing connections with the country and his personal friendship with Hauge make him singularly well fitted to carry out the task on which he was engaged. He enjoyed the confidence of the Norwegians to a greater degree than probably any officer one could name and it is not surprising that the Norwegian Authorities should have been profoundly disappointed on learning that he was not returning . . . We hope that when the position becomes clearer it might be possible for General Thorne to go out to Norway under NATO auspices. The Chiefs of Staff may think it worthwhile to convey this suggestion to Field-Marshal Lord Montgomery, pointing out the political advantages of retaining General Thorne's services in some form.'

Andrew waited until 9 April before trying to pacify Hauge, who was seeing Montgomery on that day. 'I feel sure that the F-M will have made it clear that his duties specifically cover all the help I might be able to give . . . it is only fair to say that the British Chiefs of Staff were delighted with my request to withdraw; so they obviously sensed that my mission might cause embarrassment to them and friction between Norway and the Supreme Allied Commander, Europe's Deputy. This is for your private ear!'

Hauge was determined to bring Andrew back. Despite an unpleasant accident to his head which he banged on a low door and which put him in hospital, he argued with Montgomery from his bed and triumphed. Writing on 9 April he told Andrew that the two men had agreed on a sensible compromise whereby Andrew should return to Norway and complete his Mission but should also act as a representative of SHAPE and should ultimately report his findings and recommendations both to SHAPE and to the Norwegian authorities. This was formally confirmed on 4 May, and as Colonel Robertson, the new British Military Attaché in Oslo, told Andrew: 'I gather the Foreign Office has succeeded where others failed . . . I need hardly say how pleased we all are. Hauge's letter to you was written longhand, against his doctor's orders, from his bed in hospital, and it would cause you great pleasure to know the number of "Thorne" flags that are waving and also the broad smile on Hansteen's face when he told me that they had won.'

On 1 May Andrew had gone to Paris to be briefed at SHAPE. On 17 May the CIGS wrote officially to invite Andrew to return to Norway, an invitation which Andrew 'accepted with alacrity and went up to London at once to the War Office to arrange details as far as possible, planning to arrive in Oslo on 1 June'. As it happened there was one final postponement, but a pleasant one. On 1 June he and Margaret were 'commanded' to attend a state banquet at Buckingham Palace in honour of King Haakon's visit. A week later they were in Oslo where they remained until 14 November, after which Andrew finally resumed his retirement.

Before he was taken ill Andrew and Trimble had agreed on the main needs of the Norwegian Army and both of them signed the Interim Report on 21 December 1950 for submission to Hauge as Minister of Defence, and a copy, with a covering letter on 19 January 1951, went to the British Chiefs of Staff. The final amplified report was addressed to SHAPE, as had been agreed.

The most far-reaching recommendation was that the Norwegian Joint Defence Staff and the Commanders-in-Chief Committee should be reorganised into a Joint Defence Committee on British and American lines. The recommendation was 'based on the axiom that in war no man can effectively be a Commander and his own Chief of Staff at one and the same time. The heads of the three Services are the Government's advisers on military matters, as such they are Staff officers and not Commanders. In war the Government will need their constant advice even more than in peace; they must therefore continue to function in their advisory capacity without interruption. Under the present system they could not do this and the Government would be deprived of their services at the very time that they needed them most.'

Further reorganisation at top levels was needed. A Director General of Training should be appointed and a strong Quartermaster/G4 Branch be set up. 'An army cannot fight a modern war without the most efficient and economical administrative machine behind it.' Andrew and Trimble bluntly recommended the retirement of officers 'who are no longer an economic proposition, are in fact harmful to efficiency and morale by reason of their age, their lack of ambition, enthusiasm and war experience'.

The Report expressed its authors' worries at 'the alarming deficiency on mobilisation of officers and NCOs'. To fill the void National Service should last for eighteen months rather than for one year and every potential officer and NCO adequately trained during that time. They felt that the best type of Norwegian youth is not always being selected and trained for leadership in war. We feel too that the fundamental difference between officer and NCO is not sufficiently understood . . . Promotion of NCOs to officer rank as soon as they are trained as NCOs is to destroy a most valuable core of men, which should be the backbone of the army . . . A good NCO is not necessarily a good officer, nor is a youth blessed with marked power of leadership and imagination always a good NCO. Therefore steps should be taken to train and retrain a corps of NCOs . . . who will need to be paid as well as, if not better than, the young officer . . . It will be found to be one of the most economical ways of producing quality and high morale.

In making these recommendations we have constantly borne in mind the overall concept of collective security as exemplified by the Atlantic Pact, but we have not lost sight of the primary duty of any Government and its Defence advisers to ensure the territorial integrity of their own country. We believe that our recommendations serve both purposes equally well and that one cannot be ensured without the other. It must be constantly remembered that the best way to defend a country is to keep the battle as remote from it as possible. In order to do that it is essential to organise and train the Armed Forces for immediate action overseas.

Back at home Andrew was keen to learn how far his proposals were being accepted. In December 1951 both the Prime Minister and Hauge had announced their impending resignations but before these took effect in January Hauge, in a long speech to the Storting on 13 December, had urged complete acceptance of Andrew's report. Thereafter progress was slow, partly due to the Norwegian Navy whose leaders disliked some of the proposed changes. However, as Colonel Trimble told Andrew, his report had become 'the international "Bible" of the Norwegian Army' and at the end of 1952 Admiral Brind assured Andrew that 'your great work is a classic and we try to keep it "off the shelf"'. In the following year Trimble reported that there was a bill before the Storting to implement many of his recommendations – '60% progress is better than none at all'. Eighteen months later Trimble again wrote to him: 'You can well consider yourself the father of the present day Norwegian Army.'

In May 1955 Andrew and Margaret were again in Norway as guests of the Norwegian Government to join in celebrating the tenth anniversary of the liberation. He remained a close friend of the Norwegian Royal Family, maintaining his ties with them and the country. In 1953 he had broadcast a short message of congratulation on the fiftieth birthday of the Crown Prince and had written a moving letter of condolence to him when his wife died in April 1954. Three years later in 1957 he expressed his sorrow at the death of King Haakon and his good wishes to King Olav V, as the Crown Prince had become.

Judging by Andrew's engagement diaries, time did not hang heavily on his hands. Golf, fishing – especially on the Spey when staying in Lossiemouth – and gardening provided his need for exercise. He had long been a member of the Cordwainers Livery Company but his military service had made regular attendance at dinners and meetings impossible. He was now free to throw himself into the Company's affairs, taking particular interest in the overhaul of its charitable funds, and in July 1954 he followed his father by becoming Master for the ensuing year.

One of the things which emerges from a study of the mass of his surviving correspondence is the unflagging interest which Andrew took in the welfare of others. Readiness to supply information about the fighting in two World Wars to those engaged in writing their memoirs; letters of congratulation or good wishes and, as the years went by, inevitable letters of condolence to bereaved relations and friends; pride in the achievements of his ever-growing family – not least those grandsons who had followed him into the Grenadiers – all testify to his abiding interest in people. To the end he retained his remarkable gift for making those who were with him, whether young or old, or who sought his help, feel that they genuinely mattered to him.

It is the great sense of unity of the Thorne family which so forcibly strikes an outsider. This did not mean that there were no family differences nor the normal minor jealousies; nor did all of them always wish to join their parents and an army of cousins for a summer holiday at Lossiemouth, as Margaret so much wanted. She loved having the family around her and being in a crowd of people and she was apt to be slightly hurt if some of her family preferred spending a holiday with friends rather than with relations. She had often, quite unjustifiably, felt that in some ways she had failed her children, and this lack of self-confidence caused her at times to be needlessly upset. Andrew had often tried to make her realise that as children grow up there are bound to be moments when they react against their parents. Now that her children had their own families and their own lives to live this in no way lessened their devotion or their gratitude to her. Despite their different paths in life there was a family loyalty, rather like loyalty to a regiment, which bound them together and which sprang from a deep admiration and love for their parents.

Andrew and Margaret were delighted when in May 1959 Peter, now Deputy Serjeant at Arms in the House of Commons, married Lady Anne Pery, daughter of the Earl and Countess of Limerick. Anne worked in a very different world from the Thorne family, for she was a Lecturer at the Imperial College of Science and an internationally distinguished atomic spectroscopist. Two months later the family unity was happily evident on 29 July at the party given to celebrate Andrew and Margaret's golden wedding anniversary. In recalling their parents' long married life together the family nowadays can only tell of one quarrel between them, a vivid memory of a unique event. On one occasion when Andrew was driving the family he skidded into a ditch. Margaret, who was a much better driver, made some uncharitable comment, to which Andrew replied in kind. Margaret immediately got out of the car and walked ahead until a swift reconciliation followed. A totally trivial incident which, because they had never before witnessed any disagreement between their parents, remained in the children's memories.

A full diary of engagements did not prevent Andrew and Margaret from wisely continuing to take holidays. They loved staying in the homes of their children and they were in Lossiemouth at least every summer, staying always at the Laverock Bank Hotel as Dunconusg had been sold as a nursing home after its release from the wartime occupation by the RAF. In 1961 they were again on holiday in Norway when they lunched with King

Olav. Two years later in May and June they went on a leisurely tour of Wales and in the following January a generous golden wedding present from all the family enabled them to sail in the *Transvaal Castle* for Cape Town, returning home at the end of February.

Holidays were enjoyable for themselves but essential for keeping well. Difficulty with his eyesight had led Andrew to sell his guns in 1957. As his partially blind eye had always forced him to shoot left-handed, the guns did not fetch the price for which he had hoped. During 1959 Margaret and, perhaps to keep her company, Andrew took a course in how to relax completely. This prompted Andrew's nephew Gerald Howard-Smith to write: 'The picture of you taking lessons in relaxation is far too good to be true!! I must confess that all my life I have looked on you as the terrible little man who never rested for a single moment but was always rushing round waking everyone else up . . . I do hope that the treatment really did help Aunt Margaret but I doubt if it could have really had the slightest effect on you. Something tells me that you are a hopeless case.' Andrew, to strengthen his heart, had adopted a low-fat diet, which led his cousin by marriage, Jimmy Murdoch, to write: 'When a holiday to this country is possible I hope to find you still debating the state of the lupin bank and the moss in the lower lawn of Knowl Hill House. You have still to convince me that your continued agility and breadth of interests stem from a diet . . . I'm sure the secret lies deeper than that.' At any rate a heart specialist gave him a good report in May 1961, allowing him 'a little butter and an occasional rasher of bacon' in return for a slight increase in the daily dose of digitalis.

For his age Andrew was clearly in excellent health. Margaret, never robust, was increasingly incapacitated by arthritis. Until about 1965 she was able to accompany Andrew not only on holidays but to official occasions such as the dedication of the restored Guards Chapel in November 1963, with which he had been closely involved, bravely advocating a modern design. In 1965 he celebrated his eightieth birthday with a family dinner party in Pansy's London flat. Among the piles of birthday cards a sentence from Pansy's message summed up his continuing ability to live life to the full: 'What with being 80 and catching a 22 lb-er and getting a 16th grandchild all in a space of days!' A fortnight later he was deeply touched at being the guest of his regiment at a special reception in his honour.

The first sign that Margaret's health was seriously deteriorating came in February 1966 when she was too unwell to accompany Andrew to the Anglo-Norse dinner in London. Then on 12 April she suffered a severe paralytic stroke, which affected one side of her body and deprived her of her power of speech. For eighteen months she endured this tragic plight, dependent on a nurse both day and night, duties which were often undertaken by Andrew and Diana. At times she could be brought into the garden or taken for a drive; for a brief while she regained her ability to write. She was occasionally taken to watch a regimental or sporting occasion, though the kindly pretence that all was as before was painful for all who saw her. At last on 23 October 1967 the long nightmare ended as she died peacefully at home. Three days later on a golden afternoon the family gathered at Sonning Parish Church for the funeral service and burial in the churchyard.

There had never been any question of Andrew's courage under fire; now he was called on to show a different kind of courage but of an equally high order. He was the first to say that Margaret's death was a merciful release, but this was small comfort at the end of fifty-eight years of a wonderful partnership. Throughout those years Margaret had been intellectually, emotionally and, ultimately, physically dependent on him. For Andrew she had been his constant companion, an unfailing support and comfort at every stage of his career; the one to whom alone his hopes and ambitions, his anxieties and self-questioning could be confessed. His children, who feared some reaction after the strain of Margaret's long illness, were amazed and deeply impressed by his triumph over loneliness. He was, of course, fortunate in having Diana, then working at the Shell Centre in London, to keep house and to encourage him to continue his active life but, as he told close friends, the process of readjustment was not easy. As ever, the secret of his courage lay in his unshakable belief that death was only the gateway to a fuller life, into which Margaret had already entered and which he would one day share with her.

The final three years of Andrew's life were as full as he and his family could make them. Each of his married children pressed him to come and stay, and he was welcomed by his ever-growing number of grandchildren. To them he never talked down, treating them as his equals. He enjoyed a grandfather's privilege of not being ultimately responsible for them and this made him more relaxed with them than he had sometimes been with his own children in their early years. Three months before Margaret died he had become a great-grandfather when Sandy and Joscelyne's daughter, Joanna, who had married John Friedberger of the 10th Royal Hussars, gave birth to a daughter, Rosanna. Peter and Anne's fourth child, Janet, born in 1968 was to be his seventeenth and final grandchild.

One thing which his family regretted was his firm refusal to write an account of his life story. As Benevenuto Cellini wrote in his autobiography: 'All men, whatever be their condition, who have done anything of merit, or which verily has a semblance of merit, if so be they are men of truth and good repute, should write the tale of their life with their own hands.' But Andrew, though presented by the family with a tape recorder, had a horror of generals who wrote their memoirs to justify their achievements, and with his innate modesty he refused to write down anything, even to set the record straight.

Increasing age never prevented him from fishing or from regularly playing golf. In February 1968 he and Diana were on holiday in Malta. Two months later he presided over the fiftieth anniversary dinner of the Reading Branch of the Grenadier Guards Association, an occasion at which his old soldier servant, Arthur Bines, himself recently a widower, was present. Early in May he was at Windsor when the Freedom of the Borough was conferred on the Brigade of Guards. Shortly afterwards he was in Edinburgh at Holyrood, the guest of Her Majesty's Lord High Commissioner to the General Assembly of the Church of Scotland, Lord Reith, when Pansy was also present as lady-in-waiting to Lady Reith. His engagement diary for 1969 shows no lessening of his activities, which included a small party at Buckingham Palace following the presentation by the Queen of New Colours to the 2nd Battalion of the Grenadier Guards; the marriage of Sandy and Joscelyne's son, Nicholas; August and September in Lossiemouth where he celebrated his eighty-fourth birthday; and, to end the year, a large family party which he and Diana gave at the Phyllis Court Club in Henley.

In April 1970 Andrew received a letter from General Sir Ian Jacob asking if he would consider depositing his Army papers in the archive of the Imperial War Museum. He replied that in due course he would try to sort out what might be of interest but at the moment 'I am off to Norway'. To his great delight the Ministry of Defence had supported an invitation from the Norwegian Government that, with Major-General Sir John Gubbins, he should represent Britain at the twenty-fifth anniversary celebrations of the liberation. In view of his age, Diana was invited to come with him.

A month before receiving the invitation he had given an interview at the Royal Commonwealth Society's Club in London to a journalist from the Norwegian paper *Aftenpost*. He was questioned about the problems which had had to be overcome and he gave his views on the leading Allied commanders as well as Hitler and Quisling. As the journalist wrote: 'He has for one month governed Norway with the full power of a dictator and he is the only foreigner since the dissolution of the Union with Sweden who has possessed such powers with the full blessing of the legitimate Norwegian Government . . . This blessing had been given very unwillingly. The Nygaardsvold Government did not want to be carried home by foreign soldiers and demanded a Norwegian G.O.C. for the Allied Forces. The British answered "No" and promoted Sir Andrew to "full" General so that no Norwegian regular officer could be above him in rank.' Andrew's natural modesty combined with a little tongue in cheek explains this unlikely account of his promotion.

He and Diana were in Oslo from 6 to 9 May and he attended nearly every event. On 7 May he, with Major-General Gubbins, laid the British wreath on the memorial to the Allied Dead in the Second World War in Vestre Cemetery. He went on to the thanksgiving service in the cathedral, decided to miss an official luncheon but attended a dinner and a gala performance in the National Theatre. His insistence on walking from the dinner to the theatre dismayed the security staff. Andrew was in mess dress and it was pointed out to him that Oslo was full of hippies with a passion for dressing up in uniform. There was every chance that he might be attacked and stripped. Andrew ignored what proved to be groundless fears. Following the theatre he went on to a supper party given by Jens Hauge. On the next day he attended a special session of the Storting, witnessed the unveiling of the Norwegian National Monument and enjoyed most of all the opening of the Home Front Museum with its fascinating exhibits. It had been a heart-warming but strenuous three days. Soon after he got home a letter came from Jens Hauge thanking him for coming but regretting that there had been no chance for a quiet talk about old times. 'The dinner-dance was a gay thing and many people . . . enjoyed themselves thoroughly. It was too much noise for me and I admired you standing up against this new kind of warfare.'

Andrew was determined to watch the Trooping the Colour on 6 June especially because George and Juliet's son, Ian, was taking part, wearing, as he told his grandfather, 'Uncle Tommie's' sword. To his dismay a little while after returning from Norway he developed a serious leg ailment and a mild recurrence of pneumonia. However, with the pneumonia cured, he bullied his doctor into agreeing that no great harm would come to his leg if he went to London. Unfortunately he had to walk a great distance to his seat but, though in pain, asserted that it was well worth the effort.

On 25 August Andrew and Diana began a four-week holiday at Lossiemouth. All seemed to be going as well as ever. At first floods had made the Spey fishing difficult but in one week in mid-September Andrew landed three salmon. The occasional golf lesson to improve his game – to the end he set himself always to reach higher standards – resulted in a bogey and a birdie on the last two holes in what proved to be his last round. Diana and he drove long distances in the hunt for information about his Scottish forebears. It was an enjoyable three weeks, with another week to go before returning home.

Suddenly on 18 September his heart began to give sufficiently serious trouble for the doctor to order him at once to bed and it was in bed two days later that he celebrated his eighty-fifth birthday. The usual family greetings telegrams and cards were supplemented by best wishes for a speedy recovery. Andrew had assured the doctor that he really felt much better but he privately confessed to Diana that he was far from well. Four days later he suffered a massive coronary attack and he was rushed to Spynie

Hospital in Elgin. George and Peter flew to Aberdeen to join Diana at the hospital, where at 9.30 p.m. on 25 September the heart of which Andrew for over eighty-five years had demanded so much quietly ceased to beat.

Andrew's body was taken to Sonning, for it was only fitting that he should lie beside Margaret. The funeral service on 1 October was for family alone, a memorial service being later planned to be held in the Guards Chapel on 29 October, the anniversary of the day on which he and Margaret had become engaged sixty-two years earlier. Among all the flowers sent to Sonning was a bunch of Scottish white heather from the Erskine grandchildren with the simple but all-sufficient tribute: 'For Grandy – who was fun.'

Index